COMPREHENSIVE ACHIEVEMENT MONITORING

A Criterion-Referenced Evaluation System

COMPREHENSIVE ACHIEVEMENT MONITORING
A Criterion-Referenced Evaluation System

William P. Gorth
University of Massachusetts

Robert P. O'Reilly
New York State Education Department

Paul D. Pinsky
Stanford University

Educational Technology Publications
Englewood Cliffs, New Jersey 07632

Library of Congress Cataloging in Publication Data

Gorth, William P
  Comprehensive achievement monitoring.

  Bibliography: p.
  Includes index.
  1. Educational tests and measurements.
I. O'Reilly, Robert P., joint author. II. Pinsky,
Paul D., joint author. III. Title.
LB3051.G655   371.2'6   75-11788
ISBN 0-87778-080-3

Published in cooperation with the Office of Research,
Planning, and Evaluation, New York State Education
Department. All rights reserved.

Library of Congress Catalog Number: 75-11788.

International Standard Book Number:
0-87778-080-3.

Printed in the United States of America.

First Printing: June, 1975.

3/7/77 Berkert Teylor 11.95

Preface

In 1967, a project to improve classroom evaluation techniques began under a grant from the Charles F. Kettering Foundation to Dwight W. Allen, Dean of the School of Education, University of Massachusetts. The techniques which developed partially out of the project are known as Comprehensive Achievement Monitoring (CAM). Since that time a large number of people have become variously involved with the techniques, as researchers, implementers, technicians, proponents, and writers. In addition, a substantial body of literature has been generated.

This document is an attempt to compile in a monograph some of the more useful and interesting concepts and applications developed in the project. At the time the project was initiated, its underlying concepts, such as criterion-referenced testing, were new ideas that had not yet achieved a high level of recognition in education. The CAM project also embodied the first large-scale attempt to find practical ways of applying a longitudinal evaluation framework as a method for ongoing evaluation of school programs.

From the beginning, the overriding concern of those involved in the CAM project has been finding more effective and generally applicable methods of approaching the problems of evaluation in the schools. The preoccupation has always been with application, and as a result it appears that the project has contributed substantially toward redirecting the testing and evaluation procedures used in the nation's schools. CAM now provides a well-known model and a mechanism for integrating testing and evaluation into the instructional activities of the schools in a generally useful and more humanistic fashion.

Many individuals participated either in the earliest development of the CAM techniques or in their use in an experimental version. The former category includes Lee Popejoy, Thomas Stroud, Aram Grayson, and Donald DeLay at Stanford University and Philip Christensen, Nate Sims, Frank Dumont, George Worle, and Malcolm Conway at the University of Massachusetts. The latter includes June Yamashita of Kailua High School, Jean Stromquist of Jackson High School, Max Lane and Ray O'Dell of Marshall High School, and teachers at Duluth High School.

Those who have contributed to making the CAM concept a practical reality in the schools are too numerous to mention here, but at least the major contributors can be recognized. Mr. John Easter of the Sequoia Unified High School District in California has directed one of the most productive and economical CAM projects in the nation. His special contribution was to create in practice the evaluation service center concept described in the implementation section of this report.

In the Midwest at Hopkins High School, a group composed of Mr. James Whitney, Mrs. Margaret Kosel, and Mr. Daniel Ekberg piloted the early CAM technology into a regional evaluation service center. This group, which now includes Dr. Donald Sension, has also made its own unique contributions in the form of training and dissemination materials used in many other CAM installations.

In New York State the success of the CAM project has been, to a large extent, due to a number of key projects which developed under local initiative into model demonstration centers. These are at Jamesville-DeWitt under Dr. Olcott Gardner, at the Erie County BOCES under Dr. Charles Adams, at Brentwood under Mr. Raymond Fournier, and at Greece under Mr. Robert Fitzgibbons. These projects currently attract several thousand visitors a year and offer unique applications of the CAM concept.

The growth of the CAM concept in New York is also the result of the technical and planning expertise provided to the schools by Education Department staff, including Mr. Howard Berkun, who provided the leadership for planning and organizing many of the local projects, and Miss Ruth Salter and Mrs. Fran Morris, who were largely responsible for developing the state objective banks in reading.

Special mention should be given to Dr. Peter Schriber, who has contributed to the technical development of the CAM project, and to Mr. Peter Treadway, Dr. Larry Benedict, and Mr. Dmitri Gat, who contributed to the task of editing this document. The final copy was formatted and composed by Gay Flannelly, and the cover design was prepared by Richards Steinbock.

Table of Contents

List of Figures

Overview

This monograph offers a set of guidelines and references to public school personnel for potential use in developing and instituting a new approach to the evaluation of pupils and programs. This approach is known as criterion-referenced evaluation. Its central focus is on objective criteria defining the desired level of performance for pupils and programs. The ideas and operations concerning criterion-referenced evaluation presented herein are intended for master teachers, school project directors, program managers, assistant superintendents for curriculum, curriculum developers, evaluation directors, and data processing personnel. Others concerned with educational evaluation may also find the monograph useful.

The monograph is intended to aid the planning and implementation of criterion-referenced evaluation at the school district level. While not specifically a "cookbook" on how to implement such an evaluation system, sufficient knowledge and direction are provided to aid the reader in planning and considering the possible installation of a criterion-referenced evaluation system.

The Model

The elements of the criterion-referenced evaluation model are labelled in Figure 1.1 (see page 21). Each element shown in this diagram is more fully explained in the sections of the monograph to follow.

Note that the model in Figure 1.1 has ten major elements. These are defined as follows:

(1) Programs: the institutional and administrative units of a school district designed to deliver and support the instructional and other services of the district to the students.

(2) Decision-Makers: those responsible for guiding accomplishment of the intended outcomes of each program unit or level thereof.

(3) Decisions: the variety of instructional, administrative, and resource allocation decisions made by decision-makers at all levels of the program units.

1

(4) Performance Standards: goals and objectives defining the intended achievement of program units.

(5) Evaluation Design: types, content, organization, and administration frequency of tests needed to generate information for decision-makers.

(6) Test Development and Production: the process by which criterion-referenced tests are developed, produced, and distributed.

(7) Test Administration: the process of gathering raw data and transmitting it for processing.

(8) Analysis and Reporting: the process of analyzing, summarizing, and displaying data to make it usable by decision-makers.

(9) Use of Data for Decision-Making: making decisions on the basis of the information collected.

(10) Revision of Evaluation: refining the evaluation process itself as its operation indicates needed changes.

The foregoing definitions make it clear that the central purpose of the model is to provide clear, relevant, and timely data to educational decision-makers at all levels of a system. The types of data of primary interest in the model are measures of the performance of the instructional programs of an educational system and of those treated by the system. The general purpose of the model is to provide dynamic means for maximizing the outcomes of instructional programs and the educational progress of individual students. The separate elements of the model are integrated in a self-correcting cycle of evaluation activities to support decision-making for the ongoing programs of a school district. Data on the performance of every important level of the system are collected and reported back to decision-makers in a format designed to support their decision-making activities. The decisions in turn direct the actual performance of the educational system to a closer approximation of expected or ideal performance. Recognized in the model is that, at best, only an approximation of ideal performance is possible, for educational systems operate in a constantly and inevitably fluctuating environment. An adequate criterion-referenced evaluation model thus must both maximize the approach to the expected or the ideal and be capable of continuous revision as conditions warrant.

History

The evaluation model is called Comprehensive Achievement Monitoring or CAM. Research and development on CAM was begun at Stanford University in 1967 and carried on at the University of Massachusetts by Dr. William P. Gorth, project director, and Dr. Paul D. Pinsky under a grant from the Charles F. Kettering Foundation to Dr. Dwight W. Allen. The result was a preliminary version of the model, on which further developmental work continued in schools throughout the country under the combined leadership of Dr. Gorth, Dr. Pinsky, and Dr. Robert P. O'Reilly of the New York State Education Department.

In the development of a broadly applicable model, Dr. Gorth as project director created the initial design of the total system and supervised its initial field trial. He expanded the measurement and statistical aspects of the model and developed the technical training materials necessary for implementation. Dr. Pinsky compiled and conceptualized evaluation methodology and models at the secondary level and authored the three generations of CAM computer data processing programs. Dr. O'Reilly devised the methods for creating and deriving the objectives and test items, produced the objective and item banks for data collection, and developed and applied evaluation designs for the elementary level. The integrated criterion-referenced evaluation system presented in this model grew from these efforts, and, in New York State, is known as Project SPPED (System for Program and Pupil Evaluation and Development).

Applications

The Comprehensive Achievement Monitoring system has been used extensively across the country. Three applications are briefly summarized.

Sequoia Union High School District

The CAM system has been operational in the Sequoia Union High School District, Redwood City, California since September 1970, under the direction of John Easter. During the 1972-73 school year, there were 80 courses, 110 teachers, and 7500 students involved in the program. Subject matter included the humanities, language arts, the sciences, mathematics, industrial arts, and physical education. The district CAM office provides three basic services to the six high schools in the district:

(1)   training in the use of the evaluation system;
(2)   objective and test-item banking and test production; and
(3)   computer processing of the student response data and report generation.

Using the system, teachers are able to determine entry level skills of students for program placement and to monitor students' progress through their courses. The information they gain from periodic test administrations enables teachers to plan instructional activities specifically suited to students' needs as a course proceeds and provide review opportunities when and for whom they are relevant. During the summer, other CAM reports may be used for curriculum and course revisions.

The Hopkins—TIES Program

An ESEA Title III project at the Hopkins School District, just outside of Minneapolis, provides the training and support resources to enable districts to get involved in CAM in a sound educational manner. Teachers create their own objective-based curricula and measurement instruments. Training sessions for non-involved teachers and interested parents are also available. Students are actively involved in structuring their own programs. Consequently, the community has become more active in the educational decision-making process.

The Total Information for Education System (TIES) data center in St. Paul, Minnesota services most of the school districts in the greater Minneapolis—St. Paul area. The non-profit agency provides administrators and instructional data processing services for subscribing districts. One such service is the processing of CAM data. During the 1972-73 school year, the TIES center monitored approximately 5000 students each week.

New York State

In New York State, Comprehensive Achievement Monitoring is an integral part of the statewide System for Program and Pupil Evaluation and Development (SPPED). CAM is monitoring individual student achievement and instructional group progress, and providing data feedback for instructional, curricular, and materials evaluation. In 1972-73, the system provided these services for 100,000 students and 2000 teachers in 65 school districts throughout the state.

The wide dispersion of the Comprehensive Achievement Monitoring model over several years in a wide variety of educational settings, which the three above exemplify, has contributed a large data base allowing continual ongoing model refinement.

Structure of the Monograph

This monograph is structured into four separate parts. Part I, entitled "Concepts of Evaluation," examines the context of educational decision-making and investigates current methods of evaluation in the light of that context.

The notion of criterion-referenced evaluation is introduced and a global description is presented of the particular model under discussion. Chapter 2 examines the implications of both conventional patterns of evaluation and the criterion-referenced model for decision-making at the instructional level. Finally, Chapter 3 presents some basic elements of criterion-referenced evaluation technology currently available and evaluates the feasibility of broadly applying criterion-referenced evaluation.

Part II focuses on "Objectives for Criterion-Referenced Evaluation." Chapters 4 through 8 deal with the educational context of objectives, different types of objectives, the derivation and selection of objectives, and the organization of objectives into curricula. This part also presents a number of different implications of the existence of performance standards or behavioral objectives in an educational system.

Part III, "Evaluation Design," details a number of different, but related, designs for evaluation. These designs meet the various needs and implications drawn in Part I and are based on the existence and organization of a performance-based curriculum, presented in Part II. This third part illustrates how various designs can generate different kinds of information depending upon the need for such data by different personnel both within and without the school. Part III concludes with a practical discussion of evaluation designs for group-paced instruction and individually-paced instruction based on actual working examples.

The final part of the monograph, Part IV, "Implementation," briefly brings the reader to the practical level of how one begins and what resources are needed to implement a criterion-referenced evaluation system. This fourth part deals with such topics as test development, the management of evaluation activities, the training needed for personnel within the system, and the data processing component of evaluation.

PART I

Concepts of Evaluation

It is probably fair and reasonable to conclude that contemporary evaluation procedures in education did not develop out of an explicit model that had in turn been generated from a broad analysis of information needs in the classroom and other educational program units. It appears that the most recognized elements of contemporary evaluation methodology developed out of the tradition that produced the products and philosophy of the normative testing movement. The familiar products of this movement include the IQ test, standardized achievement tests, and the classroom test built on the normal curve. The elements of normative testing were in turn developed in a context of very limited purpose, currently exemplified in the measurement and evaluation practices of the college admissions officer, the school psychologist, and the guidance counselor.

This section of the monograph first attempts to generate a broader analysis of the testing and evaluation needs of those involved in the management and presentation of educational programs and those treated by such programs—the students. The discussion further analyzes the extent to which contemporary testing and evaluation procedures actually fit these needs. In a final analysis, the required elements of a more adequate measurement and evaluation technology are identified, and the availability of a working, supporting technology is examined.

Chapter 1

The Evaluation Context and a Model

In this opening chapter, the context in which educational decisions are made and the kinds of decisions necessary for the effective management of instructional programs are explored. The implications of this context and related decisions for an evaluation model are drawn. The different needs for evaluative information in support of decision-making in the educational context are assessed. Finally, the model for criterion-referenced evaluation briefly introduced in the Overview is presented in more detail.

The Evaluation Context

The context in which educational decisions are made is an educational system or district. There are, of course, variations among educational systems. They vary in size from those having responsibility for fewer than 20 students to those with more than 100,000. Their physical facilities range from a one-room elementary building to hundreds of acres and hundreds of thousands of square feet of general and specialized purpose plants. There are public and private educational systems, and secular and sectarian systems within the private sector. Some educational systems offer generalized content, others, very technical and specific content. There are many age groups served. Some serve a clientele whose attendance is enforced, others, a clientele which attends voluntarily. Some have a tax-raising authority, others have large gift-seeking departments. Their explicit and formalized governance structures range from frankly autocratic through technically oligarchic and democratic to consensual.

There are, on the other hand, great similarities among educational systems as well. They all have as a purpose the increase of their clients' skill competence

9

in the content areas in which they offer programs. While program contents vary widely, the goal of all educational systems is raising the level of the clients' performance of the skills associated with the content. Most educational systems are functionally oligarchic. Most have a formally designated chief executive officer, below whom are installed larger ranks of less responsible personnel in various levels of authority. Where such formalized ranking is not present, there is an informal functional hierarchy, which is necessary for a system to retain purpose and directed movement beyond that which is required for self-perpetuation. It is this commonality and continuity of purpose and functional structure among educational systems that allows the formulation of a generalizable model for evaluation.

All educational systems share in having some degree of imperfection in the extent to which they accomplish their goals. It is not possible nor appropriate for an educational system to be perfect, for perfection is static. The societal context in and for which an educational system operates its programs continuously changes. With changes in the societal context, the demands on and expectations of an educational system change. Thus goals change, as the goals are reflective of the milieu in which a system operates.

Similarly, the clientele of an educational system is constantly in flux. New students move into the system with skills and needs which differ from those of prior students. These new students learn differently and uniquely. The system must move to account for this different set of skills, needs, and learning styles in its new users. The system staff also continually changes, bringing new skills and competencies and new attitudes and personal agendas into the system. New theories and discoveries expand the potential services of a system. They must be digested and incorporated. New instructional resources are continually available to a system. These must be tested in its programs and accepted or rejected.

An educational system is, therefore, constantly altering its own structure and content in response to some internal or external change. There is inevitably a lag between the actual need for change and the system's response to it. All systems, educational and otherwise, share this response lag, for adaptation requires time. The changes in conditions, demands, expectations, and resources must be perceived, recognized, and reviewed for implications to the respondent system. The implications must be studied in light of the structure and context of the system. Plans must be laid for changes to be effected in the system in response to the implications.

The sources of the stimuli that keep an educational system from achieving its goals lie both within and without the system. To react to stimuli which originate outside the system, there must be an attitude of awareness to the setting within which the system is operating. Basically, the staff of the system must be sensitive to changes in the setting, and willing and able to respond to them. To respond to internal changes or processes that affect the system's performance, there must be a portion of the system itself that concentrates on gathering, analyzing, and using data about the system's operations and goal achievement. It is for this purpose of monitoring the achievement of the system's own goals that an evaluation component is established.

The evaluation component regularly collects data about system performance, analyzes that data, and organizes it into patterns usable for the decisions needed. Then it reports the data to the appropriate decision-makers for their use in directing the system to as close an approach to optimum performance as is possible. A comprehensive evaluation component must fulfill this service for the educational system as a whole and for its internal sub-systems. It must simultaneously provide the data needed for its own dynamic revision as well as for decisions at all levels of the system. The data must be available in a continuous flow as requested by decision-makers of varying degrees of functional responsibility. The roles and locations of the decision-makers and the nature of the decisions they make govern the need for data and the consequent design of an evaluation component.

A major purpose of any evaluation system thus must be to provide reliable, timely, and relevant data to decision-makers who decide what, if any, changes to make in an educational system's programs. The decisions to make or not to make changes will be based on how successfully the system is achieving its stated goals. The existence of stated goals is assumed because it is impossible to judge the success or failure of an educational system without knowing the goals toward which it is directing its efforts.

Let us turn now to the various decision-makers who must have data, the kinds of decisions they must make, and the generality of impact their decisions have. This investigation of decision-makers and decisions should illuminate the parameters and requirements for an effective evaluation system.

Decisions and Decision-Makers

There is a seemingly endless variety of individuals and groups who make decisions having an impact on an educational system. Each needs a certain amount of data on which to base each decision. It is important that all potential decision-makers associated with the system be identified and that a conscious identification be made of their appropriate decision-making responsibilities in managing educational programs.

Generally, educational decision-makers can be grouped on the basis of a focus on a particular set of common decisions. Teachers, for instance, may be regarded as a unique educational decision-making group because they are primarily concerned with instructional decisions. Curriculum coordinators are another distinct group focusing on a different set of decisions. Boards of education have yet another set of decision-making responsibilities. A cross-section of the major decision-making groups and individuals associated with a school district includes:

1) the teachers — as faculty;
2) the teachers — as individuals;
3) the principals;
4) the superintendent;
5) the assistant superintendent for curriculum and instruction;
6) the school committee;
7) the parents — as individuals;
8) the parents — as a group;
9) the voters — who vote bond issues, who elect school committee officials; and
10) the students — both as individuals and in various groupings.

This list is not meant to be complete. It has left out some district-level decision-makers, state-level decision-makers, and federal-level decision-makers. Each of these people or groups makes decisions about the same levels of the school system. Each, however, makes different types of decisions about programs from different perspectives. Therefore, each needs different kinds of data, and their differing data needs must be accounted for by an evaluation system.

Varieties of Decisions

The decision-makers occur at varying places in the structure of a system. Their operational responsibilities in the system specify the types of decisions they will make. For instance, a classroom teacher often makes decisions about placing individual students into appropriate units of instruction in a program, based on an assessment of the needs and skills of the student, while a district superintendent rarely, if ever, would make such a decision.

Here are listed some of the types of decisions that must be made in relation to the effective operation of instructional systems. Some are made by large subsets of the set of potential decision-makers; others are made by smaller subsets. None is made by the entire set.

Type 1: Selection — to accept or reject an individual for a program or course.

An example of Type 1 decisions would be to examine a person's skills and decide to accept him into a Follow Through program or a counseling program, or into a college or university.

Type 2:   Static Placement — to assign an individual to a level of a program or course.
An example of Type 2 decisions would be to assess a person's skills and decide at what level he should enter an elementary school program.

Type 3:   Dynamic Placement — to assign an individual or instructional group within a program or course with a number of variables — level, administrative unit, leader, peers — in a continuous fashion.
An example of Type 3 decisions would be to assess a student's mastery of a unit and recycle him for additional work on some objectives. Another would be to determine which objectives to stress for a given individual or group in a unit based on a preinstructional measurement.

Type 4:   Certify Individual Competence — to evaluate and report an individual's standing in relation to a skill, set of skills, or area of professional practices.
Examples of Type 4 decisions would be to prepare student report cards and to pass a student from one level (grade) of an instructional program to the next, or to certify an M.D. for practice.

Type 5:   Formative Program Evaluation — to evaluate the internal structure of an instructional process or product for the purpose of revision where necessary.
Examples of Type 5 decisions would be to revise a unit by adding emphasis to a key objective and to develop alternative methods of teaching an objective where extant methods are failing.

Type 6:   Summative Program Evaluation — to determine the most effective and efficient programs in content areas.
Examples of Type 6 decisions would involve comparing basal

reading series and selecting or endorsing one for use, or comparing two instructional strategies or programs and endorsing the more effective.

Type 7: Curriculum Validation — to determine the feasibility of teaching any objective or skill in a program, independent of methods or materials.

One example of Type 7 decisions would be to examine a skill's prerequisites, relation to other skills in the curriculum, appropriateness for students of given ages, and add to it, modify it, or delete it from a curriculum. Another example would be to decide to give an objective a certain level of emphasis in a curriculum.

Type 8: Evaluate Administrative Units — to assess the effectiveness of any administrative grouping in program areas.

An example of Type 8 decisions would be to evaluate buildings X and Y in the reading area and allocate more money to building Y.

Type 9: Item Validation — to determine the extent to which test items or tests reflect and measure the appropriate behavior.

An example of Type 9 decisions would be to determine if test items seek responses representative of a larger, more generalized set of behaviors and are indicative of performance in the larger set, for the purpose of revising the test items or test as needed.

These nine types of instructional or program-related decisions all must be made by one or more of the potential decision-makers in an educational system. It is obvious that to make them, the decision-makers must have data. They also must have standards to guide them in reaching a decision. For instance, for the example of a Type 4 decision above, it is necessary that performance standards be established so the requirements for passing to a higher level in a program are clear and a judgment about a particular student's fulfillment of the requirements can be reached.

Who Makes Which Decisions? How Often Are They Made?

With the potential decision-makers identified and the types of decisions they must make clarified, it now becomes possible to associate the decisions with particular decision-makers. This is necessary to insure that the appropriate data are delivered to the decision-makers. For instance; it is clear that district superintendents do not ordinarily or frequently make Type 3 decisions. Likewise, it would be irrelevant to supply data for Type 5 decisions to students (except as part of an evaluation team, which is not usually a "student" role). Therefore, in a criterion-referenced evaluation model the information for each type of decision is reported only to those needing it for decision-making.

Type 1 decisions are not common in the normal course of instructional programs. Some data gathered about an individual through a criterion-referenced evaluation model might be helpful for decisions of this type, but it would be improbable, at the public school level, that these data would have much impact on such a decision. In cases where Type 1 decisions are needed in the public schools, the school psychologist or a special programs teacher or administrator would be the likely decision-maker. The data needed for such a decision would be of a more psychological, physical, or sociological nature than that which is relevant to the outcomes of instructional programs. Generally, Type 1 decisions, though often made in educational systems, can be considered largely outside the scope of normal instructional or program evaluation activities.

Decision Types 2, 3, and 4 are made by teachers, parents, and students. Teachers are usually the final arbiters in those decisions which involve dynamic placement and progress, but students and parents would be included for their insights from different perspectives. These decisions occur with a high frequency and require much support from a criterion-referenced evaluation model.

Decision Types 5, 6, and 7, those involving curriculum, course, and program validation, are generally made by teachers, curriculum specialists, and principals. These decisions occur less often than Types 2, 3, and 4.

Type 8 decisions, which concern the effectiveness of administrative groupings in units within a system, are made by boards of education, superintendents, assistant superintendents, principals, evaluation teams, and voters. Type 8 decisions, generally related to productivity of the system or its parts, occur less frequently still.

Finally, Type 9 decisions, those involving the efficacy of the evaluation system, are made by evaluation specialists based on feedback about the content and process of evaluation methods. Decisions relating to the evaluation process itself are usually made less frequently than those relating to programs.

These discriminations of decision-makers by decision types serve to inform the designer of an evaluation system of the general requirements for data each decision-maker will need. They must, therefore, be included in the planning of any evaluation system that is to be effective.

The Impact of Decisions

There is one further dimension of the matrix of decision-makers and decisions that must be explored to set the contextual framework for an evaluation system. This dimension is that of the generality of impact of decisions to be made. By generality of impact is meant the size of the program unit a decision will affect: Will a given decision have an effect on just one person or class, on a group (e.g., a level or grade), or on a set of groups (e.g., a district)? Through determining the generality of impact of the types of decisions, the level of detail of the data needed for each decision-maker can be ascertained. For example, a decision affecting one student (e.g., Should a student progress to the next instructional unit?) requires very detailed data (Has that student mastered all the prerequisites?). Or, a decision that affects the entire district (e.g., allocation of state funds) requires data generated on a highly aggregated group basis (e.g., average reading achievement of all eight-year-olds in the district).

For purposes of this dimension, educational decisions can be divided into three categories of generality of impact:

Category I: Decisions about individual students or classes based on diagnostic test data.

Category II: Decisions about courses, programs, or curricula based on large group data (building, level, or preferably, district).

Category III: Decisions about schools, districts, regions, or statewide systems based on data gathered from groups larger than districts.

Each impact category of decision-making requires different aggregations of data because each affects a different size group. This can be better seen by examining some of the questions underlying possible decisions in each category of impact.

Some Examples of Questions Underlying Category I Decisions (e.g., those decisions to be made by a classroom teacher or teaching team. . . .):

(1)   Which students mastered the prescribed subject matter?
(2)   What objectives of instruction did each student know prior to instruction?
(3)   What learning did each student retain after instruction?
(4)   Which students need additional work on what objectives?

(5)   Which students do not need to go through a particular learning sequence since they can already perform the skill to be taught?

These Category I questions require data about how individual students or particular classes or other groupings perform in relation to specific learning objectives.

The data needed for Category II are considerably different from those needed for Category I. Examining some sample questions should show this difference.

Some Examples of Questions Underlying Category II Decisions (e.g., those decisions to be made by a teaching team, on a departmental basis, or by a curriculum coordinator. . . .):

(1)   What objectives should be added to the curriculum? (Or deleted?) (Or modified?)
(2)   Which objectives are few or none of the students meeting?
(3)   What instructional materials and programs work better in terms of student outcomes at each stage? For which types of students?
(4)   Which instructional modes work in having students achieve which objectives?
(5)   Which program units or levels in the educational system are in need of additional resources in order to achieve program objectives?

These are some typical Category II questions. It can be seen immediately that this category of decision-making has a wider generality of impact in that the focus is no longer on the individual student or class but rather on group data in general. Each of the decisions implied by the foregoing questions is appropriately based on large group data, as contrasted with the individual and small group data generated in the transitory context of a particular classroom.

Note that the impact of decisions in this category is more stable or general as contrasted with the more ephemeral day-to-day decisions relating to single students or particular classrooms. Here data are needed that allow the decision-maker to generalize beyond a particular individual or classroom group.

Some Examples of Questions Underlying Category III Decisions (e.g., those decisions to be made by such groups as the superintendent, regional director, or state department of education personnel. . . .):

(1)   To what degree are the pupils of the state attaining the goals toward

which public education is directed?

(2) To what degree are the pupils of each district attaining the goals toward which public education is directed?

(3) Which districts are attaining unusual success and what factors appear to be responsible for that success?

(4) Which schools are attaining unusual success and what factors appear to be responsible for that success?

(5) When new educational programs are introduced into the schools, do subsequent changes in pupil achievement indicate that the program is accomplishing its purposes?

Category III decision-making presents a yet larger picture: the concern is with generalizing to larger aggregates of individuals and of groups of individuals. One might say that the kind of data needed here are of "groups of groups."

If the decision is in Category I, then the evaluation model must collect detailed data for each individual student, classroom, or other instructional group.

If the decision falls into Category II, then the model must collect data on larger groups, such as those in a specific course, program, or curriculum.

If the decision is in Category III, then the model must collect data on aggregates of groups. (Sampling plans may have to be incorporated in order to collect data on these large aggregates.) The category of impact into which a particular decision falls further defines the generality of the data that need to be collected for it and so defines some of the parameters of an evaluation model applicable at several levels of the educational system.

To summarize the discussion at this point, several types of decisions typically made in the educational context have been reviewed in relationship to the effective management of educational programs. Some decision types are made much more frequently than others, while one is rarely made in the course of normal program operations. Although there is some overlap, generally there are one or two decision types made frequently by each decision-making group and not by others (e.g., Type 4 decisions are made by teachers). Finally, decisions may be categorized by the extent to which the relevant data base is generated on smaller or larger groups of people.

Implications for an Evaluation Model

The educational context of decision-making, the types of decisions, and the needs of decision-makers generate several implications for the planning and implementation of an educational evaluation model useful for optimizing the operation of educational programs.

First, the effectiveness of an evaluation model will be limited by the clarity of the structural and functional conceptualization of the educational system. In order for decision-making responsibilities to be allocated appropriately at each level of program operation, the structures and functions of the system must be explicitly and clearly identified. Without an explicit exposition of a system's program structures and functions, some decisions may be allocated to the wrong personnel or even simply not be made. Further, the decisions to be made must be clarified and associated with specific decision-makers.

Secondly, the goals and performance standards at each level of the system must be determined and formalized. This process of goal and performance standard identification is prerequisite to an assessment of the system's achievement. It simply is not possible to determine if a system is meeting its own goals if there are no goals or performance standards against which to measure the system's operations.

The goals must first be identified on a global and comprehensive level. They are then made successively more precise and specific down through the functional levels of the system until the learning outcomes of each program and instructional activity are precisely identified. As they are defined, the goals and other levels of performance standards should be associated with the appropriate decision-making level of the system structure. In this way, responsibility and accountability for decisions can be allocated to the proper personnel.

The third implication of the context and the decisions is that the evaluation model must include a data collection component that yields reliable, valid, and timely information about goal achievement. These data must be provided to each decision-maker at appropriate points in time, must be aggregated to the proper level of generality, and must be relevant to the decisions in question.

To be reliable, the data must be an accurate and stable measure of the behavior of concern to the decision-maker. Therefore, the samples of behavior elicited from respondents must be large enough to insure a large statistical probability that data about it are correct. Data produced by a single response to a request would be unreliable because the response might have been randomly chosen but coincidentally correct. Reliable data must come from a sufficiently large sample of behavior from the appropriate population unit. Thus, for reliable data from an individual, a large number of requests about the same goal must be asked. For reliable group data, the requests can be spread across the group, allowing fewer responses from each individual. The size of the group from which responses are sought depends on the generality of impact of the decision to be made.

The validity of data depends on the relationship between the estimates of performance, the measures used, and the performance standards being measured.

There must be a direct correlation between the test items used to measure achievement of goals and the content of the goals. The relevance of the data collected for decision-making, and therefore the appropriateness of the eventual decisions, is determined by the extent to which the measurement procedures actually assess performance related to the goals of the system at each level.

The validity of particular measurement procedures is in part a matter of judgment for content specialists in the goal area being measured. In fact, no entirely objective judgment of validity is possible, for the opinion of the content specialist always remains as one of the standards by which the validity of data collection instruments can be assessed. Therefore, it is necessary to involve content specialists heavily in the development of the data collection procedures and to incorporate editorial quality control checks into that development process.

The timeliness of data for decision-making is very important if the data are to be useful. The decision-maker must indicate the temporal parameters within which data are to be collected, analyzed, and reported. The frequency of data collection and reporting must also be determined by the decision-maker. Generally, the appropriate time framework and frequency of data collection are a function of the generality of impact of each decision. Data used for daily instructional management are needed much more often and within stricter time limits than data used for materials evaluation, for instance. In the first case, data must be gathered very frequently and the analysis made available to the teacher within 24 hours at the minimum. Evaluative information about instructional materials, on the other hand, might be collected over a time span of a year or more at regular intervals and reported back to the decision-maker at the end of a long assessment period. Thus, an evaluation model applicable to several program levels and several decision types must be capable of one-day data turn-around and adjustable upwards as is necessary or convenient for decision-makers.

A final implication for an appropriate evaluation model is that it must be able to accommodate change in the system it serves, in the content it processes, and in its own structure. An evaluation model that is effective will have to adjust to changes in the system it serves because that system is not static and evaluation must be carried on regardless of the structural or programmatic changes of its context. It must be flexible enough to change the content and format of the data it incorporates while retaining its own integrity. The model should be self-adjusting, continually examining its own processes and products and resolving any appearing discrepancies from its specifications. In addition, it should be able to incorporate alterations to itself from the outside without difficulty, so that the evaluation process can continue in an uninterrupted fashion.

The major implications of the educational context and decision-making

processes drawn in this discussion define the parameters for an effective evaluation model. The brief introduction to the model given in the definitions of the
Overview may now be expanded and the model's components more fully described.

The Criterion-Referenced Evaluation Model

A criterion-referenced evaluation model which accounts for the major implications of the program-related evaluation needs of an educational system or
district is portrayed in Figure 1.1. The first four components of the model have
been sufficiently elaborated to permit the discussion to focus immediately on
the less familiar components, beginning with evaluation design.

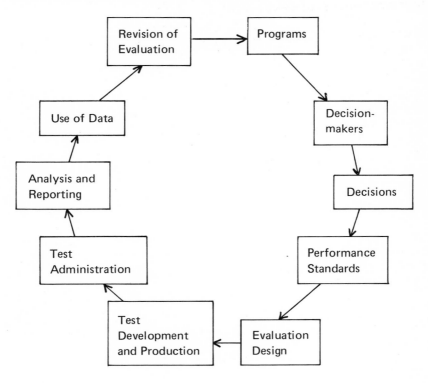

Elements of a Criterion-Referenced Evaluation Model

Figure 1.1

Evaluation Design

Evaluation design in the criterion-referenced evaluation model is generated through a process involving all relevant levels and types of decision-makers in the educational system. The outcomes of this process reflect the content and structure of the program area, the levels, and the units to be evaluated and the level of generality of the decisions to be supported through the evaluation design.

The evaluation design itself is a concrete and detailed plan showing how all the relevant types of data defining educational system performance are to be systematically collected in a certain time frame. The design accounts for the analysis of each unit of performance data and how such data are to be formatted or portrayed conveniently for decision-making. The basic elements of the design are questions or observations in the form of tests or schedules and a sampling plan for gathering student responses to them.

Figure 1.1 shows that the evaluation design component of the model is derived at that point in the cycle where an organized set of performance standards is available to define the expected outcomes of the program units of interest. The test administration cycle and data collection instruments then generated are a direct reflection of the underlying design or structure of the program unit and of the information needs of the participants in it. This structure is in turn a reflection of the organization of the behavioral content of the curriculum and the style or model of instruction which is applied to it. Many educational systems have unique structural elements and unusual approaches to instruction, with the result that the evaluation design will often require some unusual tailoring.

Test Development and Production

The outcomes of evaluation design include the selection of the types of tests needed, designation of the number of parallel forms of each type to be used in data collection, and specification of the content to be included in each test. From these portions of the design process, the actual tests can be developed.

In the design process, a detailed table of specifications is developed for each test document needed. Tables of specifications are exact prescriptions for tests. From the tables of specifications, each test is developed for use in the model.

Production of a test form is done by assigning test items to forms according to the tables of specifications developed in the evaluation design. Test items may be written by the decision-maker seeking the information (for example, a teacher) or by specialists employed for that purpose. Another option is to use an item bank, several of which are commercially available or in the public domain. Test items must conform to rigid standards with respect to the exactness with which they reflect the performance unit for which they are meant.

Actual assembly of test forms may be accomplished in a number of ways, ranging from the decision-maker assembling tests to the establishment of specialized test production departments in large-scale applications of the model.

Test Administration

The test instruments developed according to the tables of specifications in the evaluation design are administered in a controlled fashion to students on the basis of when and how often the decision-maker has stipulated a need for data.

In addition to the frequency of test administrations, the evaluation design also identifies which test forms are to be given during each administration. In designs calling for the use of item, objective, or student sampling techniques, the assignment of particular test forms to particular students must be done prior to actual test administration. The evaluation design will also indicate the sampling techniques to be used.

Analysis and Reporting of Data

The timely analysis and reporting of data for decision-makers' use is extremely important for the effective operation of an evaluation model. Unless the raw data collected can be analyzed and returned to the decision-maker at the appropriate point in time, the whole evaluation system may be useless. For profitable use in making many instructional management decisions, data must be analyzed and returned within a 24-hour period.

Modern data processing technology is necessary to support the rapid analysis and reporting of information required for daily instructional management. The tests used to collect raw data must be collected and transmitted to a data processing center immediately and the results tabulated, compiled to the appropriate level of aggregation, formatted into usable reports, and returned to the decision-maker as quickly as possible.

The level of aggregation of data and the report formats are determined beforehand, as noted in the evaluation design stage of the cycle. In general, these specifications are determined by the type of decision being made and the category of impact into which it falls.

Use of Data

The generation of usable data for making decisions and the exercise of those decisions embody the whole purpose of the criterion-referenced evaluation model. The very existence of a need for a decision implies a related set of questions for which answers must be obtained. The broad aim of an evaluation model is to generate a factual basis for producing possible answers to the questions of interest.

When the appropriate questions are asked through an evaluation design that provides reliable information at the necessary level of aggregation, the results of the evaluation process provide decision-makers with data on which to base informed and realistic decisions. Decisions based on alternative answers to appropriate questions suggested through a well-planned evaluation design enhance the system's achievement of its goals.

In more concrete detail, the decision-maker asks a relevant set of questions about his instructional program and the students involved in it. An appropriate evaluation design, together with the required tests, is applied to yield data needed for decision-making. The resultant data suggest one or more answers or causes of the events implied by the question. The decision-maker analyzes all probable causes, chooses the most likely cause — the probable answer to his question — and selects the best alternative action. This action is the decision.

Revision of the Evaluation Process

The need for flexibility in the evaluation model has been pointed out previously. Conditions change, goals change, curricula change. The evaluation system must be able to adjust to alterations in its context or in the content it carries.

As the context in which an evaluation model operates changes, the model is called upon to present different information in different ways to the decision-maker it serves. The evaluation process itself introduces a new element into the system and, as the results of the process are used in decision-making, the environment is continuously altered by those decisions.

Different or new priorities or new decision-makers introduced into the system lead to changes in the content the evaluation model carries. New goals and objectives, new test items, new evaluation designs, different reports and new levels of aggregation of data, changed formats for data reporting — all must be incorporated into the evaluation model without interrupting its ongoing service to decision-makers. The evaluation model must incorporate changes or additions as dynamically as the context or the information needs of decision-makers change.

The merger of the evaluation components described above defines an integrated and cohesive criterion-referenced evaluation model which accounts for the implications of the educational setting and is capable of serving the needs of the educational community. More detailed information about the components and the processes involved in implementing the model are presented in latter parts of the monograph.

Summary

Chapter 1 constitutes a review of the educational environment and the needs it generates for an evaluation model appropriate to the effective management of instructional programs. The external and internal contexts of educational evaluation have been explored. A discussion of decisions and decision-makers has illustrated the necessity of clear, concise, and appropriate data for educational decision-making. The implications of the data requirements for each decision-maker have defined the general parameters of an adequate evaluation model. Finally, the components of an evaluation model suggested by these implications have been determined and described.

The discussion in Chapter 1 has been of a general nature in regard to evaluation needs. In the next chapter the specific classroom situation will be examined in light of its evaluation requirements, and the contemporary evaluation methodology will be critiqued in the light of those requirements.

Chapter 2

Evaluation and the Classroom

To this point in the discussion, the implications of the educational context for the design of an appropriate evaluation methodology have been explored. The major components of a proposed methodology, in the form of a criterion-referenced evaluation model, generally appear to fit the broad needs for productive management of programs in an educational system. The present discussion is a further elaboration of the contrast between extant evaluation methods and actual needs. However, the focus of this discussion shifts to a more specific level of the educational context — the classroom — and the evaluation and testing methodology and technology ostensibly used to evaluate and manage instructional programs and individual progress in the schools.

Throughout this discussion, it should be kept in mind that gaps and inadequacies in evaluation and measurement procedures at one level of operation are felt throughout a system in the form of reduced capability to manage programs. An adequate evaluation methodology must be a coherent whole which accounts for every level and type of decision and supplies each decision-maker with appropriate evaluative information. Thus, if inappropriate evaluation designs and measurement procedures are used at the classroom level, the ability of the curriculum coordinator or the superintendent to manage programs in a larger sense will also be reduced. This results, obviously, from the fact that evaluation data for program management at higher levels of a system are largely aggregated compilations of data from lower levels.

The Classroom Context

In the context of the conventional American classroom, teachers and students are continuously involved in making decisions. These decisions, previously

27

classified into Types 2, 3, 4, 5, and sometimes 7, include initial and continuous placement; periodic monitoring of each student and of groups through the curriculum; managing and evaluating instructional activities, strategies, and resources; and assessing the curriculum itself. Evaluation and measurement procedures that provide adequate information for all these decisions are necessary for efficient management of the instructional environment and the individuals engaged in it.

The background of decision-making activities in this context may be conveniently analyzed in relation to a concept here called an "achievement pattern." The elements of an achievement pattern account for the objectives to be learned, the passage of time and events before, during, and after instruction, and the levels of performance students demonstrate on objectives over time.

The Ideal Achievement Pattern

Conceptually, what would a teacher desire as the ideal achievement pattern in relation to an objective by students? (Obviously, ideal situations are rare in reality, but for the purpose of illustration an ideal pattern is first considered.) Students would ordinarily be expected to learn objectives which they have not yet achieved but whose achievement is possible at this developmental stage. The teacher's selection should then not include objectives already mastered by students or those still out of their reach. Secondly, students should learn objectives to expected degrees through instruction. That is, learning should be facilitated by the instructor, or by a variety of instructional activities and materials, or by some other procedure planned in advance. Achievement of objectives should thus be related in time to the point at which instruction is completed. Thirdly, students should retain all the skills and behavior associated with objectives at least until the end of the course or program during which they are taught.

In the situation described, the achievement pattern for a specific objective would be considered ideal because:

(1)   The objective seems appropriate for the student because it has not been achieved before instruction and it was not too advanced for achievement. Therefore, it is associated with ideas and concepts new to the student prior to instruction and the educational activities can be maximally beneficial.

(2)   The instruction was effective because the student learned from the planned instructional activities.

(3)   Teaching was also effective in that after instruction the student retained and was able to use, for a relatively long time, the ideas and

skills associated with the objective.

Figure 2.1 is a graph of an ideal achievement pattern to aid visualization of the situation in more concrete terms.

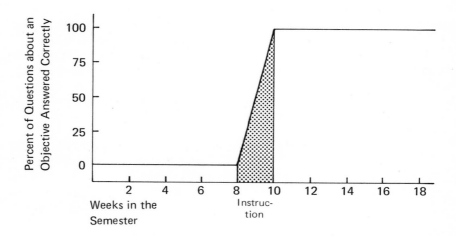

The Ideal Achievement Pattern

Figure 2.1

The graph shows one student's performance on a set of test items related to an objective tested repeatedly over the time of a course. Assuming that instruction on the objective is given during weeks 9 and 10, the graph shows that prior to instruction the student is able to answer no (or very few) questions relating to it. During instruction, the percentage of questions answered correctly rises rapidly. And after instruction has been completed, the student can answer correctly virtually all questions pertaining to the objective. The percentage of questions a student can answer correctly is a way of displaying his achievement of an objective.

As shown in Figure 2.1, an adequate evaluation of a student's achievement of an objective may well account for performance before and long after instruction, as well as immediately after instruction.

This ideal achievement pattern represents what most teachers would consider optimal student learning. In fact, much instructional activity seems to be planned and carried out as if this situation were the general rule in education.

Other Achievement Patterns

Obviously, all the achievement patterns encountered by teachers in their daily classroom duties are not ideal. In fact, few are. What characteristics would make an achievement pattern less than ideal? That is, what characteristics might imply that a student may be having problems in some part of the educational program, perhaps with the curriculum, perhaps with the instructional methods or materials or with the instruction itself, so that he does not learn an objective adequately? Generally, one of three characteristics can be identified in an unsatisfactory achievement pattern:

(1)   The pattern could show that the student had achieved the objective prior to instruction. This is unsatisfactory because time would be more productively spent on unrealized objectives.

(2)   The pattern could show that the student never achieved the objective during the course. This would indicate ineffective instruction or materials or erroneous student placement.

(3)   The pattern could show a slippage in achievement of an objective after the student initially learned it. This characteristic would indicate either a lack of long-range instructional impact or some occurrence or circumstance after instruction that interfered with achievement.

If a student has already achieved an objective, he should be allowed to withdraw from its instruction. If a student is scheduled to learn an objective, he should be helped to learn it without confusion and should remember it at least until the end of the course. Thus, an achievement pattern which shows a student has learned an objective prior to instruction, or which indicates lack of achievement immediately or well after instruction, clearly implies a need for change.

Let us look in more detail at several variant achievement patterns. They are presented in Figures 2.2 through 2.6 and are labeled alphabetically for the purpose of discussion. Each pattern displays a characteristic that implies incomplete student learning, inappropriate design of the educational environment, or unsuccessful instructional planning.

Pattern A, below, represents the achievement of an objective by a student who passed through a course without ever learning the objective. Instruction occurs during weeks 9 and 10, but the student never learns the objective. Possibly the instruction did not facilitate learning or the student was wrongly assigned the objective. It is also possible the student chose not to learn.

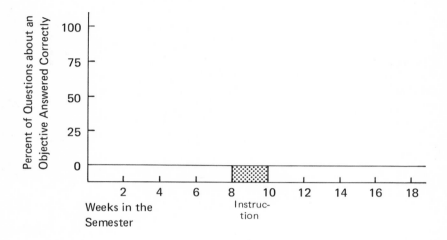

Pattern A

Figure 2.2

Pattern B, presented in Figure 2.3 below, illustrates another situation which teachers encounter. The student learns the objective through the instructional activities but is unable to retain the skills or concepts until the end of the course. The loss of skills or concepts could be due to later activities which confused the student or to insufficiently thorough teaching at the time of instruction. The situation is unproductive because the student leaves the course unable to use skills or concepts chosen for their importance.

In Pattern C, Figure 2.4, the student begins the course having already achieved the objective. Because the teacher does not discover this prior to instruction, the objective is taught unnecessarily. Time is wasted teaching an objective the student has already learned.

In the situation portrayed in Figure 2.5, Pattern D, the student has already achieved the objective but is confused by instruction and forgets it. Had the

32

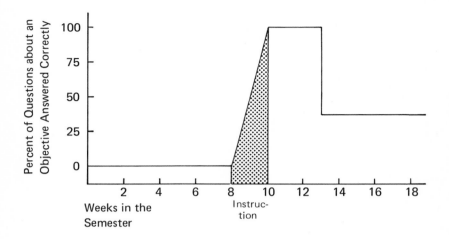

Pattern B

Figure 2.3

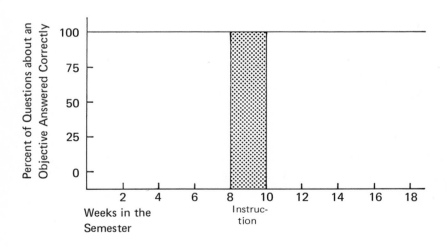

Pattern C

Figure 2.4

teacher discovered that the student had already learned the objective, the confusion created by redundant instruction could have been avoided. This situation not only illustrates the advantage of having prior achievement information but also indicates a need for continuous examination of the objective-directed performance.

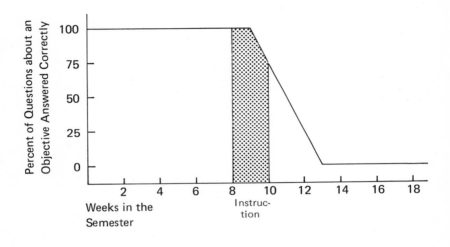

Pattern D

Figure 2.5

Finally, Pattern E, in Figure 2.6, shows that although the student has not learned the objective by the beginning of the course, some event, either outside the course or activity on a prior objective, results in its achievement before the instruction planned for it. Discovery of this pattern may not only save instructional time that would otherwise be wasted teaching an already learned objective, but also may reveal an unforeseen relationship between objectives in a course.

Achievement patterns illustrate a student's performance on an objective over time. The examples are only a small subset of all the patterns possible, but they serve to show the value of continuous information about a student's achievement of objectives for instructional planning. Yet, as informative as the achievement pattern for one objective is, it is clearly a small portion of the

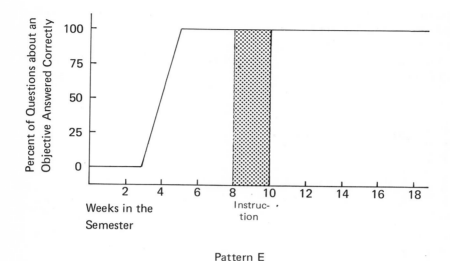

Pattern E

Figure 2.6

information needed from a comprehensive evaluation model applicable just to the classroom level.

A typical semester course will contain from 30 to 100 major objectives. At the elementary level the number may be somewhat smaller, while it may be larger at the secondary level. The achievement pattern may be considerably different for each objective. Some objectives might be learned ideally, while the achievement of others might result in other patterns. Thus, to obtain a clear picture of a student's overall performance or progress in a course or program, a continuous achievement pattern for all objectives is often necessary. An evaluation model that can collect, analyze, and report such complicated data is needed for adequate student achievement, instructional planning, and course revision.

Group Achievement Patterns

The description of achievement patterns above dealt with a single student's learning in order to introduce as clearly as possible a concept with the potential for a high level of complexity. In reality, instruction is usually carried out in a group context. This further complicates the problem of obtaining evaluative information for instructional planning and management. In addition to data relevant to individual assessment, group achievement information is needed to make reasonable instructional decisions for the group. Clearly, the number of possible combinations of individual student and group achievement patterns on each course or program objective could create a very large and diverse set of achievement patterns in one classroom.

However, in most classroom situations, various student groups often display common achievement patterns for a specific objective. The majority of a particular group's members thus comes to the objective with approximately the same level of achievement; therefore the instructional impact is about the same for most individuals. This sets the stage for teacher examination of group data as a basis for making limited generalizations about the effectiveness of instructional activities. Teachers will thus often find group data useful for ongoing instructional planning and revision.

To generate data for Decision Types 3, 5, 6, and 7, group achievement patterns can be extrapolated by compiling individual patterns or by taking samples of achievement from the group. For example, a group achievement pattern might show that 80 percent of the students in a class learned an objective several weeks prior to its instruction. This would indicate that instruction on an earlier objective might have had an unexpected relationship to the objective in question and might lead to some reorganization of instructional plans for the rest of the course. Other examples might show that very few students in a group learned an objective when instruction was given, that retention was low for a particular objective, or that one teacher had marked success teaching an objective in comparison to others. Such data would indicate needs for ongoing course revision.

Implications of Achievement Patterns for an Evaluation Model

The availability of timely performance data allows productive decision-making relative to students and instruction. Appropriate performance data may include student achievement measures on important objectives taken before, during, and after instruction. Furthermore, group data over the entire instructional time frame must be available for evaluation of the effectiveness of instructional methods or materials or of the curriculum itself. Only with such data can informed selection, endorsement, or revision be undertaken.

An adequate evaluation model would ideally collect data on each major objective during the total time of a course or program. Each of the objectives in this time frame may be associated with a different achievement pattern. There is no satisfactory way of generalizing the performance data on one objective to others. Achievement data on each important objective should thus be separately gathered.

Moreover, the collection of data related to each objective must also occur for individual students at several times during the course or program. Student achievement of an objective may change at any time during a curriculum sequence, not only when pertinent instruction is given. Therefore, measuring individual learning of objectives only at or near the point of instruction provides incomplete evaluative information for managing the total course of a student's program.

Current Measurement and Evaluation Methodology

The concept of the achievement pattern implies an evaluation model which periodically makes performance estimates available to decision-makers on all important curriculum objectives. This principle is known as time sampling. Time sampling is relevant when the performance of interest is likely to change gradually over time or goes through a series of "ups and downs" due to the influence both of known or controllable and of unknown or uncontrollable factors. This description seems to fit most learning situations.

Individuals and instructional groups vary in rates and styles of learning. While one group learns an objective in two days, another may take two weeks. The dynamic and fluctuating character of performance in a given situation is one important factor for the teacher to be aware of and consider in the instructional process.

Current Data Collection Design

Present evaluation procedures appear most inadequate when confronted with the foregoing data needs for productive program management. Usual practices for gathering performance data from students, individually and as groups, imply no continuous past or future. They operate only in the ephemeral present. Seldom is achievement monitored over a time frame of more than three to four weeks.

Consider, for example, the usual practice of giving a test following instruction in a course, program, or project. In this posttest design, part of the content of a unit is typically sampled at the conclusion of a unit. At the classroom level, the test deals only with the content of the immediately preceding unit. This approach is inadequate for several reasons. If, for instance, objectives in the unit had already been achieved, instruction would proceed on them anyway. If retention of the skills taught in the unit were poor and achievement fell off, a posttest would not reveal the impending slippage. In short, a simple posttest design fails to collect enough important information about learning. Such an approach is inefficient in terms of both comprehensively facilitating teaching and measuring achievement for the classroom teacher and for decision-making at other levels of a system.

Another approach to evaluation commonly practiced is the combination of a pretest and a posttest. Although this design eliminates some of the shortcomings of a posttest-only design, the total time frame involved is still not sufficient. Preinstructional achievement of objectives would be revealed, but any failure to retain skills would go undetected by the evaluation methodology. Again, the teacher's instructional decision-making would be based on incomplete achievement data and would remain, therefore, susceptible to considerable error.

These two approaches to evaluation, posttest-only and pretest followed by posttest, represent the prevalent modes of gathering data for contemporary instructional decision-making. Although this discussion has focused on the classroom level, these designs are also commonly used over longer spans of time for gathering decision-making data for other levels of educational systems. Regardless of the time frame in which data are collected, however, these designs are often inadequate. Collection of data about performance on each important objective must occur several times during a course or program to reveal achievement patterns for individuals and groups. Data gathered only once or twice do not provide sufficient grounds for decision-making at any program level.

Current Measurement Instruments

We have seen that the designs employed to gather data for evaluation are limited in that they restrict evaluation activities to a very short time frame. Therefore, the achievement patterns that longer-range data collection would reveal cannot be ascertained and much valuable information about student learning is lost. But, what of the content of the testing instruments generally used to collect data on the performance of the educational system? The question may now be generally posed: How relevant are the tests typically used to assess performance in the school setting to decision-makers' information needs?

Most decisions made in regard to instruction are associated with student achievement of specific learning objectives or groups of objectives. Although this connection seems apparent, it has been a major theme in the research and practical literature of evaluation only since 1963, when Glaser (1963) articulated the relationship.

Until the early 1960's, measurement procedures were primarily concerned with identifying differences among students in broad topical areas. This emphasis developed out of the tradition of testing for selection purposes. As applied in education, students' relative standing in wide areas of content was determined to support decisions about entrance into educational programs. A testing technology designed to gain the widest possible spread in student performance was applied to aid the selection process.

The comparative information collected through the use of such tests for making Type 1 decisions was eventually also used for summative program evaluation and curriculum validation. The appropriateness of these data for these purposes was assumed. Also assumed was the general relevance of the model for other types of decisions. In fact, this model is irrelevant to most types of educational decisions, especially the high frequency and high priority types that must be made in support of instruction at the classroom level.

The general irrelevance of the data gathered in current testing practices is partly the result of two questionable assumptions. First is the assumption that student competence at specific skills or concepts can be judged on the basis of comparative levels of achievement. The second assumption is that data collected about student achievement in broad content areas are generalizable and may be used to judge achievement of specific goals. Neither of these assumptions is apparently justified.

Data about relative student achievement may be useful in making such decisions as allocating entry positions in programs for which there are too many adequately qualified contenders. Colleges and universities, for example, must be able to select those candidates for entrance who seem most generally or broadly capable. However, achievement of a specific goal or task is based on competence at that goal only, and has not been shown to rest on general performance relative to a group. Similarly, achievement of a particular objective or group of objectives is most unequivocally judged on the basis of performance of tasks directly related to it, and possibly not at all on comparative performance on a related but very general measure. The use of relativistic comparisons of performance in general content areas provides no obvious or direct support of the decision-making in which educators continually engage in the operation and development of educational programs.

The performance data on which educational decisions rest are thus often gathered with instruments designed to initially support selection decisions. When information is required for ranking students in general achievement or aptitude, it is reported in relation to norms of achievement. Tests designed to discriminate among students in relation to norms of achievement are called norm-referenced tests. There are two common varieties of norm-referenced tests. The first of these is the "usual classroom test." The second is the "standardized test."

Usual classroom tests. Tests given by a teacher during and at the conclusion of instruction on a certain content area are classified as usual classroom tests. They are most often constructed by the teacher at the end of the instructional period and generally focus on an unspecified sample of the content taught. Often the tests include several trick or unusually hard items to insure that results produce a range of scores wide enough to permit assigning grades in a normal distribution.

Usual classroom tests have two major disadvantages. First, they are designed to sample across the content of units, major topics, or whole courses. They are not designed to yield the information needed by decision-makers dealing with specific objectives or higher-order performance units within courses. Secondly, the data are used primarily for ranking students and assigning general grades. Ranks are usually useful, it will be recalled, only for Type 1 decisions. Type 1 or selection decisions are made infrequently, and data for them have a low priority in the school context.

These disadvantages seriously limit the appropriateness of such tests for instructional decision-making. Even the assignment of grades could be improved if the data collected were systematically related to the specific instructional objectives. For instance, it would be more relevant and useful to report that a student learned 80 percent of the course objectives than to find he had earned a "B" ranking.

Standardized achievement tests. These tests are usually constructed to relate to broad topical areas, e.g., reading. The items selected, after a field test, are those which maximize the differences between high and low scoring students (Thorndike, 1971). Standardized achievement test results are usually given in terms of the student's percentile ranking in the group used to norm the test. This process of relating an individual's score to the norm is similar to ranking students within a class or course, except that the group to which the student is compared is the very large sample used to create the norm.

Although standardized achievement tests are developed in a highly professional manner, the data are of limited use for most instructional or program-related decisions. Since the content of such tests is not specifically related to any explicit set of goals or objectives, the data have little bearing on the ongoing instructional decision-making tasks which teachers and program managers must perform. For decisions at other levels of an educational system, such as comparative studies of instructional materials, the data yielded by standardized norm-referenced tests may be more useful, but again the usefulness is limited by the lack of a clear relationship between the system's goals and the test's content.

For instance, a teacher may want to check on the effectiveness of his teaching of certain skills to a class. He could administer a norm-referenced test at the beginning and end of the course. The percentile ranks of his students at these two times would reveal a gain, loss, or no difference of achievement compared to the norm group. However, there would be no information about instructional objectives on which students did poorly or very well, except as might be provided at the test maker's discretion. There is typically no information provided confirming that any students achieved the particular arrays of objectives and higher-order content units typically chosen in a course or program. There would be no specific information that any student had in fact learned anything absolute from the course, merely that he or she had moved from one rank to another, or not moved, in comparison to the norms of achievement. Neither course evaluation and revision information nor curriculum validation data would be forthcoming from the testing results. In short, very minimal sound decision-making benefits would accrue from the data generated at the classroom level by either usual classroom or standardized norm-referenced tests.

If educational evaluation procedures are based on normative concepts applied in classroom testing and the annual administration of standardized achievement tests, then it must be concluded that few if any relevant educational decisions are thereby supported at any level of the system. Relative or normative performance data accumulated from one level of the educational system to another do not thereby become more useful. Most of the relevant decisions at any educational level are appropriately based on absolute — not relative — criteria. The relevant questions are: Has the student achieved the objective? Or, how much of the objective or task has he achieved? Not relevant in most cases is: Has Johnny achieved a higher rank in the content or skill area than Mary? Or, does school A rank higher than school B?

In summary, norm-referenced testing, because its purpose is to compare students' performance in generalized content areas, does not provide data relative to student achievement of specific learning goals. Therefore it is largely inappropriate for gathering data to support goal-oriented decision-making. The predominant mode of data collection for evaluation incorporates student ranking and relative achievement differences. It supports selection decisions and some comparative evaluation activity. However, norm-referenced testing does not provide data relevant to many of the different decisions necessary to operate educational programs.

Contemporary Support Technology

Any system for evaluation includes some technical support components. Tests must be constructed or purchased; they must be scored after administration. Records must be kept of student results and decisions arising from them.

The effectiveness of a system for generating data is prescribed by the efficiency of its operating technologies as well as by its design or content relevance.

Test Development and Production

At the classroom level, the development and production of tests is generally left to the teacher. Evaluation design and test item development are appropriate activities for teachers, but typing, pasting, and mimeographing are more properly assigned to clerical support personnel. Teachers' time is valuable and should be spent teaching. Nor does the conventional context of test production allow for systematic and continuous refinement of testing procedures. A different mode of test production is needed to maintain long-term information on test items and forms and thus promote such revision of test elements as may be indicated. Centralizing the test development process, for example, can provide a convenient way of producing high quality tests and of making the curriculum a matter of permanent record. This could generate valuable information for program review and revision.

Test Scoring and Analysis

The tabulation of test scores, analysis of raw scores, and reporting of results often present serious problems, particularly to teachers. The usual classroom testing previously described typically involves hand scoring which may take from several hours to several days or weeks. Quite often the scoring takes the form of check or correct marks and a single grade computed by the teacher, e.g., 12 items correct, B-. With large classes, or with general or open-ended questions, such scoring can consume a very large amount of teacher time. While such scoring is in progress, the teacher has already moved on to the next unit of instruction. Even more problematical is the extent to which such unaided manpower can provide the means for analyzing and aggregating individual student data into the group data needed to support decisions about instruction and curricula.

In various educational systems, some tests are being scored by optical scanning machines or with marksense computer card forms. The analyses may then be accomplished by computer, as is frequently the case for the annual administration of standardized tests. Nonetheless, the turnaround time may still be as long or longer than with hand scoring because of demands made on a school system's computer for chores other than test analysis. Such test scoring and analysis arrangements are typically inadequate and too slow to provide data to those different decision-makers needing it.

With standardized tests, commercial scoring services are usually considerably slower than with the usual hand-scored classroom tests. In cases where the tests are sent out to be scored, it may be several weeks or even months before the data are returned. Whatever data may have been useful for instructional decision-making will thus be nearly useless by the time the teacher gets them back.

A comprehensive evaluation model must provide scoring and reporting of test results within a day or two for much of the most productive instructional decision-making. Such a capability is extremely rare and usually impossible, given current evaluation practices and supporting technologies. However, this capability should be one of the most important specifications for an efficient evaluation model.

Record Keeping

Records are kept in two dimensions for educational decision-making. First, there is the time framework of record keeping. Historical data are kept for individuals and for groups and sub-groups of many different characteristics. The longitudinal records are the foundation of much research and development, of much confirmation and denial of hypotheses, and of much decision-making.

Secondly, records are kept of varying aggregations of people, ranging from individuals to states and nations. Teachers need data about each student, about any instructional sub-groupings of the class or course, and about the whole class. Decision-makers at other levels of educational systems need data gathered from these and other groupings.

Currently used record keeping techniques maintain "paper-based" files of historical data on individuals, but rarely on groups or other levels of interest. In any event, most of this data is irrelevant to common educational decisions and little is of value to anyone, even the teacher who posts it in the form of permanent record files and class record books.

The most common record keeping in education is done in the teacher's grade book. However, such data, gained through usual classroom testing and consisting largely of student rankings, tell little about what students have learned, retained, or forgotten. They are of little help to a teacher making decisions about how a student has progressed from some point in the curriculum, about what revisions might be advisable in instruction, about which objectives to stress in teaching, or about other instructional concerns.

Another common record kept about students is the anecdotal file, in which supposedly helpful information is passed from one teacher to the next. This sort of information is very apt to be opinionated or prejudiced and its inclusion in permanent records is highly questionable.

Noticeably missing from most record keeping procedures are data about student achievement of specific learning objectives. This information would be of value for decision-making at all levels of programs. It would be very helpful to a student's new teachers. Unfortunately, such records are rarely kept.

An efficient record keeping system needs to be comprehensive enough so that at any point in time a teacher can determine for any individual or group which objectives have been achieved, which have been forgotten and by whom, which need reteaching or review, and which instructional activities seem to be working and which do not. The system must be easy to use and update. A record keeping system must be very detailed at some levels and highly aggregated at others. It must also be concise enough to retain its purpose of providing specific information rapidly and succinctly.

Standard record keeping practices obviously fall far short of the criteria for efficient and effective data storage and accession. Consequently, they do not serve efficient and effective decision-making.

Summary

Successful operation of educational programs requires information on which to base decisions. The primary context in which the information requirements of educational decision-making have been examined is the classroom. The teacher needs a continuous flow of individual and group data on achievement of instructional objectives. Without these data, many high priority and frequent decisions cannot be based on reliable grounds.

Decision-making at other levels of educational systems also depends on reliable, relevant data regarding student achievement. In the absence of these data, decisions must be reached on the basis of data collected through inadequate evaluation designs with largely irrelevant testing instruments.

Present methods of evaluating students and programs rest on an archaic set of assumptions about the relevance of data gathered with norm-referenced tests. The technology supporting the prevalent evaluation techniques is outmoded and inadequate. The assumptions and techniques must be replaced with new approaches grounded in more supportable theories about the relationship between instruction and evaluation. The new approaches must be supported by technology adequate to the task of supplying the needed data in a usable and timely fashion. Until educational decision-making is supported by an adequate evaluation model, programs will continue to be managed on the basis of incomplete information gathered by irrelevant techniques underlaid by questionable assumptions.

The components of an adequate evaluation model have been presented in this chapter. The technology to operate the model now exists. Its various aspects are discussed in the next chapter.

Chapter Three

Technology for
Criterion-Referenced Evaluation

Previous chapters illustrate the need for the right types of data, gathered in the context of an appropriate evaluation design, as a foundation for educational decisions concerning instruction. The inability of current measurement and evaluation procedures to provide appropriate data makes them largely inadequate for the decision-making needed in school systems. The failure to identify explicitly the responsible units, decision-makers, and decisions in the program structure of many educational systems further hinders the efficient flow and use of collected data. Continued use of outmoded data processing techniques precludes the availability of data within a usable time frame. Yet the management, design, data collection, and data processing technologies which would allow development of efficient and adequate decision-making processes for educational systems largely exist. The present chapter briefly explores these technologies and analyzes their availability and suitability for supporting the broad implementation of criterion-referenced evaluation.

An adequate management technology for criterion-referenced evaluation should facilitate documentation of an educational system's program structure and identify all decision-makers and their responsibilities. The evaluation technology should incorporate the new designs needed for measuring performance for courses, programs, and educational units at different levels and with different structures. The associated data collection technology should apply the principles of criterion-referenced measurement in a fashion to assure localized production of tests tailored to the needs represented by a given evaluation context with several levels of decision-makers. Finally, an extensive application of computer hardware and software technology must be applied to manage the continuous flow of a large amount of raw performance data, reduce the data to an electronically processible form, and produce the various reports needed by each level of decision-making. In recent years, these technologies have been refined to the point where they can be broadly and economically applied in support of criterion-referenced evaluation.

Management Technology

Management technology is the body of skills and concepts which allows systematic analysis of the structures and functions of an organization and revision of those structures or functions which inhibit the organization's progress toward its goals. The discussion in the first chapter about the inner and outer contexts of educational systems drew on management technology for an analytical perspective from which to view educational decision-making. Procedures for defining educational program structures and functions have been outlined by Hartley (1968) in his work on PPBS and by others. The Western New York State PPBS model (Kiser & Murphy, 1972) offers suggestions on defining a district's program structure in terms of its responsible units, its program categories, its levels, and the resources allocated to it.

There are also materials available to guide the process of creating subdivisions in the responsible units of a school district. Specific responsibilities can then be assigned. The decision-makers can be identified and the decisions they must make related directly to their positions in the levels of the educational system. This process can be utilized at any level of an organization.

A literature has also developed concerning the concept of management by objectives (MBO). This literature attempts to interrelate personnel at each level of an educational system with their responsibilities and their decisions. The concern of the MBO literature has been to establish a procedure by which management can create objectives for organizational operations. By creating these objectives and allocating decision-making authority and accountability to the organization's personnel, management is able to clarify the roles and responsibilities of personnel and to pinpoint the source of malfunctions in the system's programs.

At the instructional level of an educational system, management of students through a curriculum is best facilitated by curricular objectives. Procedures for writing and preparing objectives for instructional use have been available for a long time (Mager, 1962). There are even materials now available for deriving objectives at different functional levels, e.g., terminal objectives, course objectives, enabling objectives, etc. (Ammerman & Melching, 1966). The types and levels of objectives needed for complete instructional management have been fairly well conceptualized, as have methods for structuring and organizing them into curricula (Skager, 1971). Methods have also been worked out for involving community groups and professional specialists in deriving and organizing educational goals.

In addition to available methods for creating objectives originally, there are now extensive banks of curricular objectives in the public domain and from commercial sources. Often other school districts are willing to share their objective-based curricula as models.

These management tools are much more widely available now than they were only five years ago. They make resources for the design of efficient organizational structures and functions much more accessible now than ever before. They contribute to the design of objective-based curricula and facilitate the decision-making process by enabling the collection and appropriate analysis and distribution of goal-oriented data. Their use is essential for the creation of a viable criterion-referenced evaluation model.

Evaluation Design

The specifications for the amount and frequency of data collection for an evaluation system comprise the evaluation design. As previously noted, evaluation designs have frequently consisted of simple pretesting and posttesting with norm-referenced tests developed in a national sample. The application of evaluation designs better fitted to the educational context was limited in part by the lack of a sophisticated data processing technology. An adequate criterion-referenced evaluation system must break away from the conventions of typical research or evaluation designs and create a new design technology suited to the specific information needs of each different level of educational decision-maker. Evaluation methods for a general criterion-referenced model must incorporate a variety of designs to fit the information needs in the many levels and structures of educational systems. Moreover, the designs applied at each level must be fully and systematically articulated.

Much progress has recently been made beyond the pre- and posttesting and survey testing designs currently widely used to collect raw data. Item and subject sampling techniques have been developed and applied which provide a means for continuous assessment of important isolated or grouped objectives and goals at many levels of an educational system. Unique combinations of traditional designs have been created for criterion-referenced evaluation in both individually and group-paced programs. Variety in the types of tests, assessment cycles, and sampling techniques has generated a capacity to tailor evaluation designs to many different situations.

An example of a situation needing a considered evaluation design illustrates the types of new designs which can be tailored to the needs of a particular context.

The situation for which the evaluation was designed is a semester-long high school biology course. One hundred eighty students are divided into six sections. There are two teachers. One teaches four sections, the other teaches two. There are 90 objectives in the course, split into six units of 15 objectives each. Instruction in the course is group-paced. The teachers wanted to assess the general achievement level of the entire course enrollment at the beginning, middle, and end of the course. They also wanted to collect performance data on each student after the end of each unit and preinstruction information on the objectives of the next unit. This would allow them to assess the effectiveness of instruction in each unit, plan for a review session where necessary, and stress some objectives in the next unit more heavily than others where preinstruction data indicated such emphasis would be valuable.

The evaluation design appropriate to this biology course called for testing the entire range of objectives three times, once before any instruction was given, at mid-semester, and at the end of the course. To obtain information on the group standing in relation to the objectives without subjecting every student to a lengthy test covering all objectives, the 90 objectives were split into three groups in an application of item and time sampling. Thus each student would get a test covering every third objective three times in the course. The tests contained 30 items, one for each of the objectives tested. Over the course of the three test administrations, each student would take an item on each objective. The 180 students would be randomly divided into three groups, each group getting a test over a different one-third of the objectives. Thus, 60 responses would be collected on each objective in the course at each test administration, a large enough sample to give good group achievement information on each objective.

Also included in the evaluation design were six tests measuring all the objectives in each of the six units and a sample of the objectives in the unit following. At the end of instruction on each unit, each student took a unit test with 37 or 38 items. Thirty of the items related to the 15 objectives in the unit, two for each objective. This measured each student's achievement of that unit's objectives and allowed the teachers to plan one class section of review in the objectives which were poorly achieved, either by the whole enrollment or by one section. It also gave the teachers information on which to base revision of instructional methods or materials where necessary. The remaining seven or eight items on the test each related to one of the objectives in the following unit, giving 90 responses to items on each objective in the following unit, again a large enough sample to give reliable preinstructional group data to guide activities in the next unit.

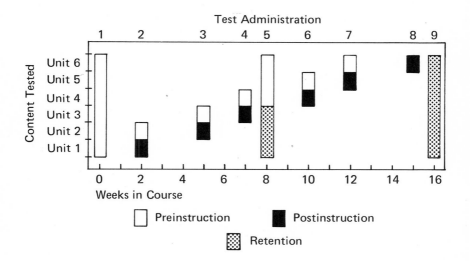

An Evaluation Design

Figure 3.1

The evaluation design applied to this biology course, visualized in Figure 3.1 above, allowed the teachers to gear instructional activities to fit the needs of the students, to make any revisions that achievement indicated as necessary in methods or materials, and to compile definitive achievement patterns for each student. Careful analysis and structuring of the course goals and objectives led to this evaluation design, which in turn generated the precise data needed for decision-making in this situation.

Progress in evaluation design has permitted greater sophistication in the collection of data for educational decision-making. When objective-based tests are administered within the framework of a thoughtful evaluation design, the data necessary for educational decisions can be collected efficiently and precisely.

Testing and Measurement

The data to be collected by a criterion-referenced evaluation system are measures of student achievement of curricular goals and objectives. To gather this kind of specific information about achievement, a new measurement instrument — the criterion-referenced test — is incorporated into the model. The tests must be produced in relationship to locally selected objectives to insure their relevance to the programs of the school district. Under most conditions, the test production should also be a local operation so that changes can be readily made and the numbers of tests needed can be provided on a timely basis. In the model, a test production capability is included as an integral component.

Criterion-Referenced Tests

A new measurement technique which emphasizes the design of tests to provide information about specific performance on objectives of particular instructional programs has been developed. In this technique, test items are not typically written for a high discrimination capability. Rather, test items and tests are developed to measure whether or not students can perform objectives to a specified level or criterion of achievement. Therefore, these tests are described as criterion-referenced.

This strategy for developing educational tests has become increasingly popular since it was first introduced by Glaser (1963). A growing literature is concerned with criterion-referenced testing, including Popham (1971), Glaser and Nitko (1971), and Gorth and Hambleton (1973).

Criterion-referenced tests are typically designed to measure whether a student or group can or cannot perform a behavior specified by an objective or group of objectives. They contain only test items related directly to previously stated desired student learning outcomes. Generally the results of criterion-referenced testing are reported in terms of whether students or groups could meet the achievement criteria or not.

The relationship between test items and instructional goals and objectives in criterion-referenced evaluation generates data which directly support decision-making activities in educational systems. Decisions affecting individual students are made on the basis of each student's achievement of the goals of instruction. Decisions affecting groups of students are made on the basis of group achievement of curricular objectives, determined by aggregating individual scores. The relative effects of different educational treatments can be determined by comparing the performance of the different treatment groups on program goals. Not only are relative comparisons of this type possible, but the differences can be seen in relation to specifically isolated skills and concepts (absolute comparisons).

The results of criterion-referenced testing are not used to rank students. The focus is on monitoring and making decisions about student learning of particular program content. Criterion-referenced test results allow teachers to judge individual competence in program goals and objectives. Decisions about modified or additional learning activities for students are more readily reached when data related to instructional objectives are available. Similar data about group achievement, compiled from the achievement of group members, enhances decisions about instruction in a group context. At still higher levels of educational systems, more highly aggregated criterion-referenced achievement data facilitate decision-making about methods, materials, and curricula.

Criterion-referenced tests and test items appropriate for use with local programs are available commercially and publicly. Among the commercial suppliers are Westinghouse Learning Corporation, CTB/McGraw-Hill, and National Evaluation Systems. Sources of tests in the public domain include the Instructional Objective Exchange (IOX) at UCLA, the CO-OP at the University of Massachusetts, the System for Program and Pupil Evaluation and Development (SPPED) in New York state, and several ESEA projects at Hopkins, Minnesota and at Downers Grove, Illinois. All of these sources maintain banks of objectives and criterion-referenced test items which may be accessed by school districts which have described their curricula in terms of performance objectives. Local item banks for test production may thus be established.

Criterion-referenced measurement techniques provide the base for data collection directly related to the needs of educational decision-makers. Though a relatively new development in education, they offer a much more relevant approach to providing the data on which sound educational decisions may be based because the data may be directly related to program goals and objectives.

Test Development and Production

Once a school district has made a decision or is in a position to access sources of criterion-referenced tests and test items, a local capability to develop and produce tests tailored to the specific needs of teachers and other decision-makers on a day-to-day basis must be established. Pinsky, White and Gorth (1972) have shown in their monograph on objective and test item banking procedures how to organize a system for local test production. The procedure involves creating files of locally used objectives and related test items. The test items are filed on separate master cards in a bank. Test masters are developed from test specification forms submitted by decision-makers. The specification forms indicate the items each test should contain and their positions within the test. Once a master has been edited and approved by the decision-maker, it is used to reproduce the appropriate number of copies for students. The test item file cards stored in the bank have space for item analysis information to be recorded. The item analysis data thus kept are useful for revision of the test items.

A local test production facility is able to respond readily to changes in courses and programs that need to be reflected in the evaluation system. Tests produced by district personnel are available on demand and in appropriate quantities. The need for storing large quantities of tests procured from outside vendors is eliminated. Local revision of testing instruments and procedures is convenient. Dependence on uncontrollable outside organizations is reduced. The availability of procedures for school districts themselves to produce high quality tests for data collection makes the implementation of locally based and sensitive criterion-referenced evaluation more feasible than it has ever been previously.

Data Analysis, Reporting, and Record Keeping

Realistic, informed decision-making in any field requires reliable, timely data. Criterion-referenced testing and advanced evaluation designs facilitate the planned collection of appropriate data, but those data must be processed from raw to usable form before decisions can be based on them. Hand-scoring techniques and cumbersome file-card record keeping have been noted as inadequate to refine the data in a workable time span. Therefore, modern data processing technology is necessary to analyze and report the data to decision-makers. This data processing technology has three components: hardware, software, and reporting documents.

Hardware

The machines that process data include the computer itself and the peripheral equipment needed to input and output the information — disc cartridge device, magnetic tape device, card reader, line printer, etc. This hardware can be made available for use in an evaluation system in three ways. First, processing services can be purchased from a commercial or university computer facility. Or, in school districts which maintain an administrative computer, the facility can be shared with the evaluation system during times when it is not needed for administrative tasks, normally at night. Thirdly, hardware dedicated to the evaluation system can be leased or purchased and a data processing staff maintained for the evaluation system. Each of these options has relative advantages and disadvantages. It is worth noting that all the options are less expensive and more flexible than they were even five years ago and that they all fit the requirements of a criterion-referenced evaluation system.

To illustrate the availability and relevance of one of the options listed above, an explanation of the hardware system incorporated into the Sequoia High School District, California, evaluation system is given.

There are approximately 110 teachers instructing 7500 students in 80 courses served by the criterion-referenced evaluation system in this district. To process the data, the district has purchased a mini-computer with a disc operating system, a card reader, and a high-speed line printer at an initial cost of about $70,000. Preprocessing data reduction is accomplished in a separate operation whereby the marks made on answer cards are converted into punches for the card reader. The data reduction equipment is leased by the district for $300 a month.

During the school day, the computer operates on-line with 16 terminals installed in the six high schools for student use. At the close of the school day, the hardware is shifted into a batch processing mode to support the evaluation system. Two thousand student tests can be scored and analyzed during the batch processing shift, with reports being returned to the teachers the morning following testing. Two full-time data processing operators are employed to run the hardware for both its uses, at a cost of $300 per week.

The present volume capacity of 10,000 student tests a week is more than adequate to support the monitoring system for this district. Data are processed through the system rapidly and efficiently to provide information when the teachers and students need it by this simple hardware configuration.

The scenario above is one example of how computer technology is now meeting the needs of criterion-referenced evaluation at realistically affordable costs. Descriptions of hardware applications under the other alternatives could have made the point as well, and the choice of this option for illustration is not an endorsement of its relative value for an evaluation system.

Software and Reports

The input forms and the computer programs that instruct the hardware in processing data comprise the software component of data processing technology. Considerable effort has been given to developing data entry formats that facilitate speedy turn-around time and economic processing of the information. There are now a number of options to expedite data input for a variety of situations. The sample reports shown later in this discussion are produced by the CAM3 System (National Evaluation Systems, 1973) used widely in the SPPED program in New York State.

A number of new comprehensive computer programs are now available.

They provide data analysis capability for a wide spectrum of information needs and thus for a range of decision-making requirements. Furthermore, the present programs operate at lower cost than their predecessors, as the experience of developing a criterion-referenced evaluation model has led to continuous refinement of the data processing function. The present programs also operate on many manufacturer's computers.

An evaluation system complex and sophisticated enough to provide information for decision-making at many levels of an organization must produce reports of analyzed data covering many areas of content in many degrees of compilation. A variety of report formats is necessary.

The output generated in this criterion-referenced evaluation model gives information for decisions about individual students, groups of students, curricula, teaching strategies, instructional materials, and other topics of concern to decision-makers. The content of the reports depends on the area being scrutinized. The formats are designed to facilitate ease of interpretation for the particular decision in question. The test of time has shown the reports in this model to be succinct and widely usable.

Figure 3.2 is an Individual Student Report generated by the CAM3 System. The student's name, identification number, class section, and teacher's name appear across the top. Below the student's name is the test administration number and date. Below the teacher's name is the course code number, and below that the number of the test form given the student. Below the test administration number and date are two lines showing the fraction of the items in the test the student answered correctly. The upper "Fraction Correct" line gives the total number of correct student responses on all items of the test; the lower line, the number of correct items on objectives for which instruction has been completed (YES ITEMS).

Below the "Fraction Correct" lines are two sets of four columns. The first column of each set, labelled QP, tells the question position on the test. The column headed OBJ signifies the objective to which that question is related. The RP column gives the response choice of the student and a plus or minus sign to indicate whether the response chosen was correct. (If a student had made no choice, a 0 would appear.) Finally, the column headed INS indicates if instruction has been completed on that objective. Over the course of several test administrations, the cumulative information on each objective would indicate the student's mastery of each as time passed.

To the right of the two sets of columns is a section showing the performance history of the student for each test taken thus far in the course. The fractions correct for the total items and for the instruction-completed (YES) items are given for each test. Below the performance history section is a

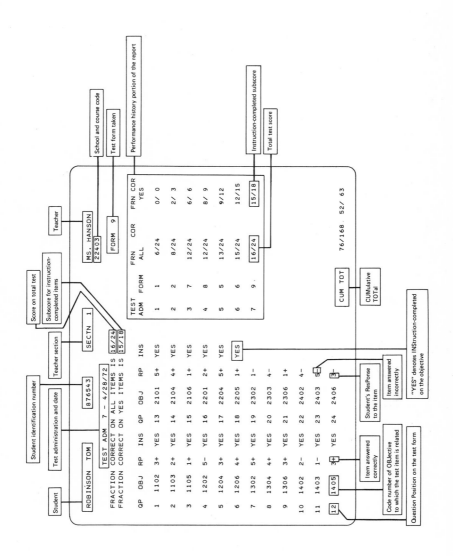

An Individual Student Report

Figure 3.2

cumulative total for all tests taken, again broken into total and instruction-completed scores.

The Individual Student Report allows the teacher to analyze each student's performance in the course and decide about review needed, appropriateness of materials and instruction, and other aspects for each student. This kind of information permits the teacher to diagnose individual progress and prescribe any corrective treatment that may be revealed as necessary.

The example presented above is one of many reports generated by the model. Its level of application is at the instructional interface of student and teacher. Other formats contribute to materials evaluation, curriculum validation, analysis of the effectiveness of administrative units, and other areas of concern. The needs of the decision-maker dictate the particular content and format of any given report, but each is specifically designed to present the appropriate data in a format appropriate for the decision.

The data processing technology used in this criterion-referenced evaluation model supports a large variety of evaluation designs, in many content areas, and at any level in the educational system. It is currently available and being used in many school districts throughout the country. Continuous advances in hardware, software, and report designs will broaden the applicability and desirability of criterion-referenced evaluation in the future.

Record Keeping

The information displayed in the Individual Student Report in Figure 3.2 is useful for daily instructional assessment and decision-making. It is also necessary for records to be kept over relatively long periods of time. Data as detailed as those in the Individual Student Report are not necessary for those long-term information needs, but records are needed that show student progress through curricula over time.

The Teacher Roster List shown in Figure 3.3 keeps records of student progress in a more concise form. It allows longer-range evaluation of individual and group progress through a course or program. The Teacher Roster List displays student achievement on tests, again broken into total and instructed fractions correct. In the CAM3 System, from which the report is drawn, it is possible to include scores for up to 50 tests. Using the Teacher Roster List, a teacher can see at a glance which group members are making satisfactory progress and which are not, possibly using the information as a basis for forming special review or reteaching groups on various portions of the curriculum

Figure 3.4 is still another of the reports generated by the CAM3 System. The Group Summary Report provides the percentage of correct student

```
┌──────────────────────────────────┐        ┌───────────────────┐
│ Information taken from performance│        │   Teacher NumBer  │
│ history portion of the individual│        │                   │
│ Student Report                   │        └───────────────────┘
└──────────────────────────────────┘
```

```
       COMPREHENSIVE ACHIEVEMENT MONITORING - TEACHER ROSTER LIST        22403
MADISON HIGH READING PROGRAM              SECTN 6      TNE  48        MS. HANSON

                           CUM                    TEST ADMINISTRATION
NUMBER        NAME         TOT      1        2        3        4        5        6

234512 CLARK SALLY S     ALL    61/120   6/24     0/ 0     8/24    10/24    17/24    20/24
                         YES    36/ 42   0/ 0     0/ 0     6/ 6     6/ 9     9/12    15/15
                         FORM      2        0        4        1        3        9

532614 DIMOND THOMAS W   ALL    99/144   7/24    16/24    17/24    18/24    21/24    20/24
                         YES    43/ 45   0/ 0     3/ 3     5/ 6     8/ 9    12/12    15/15
                         FORM      4        5        1        3        2        8

412356 HENDOM ROBERT P   ALL   111/144   8/24    20/24    21/24    23/24    19/24    20/24
                         YES    45/ 45   0/ 0     3/ 3     6/ 6     9/ 9    12/12    15/15
                         FORM      3        1        7        4        5        3

234765 KELLY ANN S       ALL    69/144   3/24    10/24    12/24    13/24    15/24    16/24
                         YES    38/ 45   0/ 0     3/ 3     6/ 6     7/ 9    10/12    12/15
                         FORM      2        6        4        1        3        9

876543 ROBINSON TOM      ALL    60/144   6/24     8/24    12/24    12/24    13/24    15/24
                         YES    37/ 45   0/ 0     2/ 3     6/ 6     8/ 9     9/12    12/15
                         FORM      1        2        7        8        5        6
```

Teacher Roster List

Figure 3.3

responses to questions relating to specified content. Therefore, it provides valuable data for formative and summative program evaluation and for curriculum validation. Information of this nature would be useful at many program levels in an educational system.

As can be seen on the report, data can be collected on single objectives or on groups of objectives. The decision-maker specifies in advance what degree of aggregation is needed, depending on the extent of curriculum content under scrutiny. Thus a teacher might want to have data on single objectives and a course unit, while a curriculum coordinator might wish information only on the major division of the content of a course.

A variety of records must be kept by an adequate evaluation model to provide decision-makers with all the data necessary to make decisions in support of educational programs. A data analysis and processing component and a record

- Designation of student group by code number
- Student group label
- Content Group Number
- Total NUMber of items related to the content group across all student's of the group
- PerCenT of items related to the content group answered correctly by the student group

COMPREHENSIVE ACHIEVEMENT MONITORING - GROUP SUMMARY REPORT
MADISON HIGH READING PROGRAM 22403
STUDENT GROUP 7200 ALL MR. SMITH'S STUDENTS

CGN	CONTENT GROUP		1	2	3	4	5	6	7
	NUMBER OF STUDENTS		85	88	86	89	90	86	88
0	ALL OBJECTIVES	PCT	35	42	46	52	60	64	68
		NUM	2040	2112	2064	2136	2160	2064	2112
11	UNIT 11	PCT	36	80	75	76	72	74	73
		NUM	255	264	258	267	270	258	264
13	UNIT 13	PCT	37	36	42	73	80	82	78
		NUM	255	264	258	267	270	258	264
14	UNIT 14	PCT	28	29	41	46	60	62	75
		NUM	255	264	258	267	270	258	264
1301	OBJECTIVE 1301	PCT	36	41	43	80	79	82	76
		NUM	42	44	43	45	45	43	44
1401	OBJECTIVE 1401	PCT	38	45	39	38	46	51	48
		NUM	43	44	43	44	45	43	44
2201	OBJECTIVE 2201	PCT	20	18	26	25	20	26	79
		NUM	43	44	43	45	45	43	44

Group Summary Report

Figure 3.4

keeping system capable of generating, storing, and retrieving information relevant to a school district's unique needs must therefore be integrated into a criterion-referenced evaluation model.

Costs and Benefits

The basic elements of technology necessary for applying criterion-referenced evaluation procedures to educational systems have been developed and are feasible for current use. The increased sophistication and relevance they offer to program analysis and decision-making in education imply both costs and benefits for involved school districts.

Costs

Implementation of criterion-referenced evaluation does add to operating budgets of school districts. The financial costs for a comprehensive criterion-referenced evaluation system involving all the students in a district in four or five curricular content areas could add as much as $30 a year per student to the over-all operating budget. A lower level of involvement, in two or three content areas, could cost $10 a year per student to generate all the reports needed by decision-makers at various levels in the district. In addition, there are initial costs associated with organizing courses and programs on an objective basis, with developing testing instruments, with training staff in the system's use, and with other aspects of beginning a new approach to evaluation. Though the developmental work on the resources to accomplish these tasks has largely been done, implementation of any already developed system does involve expenses.

In addition to financial costs, there are social or organizational costs involved in the implementation of a criterion-referenced evaluation model. Changes in individuals' lives demand an expenditure of their energies and emotions. Such expenditures often are taxing to the point of individual and organizational discomfort and friction. Nevertheless, change cannot be avoided. When it is, stagnation and organizational breakdown inevitably occur. The advantages of criterion-referenced evaluation almost mandate its future widespread use. A foresighted system will anticipate each change and plan organizational activities and training programs that enhance the acceptance of the changes in people's roles and behaviors and the use of the new technologies. Considerable thought should be given to the need for orientation and training before any decision for implementation is reached.

Benefits

The costs associated with criterion-referenced evaluation are, of course, accompanied by benefits. The goals of the system are explicitly formulated and their achievement regularly monitored. Feedback on performance is presented in absolute terms. More clarity is introduced into the district's programs. Decisions are based on a foundation of concrete data. Role expectations and responsibilities for system personnel and clientele are made more definite. Programs operate more efficiently and productively. Their goals and content can be made more relevant. Participation in the goal setting process can be widened.

Criterion-referenced evaluation aids in managing a district's programs more efficiently at every level. It should therefore generally make programs more productive as shown by several reports disclosing that after involvement in the model, student achievement on standardized and other tests improves relative to non-CAM student achievement (Adams, 1973; Sequoia, 1973). Other studies tend to show that simply using performance objectives to guide instruction heightens achievement (Duchastek & Merrill, 1973; Rothkopf & Kaplan, 1972; Kaplan & Simmons, 1974; Dalis, 1970). The availability of rapid, direct performance feedback should have an even greater effect because information is thus provided for the day-to-day management of instruction in the classroom and for higher-level decision-making about the programs, program units, processes, and materials used in a district. The effective implementation of criterion-referenced evaluation will ultimately direct attention to achievement of the broad goals of the district, giving clear guidance to the decisions necessary to continue and improve program operations at every level.

A system of criterion-referenced evaluation will also make a district's operations more humane, for it necessitates clear formulation of the expectations for each person and allows a definitive statement regarding achievement of those expectations. This clarity should emphasize the individualization of expectations and achievement to reduce the anxiety inherent when goals are undefined and performance measures are relative.

Because goals and expectations are clearly stated when a criterion-referenced evaluation system is operative, analysis of the relevance of the district's programs to the needs and desires of its constituencies is more readily done. Additionally, the district with clarified goals and processes should be able to respond more coherently, directly, and decisively to any deficiencies such an analysis might reveal.

In the process of goal setting for a criterion-referenced evaluation system, all individuals touched in any significant way by the educational system must necessarily become involved. This wide involvement takes away much of the hiddenness of important decision-making generally apparent in organizations. People thus gain a voice in the setting of goals and standards that affect their own lives. In terms of student and parent involvement, this should work to eliminate much of the bitterness and confusion many feel about the functioning of the schools. In terms of teacher accountability, a subject of much current educational discussion and rancor, this should engender teamwork between teachers and management in the establishment of appropriate standards for staff evaluation. By recognizing everyone as a decision-maker and outlining the decisions each must make, a criterion-referenced evaluation system can justly allocate authority and accountability.

A criterion-referenced evaluation system integrates technology into a school district's operations rather than imposing it over them. The uses of technology in criterion-referenced evaluation are beneficial to the users. For instance, testing becomes a diagnostic tool and servant for both teacher and student rather than a means of comparing or ranking students with each other in a competition which no one wins. For too long, testing has been perceived by students as the club with which teachers separate the worthy from the worthless. The damage to self-images that has resulted from this inappropriate use of measurement cannot be estimated. Criterion-referenced testing allows teacher and student to see each other as partners on a team cooperatively working toward a goal.

The establishment of goals and objectives for an educational system increases the system's efficiency. By clarifying the expectations of personnel and clients, a criterion-referenced evaluation system facilitates goal-directed behavior. Behavior that is not aimed at system goals becomes too obvious and irrelevant, and tends to diminish. One not unexpected manifestation of this already noted is that average student achievement levels have risen in classes using criterion-referenced evaluation systems. This gain in performance levels seems related to the student's understanding of the purposes of instruction, to the presence of direct performance feedback, and to the more efficient nature of instructional programs aimed at definite goals. Thus, there is evidence that both staff and client efficiency rise.

A criterion-referenced evaluation model is implemented in a school district to increase the availability and usefulness of information for decision-making at all levels. In addition to this result, criterion-referenced evaluation also brings a number of other benefits to the operation of educational programs. The benefits may have far wider consequences than simply a considerably increased ability to formulate decisions based on solid evidence.

The benefits of criterion-referenced evaluation must be measured against its costs. Each educational system's leadership must consider whether a more efficient and humane operation is worth the additional financial expenditure. The social costs of implementing criterion-referenced evaluation procedures must be measured against the social costs of continuing to rely on outmoded theories and techniques of evaluation and decision-making.

Summary

The management, data collection, and data processing technologies needed to support criterion-referenced evaluation are developed and available at reasonable expense. Their costs and benefits must be balanced against each other. Though the costs, in financial and social terms, may initially be high, the benefits are considerable and lasting.

The first Part of the monograph has introduced the concept of criterion-referenced evaluation and given an overview of a model. The context of educational decisions and the needs for data to support decision-making have many implications for an effective evaluation model. The data needs of educational decision-making at the instructional level are for quite detailed information; at higher levels they are for more aggregated achievement data. A criterion-referenced model gathers appropriate data and incorporates a technologically based capacity for analysis and timely distribution of data at all levels. It, therefore, appears adequate in theory. Its current application in many school districts shows it to be adequate in practice as well.

The remainder of the monograph describes the model's components more thoroughly, beginning, in Part II, with the role of objectives in evaluation.

PART II

The Organization of Objectives for Criterion-Referenced Evaluation

The derivation of an appropriate evaluation design is based on a thorough analysis of the unique structure and elements of a given curriculum in a program area. The effective application of evaluation design principles requires that this underlying structure and its components be made explicit and that its contents be presented in a new format with measurement implications.

The new format is the language of the behavioral or performance objective presented in a logical sequence which may preserve much of the scope and order of the former curriculum. The new curriculum format, with its expressed implications for measurement and evaluation, is composed of different types and levels of objectives organized hierarchically into a so-called program structure.

Another major element integral to the curriculum structure is the philosophy of instruction in the form of an applied instructional model. The instructional model, for example, determines whether instruction is to be group organized and paced or individually paced, will incorporate reinforcement, and so on. The curriculum structure and its contents in the form of topics, objectives, and specific content, together with the instructional model, directly imply much of the structure and elements of an appropriate evaluation design.

The present section focuses on an analysis of the elements of the program structure and how they are to be derived or generated and organized for the purposes of designing instruction and evaluation. Chapter 4 discusses the various levels of the management structure of educational systems and shows how the structure, decision-makers, and performance standards interrelate at each level of a system. As seen in this broader context, performance standards and evaluation activities converge to assist educators in carrying out major management functions. The subsequent chapters of Part II focus on types of performance objectives and on their development, derivation, classification, quality control, and organization in the context of the program structure.

Chapter 4

Objectives and Evaluation
in the Context of Educational Systems

As has been previously pointed out, the primary purpose of an evaluation system, whatever its context of application, is to provide a rational basis for decisions. The evaluation system must give a clear portrayal of reality. The most useful picture of reality for educational decision-making comes from assessing a system's achievement in terms of its performance standards and goals. The goals of a system, if their achievement is to be objectively measured, should be established in terms of externally manifested and observable behaviors. Only then can achievement be assessed through measurable phenomena. Thus, the evaluation process is dependent on the existence of performance standards or objectives for the educational programs within a system.

Educational objectives and the evaluation processes they make possible do not, of course, exist in a vacuum. There is a context of educational functions which gives meaning to the objectives and the evaluation process. It is the purpose of this chapter to briefly elucidate this functional context and to place educational objectives and evaluation into the appropriate perspectives.

Educational System Functions

The functional context of performance objectives and evaluation is shown in Figure 4.1. Planning and decision-making are depicted as the overriding management activities relating to all three broad instructional system functions, program structure development, instructional systems design, and program delivery. These three operational functions are the vehicles by which educational programs on a broad scale, or even whole educational systems, are designed, developed,

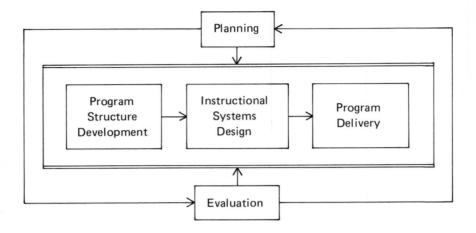

The Context of Performance Standards
in Relation to Evaluation and Other
Major Educational Functions

Figure 4.1

and implemented. Planning/decision-making provides the direction for all three functions. Evaluation monitors the effectiveness of the planned programs and refers the results back for further planning and decision-making. The cycle continues in a pattern of planning—implementation—evaluation. Effective planning decisions are thus dependent on a viable evaluation system.

Planning/Decision-Making

Through planning and decision-making, information from various sources is gathered, processed, and channeled for the formulation, installation, and management of instructional programs in an educational system or district. Planning/decision-making includes such activities as analyzing students' needs in terms of goals and objectives, obtaining information on resources and costs for programs, setting goals, and analyzing and selecting alternative instructional methods and materials for teaching objectives.

Adequate planning for a program involves several levels of planners, often simultaneously performing similar activities. For example, the objectives for a reading program may define a set of minimal standards for students completing sixth grade. A subsequently discovered discrepancy of actual performance from expectations becomes the basis for the generation of modified goal statements for several levels and units of the educational system.

Consider the following goal statement where it is assumed that half the students failed, at the conclusion of the program, to achieve the objectives to expected standards:

> By the end of the 1974-75 school year, the discrepancy in performance on minimal reading objectives will be reduced to 25%, and to 5% by 1975-76.

Note that the ability to determine such discrepancies, to plan interventions and, subsequently, to monitor the extent to which revised goals are actually met, is dependent on an evaluation system which measures actual program effectiveness relative to expected performance on objectives.

Program Structure Development

The program structure identifies the levels of a program, the organization of the goals and objectives of the educational system, and the resources devoted to achieving them. Part of developing the program structure is explicitly recording the performance standards against which the effectiveness of the system is to be measured and from which any discrepancies in performance are to be determined. That is, the process of establishing the structure of a program includes setting down the goals and objectives of the system, extending to the level of outcomes of each particular course of instruction.

In the jargon of planning, the levels of a program begin with the system. The system includes all activities and resources in a school district. The next level, the program unit level, includes all activities and resources in a building or other subdivision of an educational system, such as the Elm Street Elementary School in the Ark City Public Schools. A program element is all the activities and resources in a content area in the program unit — for instance, the reading program for the Elm Street School. A subprogram element is a level in a content area, such as fifth grade reading (or a particular course at the middle or high school level).

Figure 4.2 shows a working example of a system's program structure. It reflects program units and elements in both instructional and non-instructional areas.

Program Categories

1. Instructional
2. Instructional Support
3. General Support
4. Community Services

Programs in Instructional Program Category

1. Elementary School A . . . N Program
2. Middle School Program
3. High School Program
4. Special Education Program
5. Continuing Education Program

Instructional Program Category

Elementary School Program
   Art Program Element
   Health Program Element
   Physical Education Program Element
   Language Arts Program Element
   Mathematics Program Element
   Music Program Element
   Science Program Element
   Social Studies Program Element
   Special Projects Program Element
   Reading Program Element
   Student Activities Program Element
   Learning Center Program Element

Middle School Program
   Art Program Element
   Typing Program Element
   Foreign Language Program Element
   Physical Education Program Element
   Industrial Arts Program Element
   English Program Element
   Reading Program Element
   Mathematics Program Element
   Music Program Element
   Science Program Element
   Social Studies Program Element
   Home Economics Program Element

Middle School Program (cont'd)
    Special Projects Program Element
    Student Activities Program Element
    Learning Center Program Element

High School Program
    Art Program Element
    Business Program Element
    Foreign Language Program Element
    Health Program Element
    Physical Education Program Element
    Industrial Arts Program Element
    English Program Element
    Mathematics Program Element
    Music Program Element
    Science Program Element
    Social Studies Program Element
    Home Economics Program Element
    Special Projects Program Element
    Driver Education Program Element
    Vocational Program Element
    Student Activities Program Element
    Learning Center Program Element

Special Education Program
    Emotionally Disturbed Program Element
    Physically Handicapped Program Element
    Mentally Handicapped Program Element
    Home and Hospital Instruction Program Element
    Learning Disabilities Program Element

Continuing Education Program
    Adult Education Program Element
    Summer Education Program Element
    Pre-Kindergarten Program Element

System Program Structure Outline[a]

Figure 4.2

---

[a] Jamesville-DeWitt PPBS Task Force, Jamesville-DeWitt Public Schools, NY.

The program structure for an educational system is initially defined in terms of several levels of performance objectives, beginning with the most general statements, called goals. Each successive level of goal statements becomes more and more detailed, as each level of the program structure relates primarily to a different decision-making group. For example, boards of education relate to overall district goals, which are relatively few in number, while teachers relate primarily to sizable numbers of specific performance objectives for one or more program subelements. The explicit structuring of the goals and objectives for a school district program would include the identification of levels, the organization of objectives within levels, and the identification of decision-makers. This structure is shown in outline form in Figure 4.3. Note that overall goals are drawn at the societal level and that the levels extend downward to individual courses in given content areas.

The vertical arrows connecting performance levels indicate the articulation of performance standards. This articulation has significance both psychologically and in terms of evaluation. At the psychological level, the various levels of performance standards should constitute a smooth developmental sequence of "learnable" and relevant objectives, thus accounting for the abilities and interests of the student population to be served. The process of evaluation will contribute in determining to what extent the objectives in a program are in fact developmentally suited to the needs and abilities of learners.

Through evaluation, the performance of the educational system is measured in terms of discrepancies from expectations found at one or more levels. As Figure 4.3 reveals, discrepancies occurring at the system level are potentially identifiable by evaluation data both at the total educational system level and at successively lower program structure levels. For example, if a set of goals referring to communications processes were notably underachieved at the system level, the sources of the discrepancy should be traceable to the individual course level. Each appropriate management group could then undertake to correct the discrepancy.

As previously noted, the documentation of the program structure would also include the identification of the resources to be applied to it (e.g., personnel, materials). Thus, the potential exists for making certain performance comparisons among program elements and units. For example, problems with the reading program may be relatively more severe than those identified for mathematics. Furthermore, problems in reading may be more extensive in one building than in others. Data available on program costs and resources will suggest where available resources might be best allocated to eliminate discrepancies between actual and expected performance.

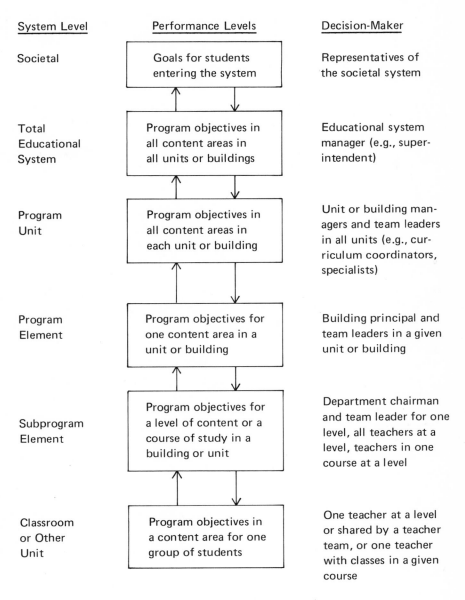

System Level	Performance Levels	Decision-Maker
Societal	Goals for students entering the system	Representatives of the societal system
Total Educational System	Program objectives in all content areas in all units or buildings	Educational system manager (e.g., superintendent)
Program Unit	Program objectives in all content areas in each unit or building	Unit or building managers and team leaders in all units (e.g., curriculum coordinators, specialists)
Program Element	Program objectives for one content area in a unit or building	Building principal and team leaders in a given unit or building
Subprogram Element	Program objectives for a level of content or a course of study in a building or unit	Department chairman and team leader for one level, all teachers at a level, teachers in one course at a level
Classroom or Other Unit	Program objectives in a content area for one group of students	One teacher at a level or shared by a teacher team, or one teacher with classes in a given course

Model of an Overall Program Structure

Figure 4.3

Instructional Systems Design

Instructional systems design requires the existence of the leveled sets of goals and performance objectives that partly constitute the program structure. Performance objectives in the hierarchy of the program structure (system, program, program element, and subprogram element) are refined further to include the levels more directly related to the organization of instruction. The remaining parts of the organizational hierarchy are described in Figure 4.4, an extension of Figure 4.3. Note that the course/classroom level of the program structure forms the functional boundary between program structure development and instructional systems design.

Figure 4.4 shows that instruction is actually designed only at the last level, the lesson, where the instructional interface between teacher and student occurs. Higher levels of organization, however, do affect the planning of instruction at the lesson level. For example, the importance of an objective is determined in part by the extent to which it is repeated in the hierarchy (e.g., arithmetic operations appear in lessons at every curriculum level), while taxonomies or other classification systems applied to objectives in the hierarchy may imply something about the types of learning involved — for example, transfer. Both the importance of the objectives and information on the type of learning represented affect the planning of instruction at the lesson level by suggesting the degree of emphasis and types of activities appropriate to learning each objective.

The role of objectives in the design of instruction is further defined in the process of sequencing objectives. One technique for the sequencing of objectives is that of structural analysis (Tuckman & Edwards, 1971), a procedure for determining precedence or independence. Procedures for identifying lower level or prerequisite objectives for a lesson may also be included. In this fashion, the activity that begins with specifying the program structure is analytically extended downward to map the sequence and interrelationships of skills and other types of performance that comprise the outcomes of an educational system. When this structuring of performance objectives is complete, the instructional manager is ready to specify, generate, or select instructional activities.

The relationship between instructional systems design and the evaluation process is evident in some of the questions underlying the decision types previously reviewed. The design and installation of instructional systems and materials is a formative process. Instructional systems have a perpetually unfinished character and must be continually revised on the basis of the relationship between actual achievement and expected performance. Evaluation of instructional design is therefore concerned with the effectiveness both of objective organization and of methods and materials used to teach objectives. It may be

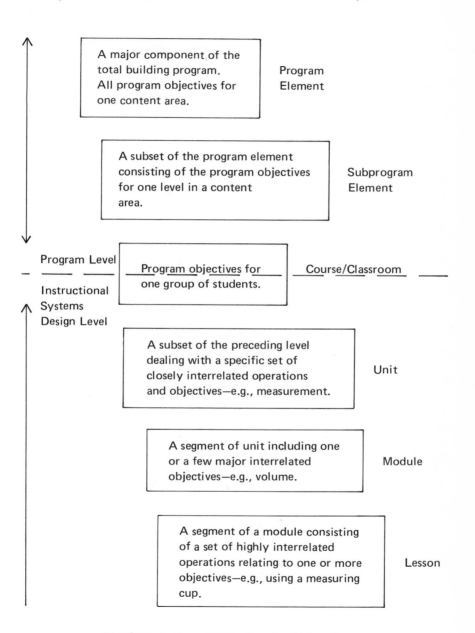

The Organization of Objectives for Instruction

Figure 4.4

expected that school districts will be greatly concerned with these types of formative evaluation so that staff may continually adjust programs at many levels to meet constant and changing needs.

Program Delivery

The final educational function is program delivery, the process by which a system's program content is actually presented to students. The individual classroom teacher, and backup systems and personnel such as librarians, are all mechanisms for delivering programs to students. The need to monitor students through the process of interacting with program content controls the focus of evaluation in the delivery function. Indeed, the very identification of explicit performance objectives to be achieved by students implies the existence of an evaluation system which delivers appropriate and timely data on students' achievement. A further implication is that there must be a monitoring segment incorporated into the delivery system to support ongoing management activities dependent on evaluative data. The occurrence of actual learning activities within an overall program structure further indicates the need for complete articulation of decision-making responsibilities, since the results of evaluation may often affect several levels of the structure.

Summary

There are three distinct operational functions occurring simultaneously in educational systems: program structure development, instructional systems design, and program delivery. Each function depends on articulated goals and performance standards to be properly established initially. Further, performance standards are prerequisite to an evaluation system capable of assessing the effectiveness of educational programs. Without an explicit set of performance objectives for each operational program level, the system's functions can neither be clearly delineated nor can its achievement be monitored and the constantly necessary revisions be made on a realistic basis.

Objectives and performance standards, necessary to implement educational programs effectively, are present in American education in several forms. Chapter 5 now turns to the various types of objectives with which an educational system may be concerned and separates performance objectives from the other types.

Chapter 5

Types of Objectives
in the Evaluation Context

The effective use of performance objectives in establishing standards for an educational system, at whatever level, requires an awareness of some important distinctions among types of performance objectives. Knowledge of these distinctions should precede such activities as deriving, selecting, and organizing objectives. Distinctions among types of objectives are important because different objectives have somewhat different forms and purposes. Such distinctions qualify the task of writing and selecting objectives, since some types of objectives are often written or selected before others. The distinctions made in this chapter first require briefly clarifying differences among three major categories of objectives in education: outcome or performance objectives, process objectives, and management objectives. The remainder of the chapter then focuses on a number of useful distinctions made among types and levels of performance objectives — the principal focus of evaluation.

Basic Groups of Objectives

Distinctions made among the three basic groups of objectives — performance objectives, process objectives, and management objectives — derive from their placement in relation to the major functions and the program structure previously reviewed. Performance objectives are distinguished by their focus on products or outcomes of the educational system at any level in the program structure. A performance objective may define a student performance outcome, thus communicating something about a student being able to add single digit numbers, for instance; or it may define the expectation that the system will produce adding skills in all or nearly all students. Performance objectives define what the program is supposed to achieve and provide the specifications for measuring each achievement.

The process objective, by contrast, defines a <u>system, activity, or procedure</u> to be installed or conducted to achieve a performance objective. At another level, a process objective describes what a teacher intends to do to achieve a given performance objective. Beginning writers of objectives frequently confuse performance with process and end up defining their own activities, such as:

> To increase the use of objectives to plan and manage the instruction of children. . . .

The third basic division among objectives is in the distinction made between their functions as system performance standards, on the one hand, and, on the other, as management tools. The management objective is given in the form of a goal statement which is referenced to one or more performance objectives at some level of the system. For example, if an overall district-level performance objective is:

> Students will possess the skills and attitudes required to enable them to continue learning on their own initiative after graduating, as indicated by. . . .

an appropriate management objective would be constructed in relation to performance discrepancies found through measures taken on indicators of the objective. Relevant standards of performance relating to this high-level outcome may be found by examining various courses at the high school level. Through subsequent measurement and evaluation, it might be found that selected skills important for independent learning are being notably underachieved. Subsequently, a management objective such as the following might be developed:

> By the end of year 2, 75% of the eleventh grade language students enrolled in regular classes will be able to locate reference books and periodicals in the school library through the use of standard reference bibliographies within two 50-minute periods.

This management objective is thus a temporary restatement of a performance standard for a given level of system operation which "promises" to make some progress over a two-year period toward elimination of the gap between actual performance and the standard. In this example, the gap indicated that only

50 percent of students were learning reference skills, while the expected standard in the program structure was 95 percent. The effort to eliminate the discrepancy proposed an increase to at least 75 percent of students by year two as the teacher-management team conducts a new set of activities and gains new resources to effect changes in the program.

The distinctions made among the three basic divisions of objectives might be summarized as:

A Performance Objective
. . . is what is expected in terms of what a student or program can do.

A Process Objective
. . . is something a teacher or administrator might do.

A Management Objective
. . . is a target statement defining how much more a program component will achieve in terms of student or group performance.

Types of Performance Objectives

Educational objectives may focus on different contexts, such as the products or processes of a system. Within a criterion-referenced evaluation system, the focus of objectives is the performance of students and program units of any and all levels of the program structure, extending from the entire district to the individual student. Each decision-making group defines objectives that appropriately reflect the level and breadth of its interests. Within a given district, attempts to state objectives for different levels will generally result in definitions which range from the general to the detailed, as shown in Figure 5.1.

The performance objectives defined for different operating levels of the program structure, it may be expected, will be named in a variety of labels (it seems unlikely that standardization of terms will occur) and will differ from locale to locale. That is, what is one district's standard for third grade mathematics performance is another's standard for fifth grade. Attempts to establish distinctions among different levels and types of performance objectives have led to a somewhat confusing array of terminology, as shown by the list of different terms for one level or type of objective given in Figure 5.2 (from Ammerman & Melching, 1966, p. 7).

This confusion in terminology is less of a problem if it is expected and if

Level of Specificity	Program Structure
General	District level
Intermediate	Program level
Detailed	Program Element level

Levels of Specificity of Performance
Outcomes in the Program Structure

Figure 5.1

it is understood that various authors are attempting to communicate subtle and useful distinctions of type, importance, level, and sequence among objectives. The process of completing the program structure in terms of levels and types of performance is essentially one of making such subtle distinctions. The task involves, for example, defining both global and specific objectives, designating terminal and interim objectives, determining sequences, and stating levels of mastery.

Enabling Objectives	
Intermediate Objective	Learning Objective
School Behavior Objective	Supporting Objective
Component Objective	Duty-enabling Objective
Subordinate Objective	Teaching Point
Subject Matter Objective	Learning Outcome
Lesson Preparation Objective	Specific Objective
Subsidiary Objective	Learning Task
Task Demand	Immediate Learning Goal
Functional Objective	Behavioral Objective

Some Equivalent Terms for One Type of Objective

Figure 5.2

Figure 5.3 shows how the concept of the program structure is extended to include the types of objectives needed to define outcomes for every level of a local educational system. At the uppermost level, objectives appear in the most general terms, often referred to as goals. The most detailed levels consist of objectives directly related to the organizational units of instruction (units and modules) and to instruction itself (lessons). The various levels of objectives have different but somewhat overlapping sources of derivation and validation.

Types of Performance Objectives	Program Structure Level	Source of Objectives
System Goals	Educational System, District	Government Legislation, Educational Literature, Community Higher Education, Education Department
Program Objectives	Program, Program Element	Objective Banks, Job Descriptions, Published Requirements, Teachers
Course Objectives	Subprogram Elements, Units, Modules	Teachers, Objective Banks, Derivation from Higher Level Objectives, Content Experts
Instructional Objectives	Lesson	Objective Banks, Content Experts, Teachers, Content Analysis, Literature

Types of Performance Standards in the Program Structure

Figure 5.3

Goals

Statements at the highest level of the program structure range from relatively brief short-hand expressions to two or more levels of statements which define the overriding purposes of an educational system. Performance standards at this level are not strictly operational, usually being defined in reference to a number of independent indicators both within and without the educational system. In a two-level system, the most general statements may appropriately be called lifelong goals, as shown in Figure 5.4, and refer to outcomes to be achieved continuously well after the student's tenure in the educational system has ended.

Lifelong Goals:
Continuous, Long-Standing, Multi-Year Purpose

    — Intellectual Development
    — Moral Development
    — Human Relations
    — Civic Responsibility
    — Self-Realization

Examples of Lifelong Goals

Figure 5.4

Statements at the goals level may be further subdivided into system goal statements, shown in Figure 5.5, which come closer to being more explicitly operational but obviously include a broad range of indicators. The sources of system level goals are philosophies of education, the broad educational literature, and the needs of the culture expressed through national, state, and local governments and institutions. System goals express broad system learning outcomes in a few statements and provide a basis for program planning.

Program Objectives

Performance objectives at the program level comprise the first set of

---

System Goals

— Every student is able to read well enough for occupational success, personal enjoyment, and personal survival.

— Every student is able to communicate with others orally and in writing to satisfy needs for expression and for life requirements.

— Every student can make effective use of school and community resources in pursuing his life interests.

Examples of System Goals

Figure 5.5

standards which prescribe or imply a set of measurement operations in themselves, in contrast to goals, which are measured by a number of general indicators. Program level goals define the performance outcomes of major areas and levels of instruction, typically defining only the end or terminal performances for a given content area. Such performance standards are thus summative and relate to major skills or competencies to be achieved by students and programs. The sources of program objectives include the formal derivation of required competencies from analyses of job performance, knowledge of human development, and projections into future needs and requirements of human society. Program objectives are established through study of the psychological, social, and cultural contexts indicated by goals.

Terminal program objectives are typically located in sequence at the conclusion of such program elements as the elementary, middle, and high schools, at the completion of training in auto mechanics or woodworking, and at the certification point in cosmetology. Examples of program level performance objectives are given in Figure 5.6. Objectives of this type might, for example, define the types of performance and content to be used in a survey of performance in the final year of the high school language arts program. A comparable but less

demanding set of standards would be used to define performance at the conclusion of the middle and elementary school levels. Program objectives define concluding behaviors for programs. They are the source of lower strata objectives
for program levels and courses.

Program Objectives

— Given a sampling of sentences at Level X requiring
   punctuation, the student will apply the major rules of
   punctuation correctly with 95% accuracy.

— Given orally a random sample of 500 non-function
   words with a high frequency in the population drawn
   from Level 1-n vocabulary lists, the student will spell
   them correctly with 95% accuracy.

Examples of Program Objectives

Figure 5.6

Course Objectives

The course level objective is again a summative objective like the program
objective. It defines end or terminal performance for subprogram elements in
content areas, such as tenth grade woodworking and third grade reading. The
application of the course objective is not limited to any fixed system of levels,
such as the typical graded program, but may be varied to fit any successive or
hierarchical plan of levels. An example of a course level objective is given in Figure 5.7. The sources of course objectives include derivation from higher order
objectives and goals, existing objective banks, and the logical ordering and structuring of more detailed objectives at the instructional level.

There are at least four basic forms of course objectives, two of which are
sampling forms and two of which are hierarchical or consist of a series of inter-

---
Course Objectives

Given orally a random sampling of 150 non-function words from Level n vocabulary lists, the student will spell them correctly by writing with 95% accuracy for 15 minutes.

Example of a Course Objective
Figure 5.7

related performances ending in a single complex unit. One sampling course objective is relatively common in mathematics and reading and consists of a single unique type of performance which varies by level on the basis of successive changes in the difficulty of the content sampled. This sampling form would be applied to objectives defining skills and related content of the type shown in Figure 5.8.

Skill	Content
Vocabulary Objectives	Sample from a pool of vocabulary words
Comprehension Objectives	Sample from a pool of paragraphs and selections
Arithmetic Operations	Sample from among examples of one type of problem at a given level of difficulty

Examples of Skills in Which Objectives Would Define Sampling of Content
Figure 5.8

Course objectives of this form obviously refer to very broad or extensive samples of content at a particular level of the curriculum. The course objective communicates that several samples of performance are to be drawn from a set of such content. Adequate performance to the required standard indicates the student can generalize to the whole set (e.g., can add single digit numbers).

Another sampling form course objective varies both the constituent objectives in a category, such as punctuation, and the related content, as shown by the skills and related content in Figure 5.9.

Skill	Content
Punctuation Skill	Objectives defining different punctuation skills together with content at different levels of difficulty.
Reference Skill	Objectives defining different reference skills together with content at different levels of difficulty.
Identifying Tenses	Different objectives dealing with different tenses and content at different levels of difficulty.

Examples of Objectives in Which Both Skills and Content May Be Sampled

Figure 5.9

The course level objective is summative for a level (subprogram element) of the educational system. It may represent achievement of a level of difficulty for a single skill for which there is a broad universe of content, or it may represent achievement of a set of related skills in the universe of content. The course objectives for a given program element define the expected outcomes for levels of the element and are frequently known as mastery objectives. The basic form of such objectives is as follows:

> Given (define the sample of constituent objectives and/or content), the student will produce (number of outputs) with (standard of accuracy) in (time standard if important).

An example of a course objective which samples content at a level is (note not only the inclusion of sampling criteria, but the additional mastery criteria for speed and accuracy):

> Given six division of whole numbers problems at the following level . . .
>
> $$447{,}528\,\overline{\smash{\big)}\,1{,}596{,}703}$$
>
> . . . the student will apply any of three division algorithms with 80% accuracy; time limit is 12 minutes.

Other forms of the course objective include complex cognitive and motor operations where the end result is all that is of interest. For example, the following objective defines both the outcome (being able to make a field wire splice) and the sequence of its constituent behaviors:

> Using rubber and friction tape, Pliers TL 13-A, and Wire WD-1/TT, the student should be able to make a standard field wire splice by completing each of the following steps in sequence:
>
> a. From one conductor, cut off one plier's length, about six inches.
> b. Mark each conductor six inches from end by inserting one conductor at a time into small hole in jaws of pliers.
> c. Close pliers.
> d. Insert long conductor in small hole about two inches from end.
> e. Close jaws carefully to remove insulation.
> f. Etc.

Likewise, the next course objective defines an end result for a science course:

> Given (number) descriptions of natural science events
> such as (example), the student will explain the causes of
> the events in brief paragraphs of 100 words or less (30
> minutes time limit).

Though this objective is composed of several separate constituent behaviors, such as recording important characteristics of an event sequentially, it is an appropriate course objective because it focuses only on the most important terminal skill: the ability to explain causes.

Instructional Objectives

The next group of objectives to be considered comes at the instructional level. Instructional objectives usually define a single, simple unit of performance accomplished quickly. The sources of instructional objectives include traditional content authorities, existing objective banks developed by teachers, content outlines, texts and other instructional materials, tests constructed for given content areas, and systematic refinement of higher order objectives.

When instructional objectives are derived through a process of refinement from course objectives, a basic generic, or content-free, format is transformed by the addition of specific content, such as words or mathematics problems. That is, the actual constituent objectives and content summarized in a course objective become the basis for defining a large number of instructional objectives, which are the immediate foci of teaching in lessons. For example, the following specific instructional objective was derived from a course objective by the insertion of the word cat, drawn from the relevant content set, into the generic objective format:

> Given the word cat orally, the student writes the word.
> (Generic format: Given a word, ...)

The specific word, cat, then becomes the focus, along with a few other words drawn from the relevant sample of content, of a particular lesson. This specific objective in turn contributes to the achievement of the longer term course level objectives which stipulate the ability to spell a large number of common words selected for a level. The course objectives, in their turn, contribute to the ability to spell common English words generally — a set of some 2500 to 5000 words referred to by the program level objective.

The following example provides another illustration of the derivation of instructional level objectives from a course objective. The course objective is:

Given samples of ungrouped subsets of the following
type, with variable numbers in any subset:

 etc.

the student will regroup into subsets by providing names
for each subset and designating their members (standard
of accuracy: 90%).

The component or enabling behaviors of this objective can be specified
more or less to the extent that both its stimulus and response sides have been
clearly described. From the objective, it is apparent that learning some verbal
concepts is prerequisite to achievement. Therefore instructional objectives need
to be derived in the following areas:

(1)   subsets;
(2)   regrouping; and
(3)   discriminating or abstracting such characteristics as "roundness,"
       "triangularity."

On the response side, note that the student is to regroup the members of
the subset and designate the basis of their regrouping in some fashion, such as by
drawing its members.

This analysis now leads to the statement of some derived instructional objectives, such as:

Given an example of a subset in a set, the student will say,
"subset."

Given examples of regrouping of subsets, and a question
requiring application of the regrouping label, the student
will identify those subsets that have been regrouped.

The instructional level objectives defined through this process of consecutive refinement from the goals of the educational system are then used directly
by instructional planners for the development of lessons.

The Hierarchy of Goals and Objectives

The process of deriving performance objectives creates a hierarchy of goals

Goal or Objective Example	Position	Program Structure Level	Decision-Maker
Intellectual Development	Lifelong Goal	Educational System	State Legislature, Education Dept., Economic System
Every student is able to communicate effectively with others orally and in writing to satisfy needs for expression and for life requirements.	System Goal	Educational System	Local Community, Board of Education, Superintendent, Relevant Experts
Given orally a random sample of 500 non-function words at Levels 1-n with a high frequency in the population, the student will spell them correctly with 95% accuracy.	Program Objective	Program, Program Element	Asst. Superintendent, Curriculum Consultant
Given orally a random sample of 150 non-function words from Level n, the student will spell them correctly by writing with 95% accuracy for 15 minutes.	Course Objective	Subprogram Element,	Department Head, Teacher, Team Leader, Curriculum Consultant
Given the word cat orally, the student will spell it correctly in writing	Instructional Objective	Lesson	Teacher, Curriculum Consultant/ Designer

The Hierarchy of Goals and Performance Objectives

Figure 5.10

and objectives, portrayed in Figure 5.10. The evaluation system utilizes these higher level objectives for decision-making at all program levels. By gathering achievement data on the higher level objectives and goals, decision-makers throughout the system structure can monitor the effectiveness of programs and plan necessary interventions. In this way, criterion-referenced achievement data on performance objectives lead to new management objectives and revisions in programs.

Summary

This chapter has extended the detail of the program structure by showing the various types of objectives that apply at each educational level. Though there is some confusion in terminology and form of objectives by level, the intent of different levels and types of objectives is to provide the increasingly general performance standards which define operations at successively higher levels of educational systems. The responsible audiences at each of these levels, teachers, parents, legislators, etc., contribute to defining appropriate performance standards. The implication is that such standards will ultimately be used to determine discrepancies in the operation of the system and constructive goal setting will ensue through the development of management and process objectives. There is the further implication that an effective local evaluation system operates simultaneously at several levels of the educational system in relation to performance standards at each level. Measurement of performance standards will thus be successively cumulative from lower to higher levels of the educational system.

Special attention needs to be given to the form of performance objectives for different levels of educational systems. These objectives have been shown to differ in terms of form (sampling versus hierarchical), specificity (goals versus instructional objectives), content (domain of content and extent of sample), and inclusion of performance condition (time and accuracy). The differences among types of objectives obviously imply differences in derivation and in the intent of measurement and evaluation.

Chapter 6

An Analytical Process for Deriving
Goals and Performance Objectives

Probably the most difficult and time-consuming activity in applying a criterion-referenced evaluation model lies in generating and deriving the various levels of goals and performance objectives that define the outcomes of selected levels of the program structure. This chapter presents a theoretical construct of that activity.

Some of the steps described are often not included in the actual practice of objective derivation, at least in any explicit or deliberate manifestation. In practice, the derivation of objectives in an educational system usually begins either on the individual course level by a single teacher or by a group of volunteers in one content area. However, the process of deriving objectives, when done on an organized system-wide basis, can follow a logical pattern beginning with the explication of the values context in which the educational system operates.

This and the subsequent chapter assume that much of the activity involved in the development of performance curricula will proceed from existing objective banks, ranging from the often rough-cut collections exchanged among school districts to the systematically organized banks available from educational institutions, projects, and commercial agencies.

It has become obvious that the most efficient method of generating a performance curriculum is through selection of objectives from an organized bank. Though users will still profit from a reading of Mager's brief text on preparing objectives (Mager, 1962), the task of writing objectives can now often be largely replaced by the more interesting and less arduous tasks of selecting and modifying objectives from an existing bank.

91

Some of the latest developments in education have contributed a number of organized banks of objectives, such as the IOX series from UCLA, the SOBAR bank of reading objectives from the Center for the Study of Evaluation (Aschbacher & Fitzgerald, 1972) also at UCLA, the Westinghouse Learning Corporation series of objectives, the SPPED or New York State bank of objectives in reading and mathematics (O'Reilly, Cohen & Algozzine, 1973), and the objectives from the CO-OP, University of Massachusetts. A considerable number of content areas, levels, and even types of objectives are supplied by the various sets now available.[1]

Typically, a bank of objectives consists of a topically organized collection presented in a book or booklets. Usually only one level or type of objective is presented and this is typically generic, or content-free. Often, the user has the task of defining, with the bank as a resource, other levels or types of objectives through the specifications of content, the addition of mastery criteria, and so on. A few banks of objectives include the different types and levels required to create a portion of the program structure and also to incorporate systematic procedures for aiding the organization of objectives and content. Technical assistance to users varies from instruction booklets, brief or elaborate, to the use of computers for printing objectives in a user-designated format.

The Derivation Process

The process of deriving and organizing performance objectives for educational programs involves several consecutive phases or stages of activity. First, the community in which the educational system operates must be considered so that its values and perceptions are reflected in the programs the system establishes. The findings and opinions of related academic and research disciplines may also be consulted at this time. Next the district staff formulates a tentative set of goals, relying on expressed community feelings and relevant expert advice. The goals are then referred to the community again for validation and prioritization. Finally, performance objectives at several program levels are derived from the prioritized list of goals through a refinement process.

Values and the Derivation Process

In the initial stages of generating a performance curriculum, recognition

---

[1] For example, the Phi Delta Kappa (1972) materials include statements at the level of goals and performance objectives at the program and course levels.

should be given to the broad problem of values and choice in deriving goals and performance objectives from any source. Stake (1970) writes that a set of performance objectives should be considered fallible, judgmental preferences which are incomplete, imprecise, and embedded in a context of values. A local bank of objectives, therefore, is susceptible to change over time as experience and the clarification of the educational philosophy and values context of the district lead to revision.

An early explanation of the often implicit values position of the community should facilitate the process of derivation since values will determine the priorities, importance, and relevance of criteria for inclusion of objectives in the set used in a given district. The statement of a community values position should thus ideally precede the actual derivation of goals and performance objectives and thereafter continue to determine their suitability. Therefore, local responsible audiences in the community are asked to contribute to the derivation process from its inception.

Audience Analysis Stage

The first stage of the formulation of goals (and eventually of selecting objectives) involves the identification of potential contributing and responsible audiences in the community. The board of education, as the "contractor" for the educational system, should define the criteria for inclusion of audiences, such as staff, lay leaders, and students. A "complete" set of audiences is then selected to insure broad representation of community decision-makers and, thus, values. Experts with special relevant knowledge, such as the developmental psychologist and the educational philosopher, may also be included in this stage. These audiences interact concerning the values position of the educational system and on the tentative goals to be placed before the community, providing the variety of perspectives which represent the broad range of community, cultural, and universal values.

One set of materials for training in goal selection presents the following list of participating audiences (Phi Delta Kappan, 1972):

(1)   Parents
(2)   Representatives of community businesses, services, religious and cultural organizations
(3)   Representatives of school-affiliated organizations
(4)   Representatives from ethnic and socioeconomic groups
(5)   Representatives from governmental organizations
(6)   School board members

(7)   Administrative staff
(8)   Classroom teachers
(9)   Classified personnel
(10) Students

The selection of appropriate audiences is also important in relation to their later support of the goals and other levels of objectives selected for the district. One obvious criterion for inclusion as a participating audience is the extent to which an individual or group participates in or is affected by the educational activities. Another obvious criterion is the extent to which audience members possess specialized knowledge about human development from psychological, historical, ethical, aesthetic, and physical points of view. The agreement of the various audiences on the goals and objectives eventually selected will also contribute to their effective participation in activities designed to achieve those goals.

Traditional Values Positions

The typical underlying value positions for the generation of educational goals have been identified by Kohlberg and Mayer (1972) as: (a) the romantic position, (b) the cultural transmission position, and (c) the progressive or cognitive developmental position. A brief definition of each should serve to indicate the influence of such positions on the choice of goals and the resulting implications for the general focus of educational institutions.

The first position originates from Rousseau's thinking and defines a maturationist view of what human beings are "believed to be" in terms of traits and the qualities of innate goodness. Generally, this position results in a long list of desirable traits defining mental and physical health, curiosity, and others, which will develop and unfold naturally given an unstructured, non-interfering educational environment. The goals typically derived from this position consist of a list of such traits defined as the outcomes of the educational system. The task of education in this tradition is to maintain a relatively unstructured environment within which development may unfold through choice and freedom.

The romantic position often influences the development of goals through a process in which the various responsible audiences convene and commune on the outcomes of education. The conventions frequently define processes or produce a lengthy set of characteristics of educational systems (e.g., "The system should encourage individuality, curiosity, wholeness. . . .") instead of outcomes.

The cultural transmission position influences the selection of goals on the basis of cultural givens. That is, if a goal is consistent with the social and moral rules of the society, contributes to adjustment in that society, or maximizes reward and minimizes punishment in that society, then its selection is appropriate (cf. Skinner, 1971). This position focuses on vocational and social adaptation to the current cultural context and implies a process of education which transmits information with the intent of generating predetermined output. There is a relative lack of focus on more universal philosophical, ethical, and moral issues or positions, except as they relate to cultural norms. The romantic and cultural transmission views converge to the extent that desirable traits are culturally determined.

The cognitive-developmental position identifies the goals of education as consistent with intellectual and moral human development. This view incorporates a theory of ordered development through stages which is justified both philosophically and scientifically. It would include the formal theories of Piaget and provide a means for integrating cognitive, moral, and ego development. Objectives dealing with such skills as reading and mathematics are justified on the basis of their potential for contributing to such development. More important, the general forms and levels of human development, which are the ultimate expression of goals, are determined independently of existing cultural norms. The cognitive-developmental view implies a process of education which is democratic, rule- or principle-centered, explicitly moral or concerned with ethical principles, non-indoctrinative, and strongly liberal in focus.

Goal Derivation Stage

After systematic consultation with the community representatives, and after concurrent or subsequent contribution from experts in such fields as developmental psychology and educational philosophy, the educational system usually formulates and presents tentative goals for the community to validate, modify, and prioritize.

Goals, as noted, are broad expressions of policy which reflect community values as they become more explicit and begin to reveal intent. Program objectives and other levels of performance standards in the school context are derived from goals chosen to achieve policy. The process of deriving these goals ordinarily starts with a set of brief concerns, such as the set from Downey given in Figure 6.1 (Stake, 1970, p. 184).

Such dimensional systems are used as a basis for generating statements of goals and eventually of the related detail which might define process. For example, from the "Possession of Knowledge" dimension one might derive the following goal as an ultimate outcome to be accomplished through programs:

GOAL: Mastery of the basic skills of communications and

Intellectual Dimensions:

1.	Possession of Knowledge	A fund of information, concepts
2.	Communication of Knowledge	Skill to acquire and transmit
3.	Creation of Knowledge	Discrimination and imagination, a habit
4.	Desire for Knowledge	A love for learning

Social Dimensions:

5.	Man to Man	Cooperation in day-to-day relations
6.	Man to State	Civic rights and duties
7.	Man to Country	Loyalty to one's own country
8.	Man to World	Interrelationships of peoples

Personal Dimensions:

9.	Physical	Bodily health and development
10.	Emotional	Mental health and stability
11.	Ethical	Moral integrity
12.	Aesthetic	Cultural and leisure pursuits

Productive Dimensions:

13.	Vocation-Selective	Information and guidance
14.	Vocation-Preparative	Training and placement
15.	Home and Family	Housekeeping, do-it-yourself, family
16.	Consumer	Personal buying, selling, investment

Dimensions of Public Education

Figure 6.1

reasoning essential to live a full and productive life.[2]

The goal is then progressively refined through the addition of appropriate detail, which includes statements short of specific program outcomes, such as:

Be able to communicate verbally and in writing in a range of common life situations.

Be able to express the self creatively through writing.

Goals are communicated appropriately with relevance to the societal or cultural context, not in terms of school or program outcomes which at best simulate the eventual context of educational policy. Consider the following additional example:

GOAL: Develop attitudes, values, and moral or ethical judgment and behavior essential to human dignity and the development of a humane civilization.

The second level of refinement may include:

Render moral judgments in personal life consistent with the liberal tradition.

Behave morally in life situations consistent with the highest levels of humane and liberal values.

Operationalization of the foregoing statements is achieved by defining levels of moral judgment and moral behavior in related situational contexts. At the

---

[2]Note that various examples of goals may differ in level of detail from example to example. With experience and time, the statements become more detailed. At the goal level they eventually are made sufficiently specific as to clearly suggest the operations by which they may be measured. Such operations are, of course, broader than those suggested by performance objectives specific to the school context.

second level of detail, it is also obvious that the value orientations of participating audiences are becoming more explicit. As these audiences define the importance of the goals in the prioritization process and allocate resources, in the later refinement processes, the related values context gains additional detail. The final level of detail is provided through the definition of processes and methods for achieving objectives.

Prioritization Stage

The foregoing discussion points out briefly again the importance of clarifying the "values context" for the formulation and selection of goals and performance objectives. The process of deriving goals in the community can have an obvious influence on the value positions which come to weigh on the final selection of goals. Such positions in turn will influence the selection of objectives at lower levels and may heavily determine the processes for achieving objectives. Procedures used for validating and prioritizing a tentative set of goals should explicitly account for the unique contributions of the various participating audiences. An appropriate procedure would seem to include at least the following steps (not necessarily in this sequence):

(1)   Construct or adopt an explicit values position consistent with that of the community, interrelating ethical principles, psychological theory, and decision process as they relate to human development.
(2)   Derive goals from (1) above.
(3)   Elaborate goals using appropriate specialized audiences.
(4)   Validate and prioritize goals within the community using survey techniques.
(5)   Communicate and validate goals with selected specific audiences (e.g., the board of education and the educational community should review the goals).

Methods for gathering judgment data from appropriate community audiences have been reviewed by Stake (1970). One of the more promising and appropriate techniques for determining priorities among objectives is the Q-sort described by Kerlinger (1967). In this technique, the respondent sorts statements on small cards into a 1-2-3-4-3-2-1 distribution (for 16 statements) which results in a set of relative priority values easily aggregated into an overall set of priorities (the most extreme positive and negative statements go into the "1" positions). These judgments in turn may be taken to indicate the feelings and attitudes of the community toward the goals and subsequent priorities may then be based on actual performance deviations from less or more important goals. The Phi Delta Kappa materials (1972) provide an inexpensive and easily used technique for prioritizing some 18 goals, although the user must accept the limitations of the prepackaged statements.

Performance Objective Derivation Stage

As previously noted, the task of selecting performance objectives ideally follows the explication of a values position and the final selection of goals. The professional staff then undertakes the task of deriving, selecting, and preparing the various levels of performance objectives which define the needed program outcome layers — the program structure.

Goals from which performance objectives will be refined are determined on the basis of perceived and expected needs within the district values context. Consistency between goals and performance objectives in programs begins with a formal process of derivation of objectives at the program level. The process involves refinement of program objectives from goals and consideration of the life situations to which the goals have relevance. Once the program level objectives have been systematically derived, it is then appropriate to make use of prepared banks to define performance standards at successively lower levels in a program. Due to the difficulties and expense involved in the formal derivation process, district personnel will frequently move directly to the levels of objectives provided in banks and will eventually work "upward" to define the terminal standards for programs. Ideally, however, the process should occur as depicted in Figure 6.2, working down from goals to instructional performance objectives.

Once derived, the goals indicate the broad range of situations within which appropriate behavior is to be displayed. For example, recall the following goals, but with the further consideration given to defining the constituent behaviors and situations of interest:

Behave morally in life situations (?) consistent with. . . .

Be able to communicate verbally and in writing in a range of common life situations (?). . . .

The specification of the behaviors and related life situations occurs largely in the form of simulations of the actual life behaviors and situations. These are in turn classifiable as performing a specific task of skill ("weigh materials using a chemical balance"), a generalized skill ("adjust the carburetor of any type of

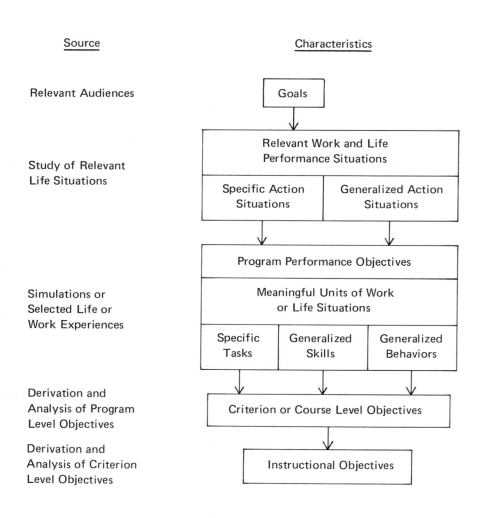

Sequence of Performance Objective Derivation

Figure 6.2

gasoline-engined land vehicle"), or a generalized behavior ("obey local traffic laws when operating a motor vehicle"). When stated as objectives, these skills or behaviors should simulate as closely as possible the intended life or work performance situations as shown in the following comparison:

Inappropriate or non-terminal (does not closely simulate real-life requirements):	<u>Using classroom notes</u>, the student should be able to convert from the English system of linear measurement to the metric system.
Appropriate or relevant simulation of life event (simulates some real-life requirements closely):	Given six common problems requiring conversion from the English system to the metric system of linear measurement, the student will correctly solve five of the problems in 15 minutes.

Given a set of terminal program level objectives derived as shown in the foregoing examples, lower level objectives can be selected or refined in a context of relevance. Objectives selected from an information bank must be justified in terms of their ultimate contribution to program objectives and through these to the goals of the system. This selection process is conditioned by the spiritual and scientific content of the district educational philosophy. For example, in defining the program structure, district personnel will set successive levels of mastery for objectives. These are not arbitrarily set, but take into account the characteristics of human development. Competence is thus gained only after a period of incompetence, practice, and consistent display of a given skill. The achievement of competence is followed by a period of practice, of over-learning, of the newly gained skill. Competence in one level of skill eventually gives way to an entirely new skill of a higher order. In summary, knowledge and theory of human development will condition the selection and modification of performance objectives.

Summary

The discussion in this chapter has focused on the ideal process by which an appropriate philosophical and organizational context is established for the derivation and ordering of goals and objectives for an educational system. Involved are an explicit statement of the values position held by the system, obtained through interaction of community representatives, system personnel, and technical experts, and the identification of system goals flowing from the values position. Following the broad goal statements, a process of elaboration begins, resulting ultimately in the refinement of various levels of performance objectives.

It is emphasized that the process illustrated in this chapter is an ideal one that seldom occurs in reality. Nevertheless, the portrayal of the ideal serves to emphasize that whether they have been explicitly, consciously, or systematically considered, the values of a community are, in the final analysis, the ultimate context in which the goals and objectives of an educational system are chosen.

Chapter 7

Selecting and Organizing
Performance Objectives for Curricula

Chapter 6 presented a theory of the context or background that should be created to facilitate a logical and representative basis for deriving and selecting goals and objectives for an educational system. It is clearly recognized, however, that this ideal process is often supplanted by a less comprehensive procedure which may begin within a single course, or, perhaps, within a given content area. The present chapter reviews a number of practical procedures for selecting and organizing objectives from available banks and other organized sources.

The procedure for deriving objectives for a course or content area assumes that the input is a set of raw objectives chosen for their relevance to the course or area content. These objectives are usually only nominally classified, of mixed, unidentified levels of importance, possibly written improperly, and varying in comprehensiveness. Therefore, an explicit plan for selection or organization should be prepared prior to the process itself.

There are four main operations necessary for selecting the objectives to be included in the final set for the course or content area. These operations are:

(1) Construction of a content outline to aid and organize selection.
(2) Designation of importance or emphasis among objectives.
(3) Evaluation of the objectives for appropriateness for the educational system and its students.
(4) Checking the objectives for completeness in relation to accepted standards for writing objectives.

The discussion of these four operations is followed by two illustrations of the objective selection process.

The Content Outline

Constructing the content outline is usually the first task in the selection process. Sources of the content outline include the existing course structure, available texts, other course outlines, and expert opinion. Ordinarily two to three levels of topic subordination in the outline are found useful for objective selection.

When a content outline is constructed as an aid in selecting objectives for a course, a framework is established into which the raw objectives may be sorted for preliminary organization. Thus, the set of raw objectives is broken into subsets relating to the content topics of the course or area. If some topics are revealed as having no objectives, then objectives must be derived for them so the topic will be included in instruction.

It is appropriate to note again that objectives relating to many content areas are widely available from outside agencies in organized banks and other forms. Referring to these sources when objectives for a topic are needed is likely to produce the needed material more conveniently than would trying to write appropriate objectives.

Once the content outline is prepared, it is used to sort the objectives into their appropriate topic or content categories.

Designating Importance

As objectives are being sorted into the content outline, its major topics should be weighted in terms of importance in the course or area. A tally of objectives actually placed within each content category should be maintained and the frequency of selection should be compared to the categories' judged importance. Generally, more important categories have more objectives or more complex objectives. Objectives within categories are then to be rated along a scale of importance, such as the following:

(1)   Very important
(2)   Above average importance
(3)   Average importance
(4)   Less than average importance
(5)   Inappropriate or irrelevant

The outcomes of the ratings and tallies include the elimination of some objectives and an indication of categories where objectives need to be adjusted in terms of content, number, and complexity. The weight of each objective in the course or area should be clearly determined at this point.

The objectives, sorted into the outline and weighted according to the importance each has for the content, then must be tested for their appropriateness.

Evaluation of Objectives for Appropriateness

Once the initial set of raw objectives has been located in the outline and adjusted to reflect judged importance, the selection committee can begin to apply more complex evaluative criteria to insure the relevance and appropriateness of each objective for the system. These evaluative criteria should be developed with the following considerations:

(a)   Appropriateness to the Instructional Area. The derivation of the content outline only assures the representation of content across objectives. The objectives should then be examined in terms of their focus on the types of skills that can be developed in the area, whether specific or complex and generalized. Are different types of objectives appropriately included? Cognitive representation? Affective representation? Psychomotor representation? Do the objectives overemphasize memorization of facts as opposed to more complex behaviors involved in application and evaluation?

(b)   Appropriateness and Attainability of Students. The objectives should be examined in terms of their developmental implications for the intended student audience. Students should have completed important prerequisites and should be ready for any new stages of development represented by the objectives. In addition, the objectives should be consistent with students' motivational patterns, needs, and interests.

(c)   Appropriateness to Goals of the System. The objectives should be carefully examined in terms of their relation to the ultimate goals of the system. Do they logically contribute to long-term goals? Do they simulate as closely as possible ultimate situations of interest? Do they more frequently reflect generalized skills and behaviors as opposed to specific?

After this evaluation for appropriateness, the objectives must also be checked for completeness.

Evaluation of Objectives for Completeness

Following evaluation for appropriateness, the objectives should be given a final check to insure that all important components are present and vagueness is eliminated. A complete performance objective is stated specifically and behaviorally and contains the behavior expected, the conditions of performance, and the criterion of success. Any number of training booklets, such as Stating Behavicral Objectives for Classroom Instruction (Gronlund, 1970), are helpful for this task.

Once the four operations described above are completed, the set of objectives should be comprehensive, precise, and ready for instructional planning and use. Two examples of the objective selection process — one simple, the other more complex — are presented below.

Simple Example of Objective Selection

The first example of procedures for selecting objectives is generally appropriate in applications that are less than system-wide. Such is the case where a single teacher becomes involved in criterion-referenced evaluation. Or the effort may be initiated on a volunteer basis level by level or course by course.

Content Outline

Figure 7.1 is part of a content outline for an eighth grade mathematics course. The sources for an outline include texts, relevant expert opinion, and, of course, the teacher's experience. The subtopics listed under each major topic might be considered as appropriate units of instruction for which lessons and objectives remain to be determined. Into this content outline must be sorted the appropriate course and instructional objectives.

When an outline is used as a selection device, available objectives are simply located within the outline and numbered to match the content number. For example, the objective in Figure 7.2 might be selected as the first objective in the subtopic "Union and Intersection" within the major topic "Sets" of the outline in Figure 7.1.

As the objectives are being sorted into the outline, a tally should be kept of the number that fall into each topic and subtopic. Noting this frequency will help in the next step, designating importance.

I.   Sets
           Subsets
           Union and Intersection
           Venn Diagrams
II.   Real Numbers
           Sum and Difference of Positive Common Fractions
           Product and Quotient of Positive Common Fractions
           Sum and Difference of Positive Decimal Fractions
           Product and Quotient of Positive Decimal Fractions
           Sum and Difference of Integers
III.   Measurement
           Linear Measure
           Metric System Conversion
           English System Conversion
IV.   Geometry
           Perimeter of Polygons in Metric System
           Perimeter of Polygons in English System
           Area of Quadrilaterals
           Area of Triangles

Part of a Content Outline Used for
Selecting Objectives for a Course

Figure 7.1

Objective Number: XXXX   Math 8
                                                             Semester 1

Major Topic: Sets
Subtopic: Union and Intersection

Objective: Given two sets, the student will list their union and intersection.

Example of the Selection of Objectives

Figure 7.2

Designating Importance

By comparing the tallied frequency of objectives in each topical category with the judged relative importance of the category, imbalance in the projected instruction will be revealed. As a general rule, more important content categories are associated with more and more complex objectives.

Each objective within a topical category should also be ranked on a scale of relevance to its topic. The results of this comparing and ranking will indicate topics or subtopics needing more or less emphasis and will show the importance of each objective to the unit, possibly leading to the elimination of some.

For instance, both objectives in Figure 7.3 would reasonably be included in the unit on Union and Intersection. The first objective, however, would be given a higher ranking on relevance as it represents an important course outcome of the unit, while the second designates an enabling behavior subordinate to the first.

Objective 1: Given two sets, the student will list their union and intersection.

Objective 2: Given a list of definitions, the student will identify the definition of <u>union</u>.

Selection of Objectives with Two Levels of Importance

Figure 7.3

Evaluating Appropriateness

Following the ranking, the objectives are then evaluated in terms of their appropriateness to the instructional area, to the students, and to the larger goals of the system.

In relation to the instructional area, each objective should be reviewed as to whether the skills developed are generalizable or complex. Generalizable skills should be favored.

For instance, consider the two objectives in Figure 7.4. The first objective represents a much more generalizable skill than the second and would therefore be considered a more appropriate course objective.

Objective 1:   Given two sets, the student will list their union and intersection.

Objective 2:   Given the symbols for union and intersection, the student will write their names.

Selection of Objectives with
Two Levels of Appropriateness
Figure 7.4

Questions should also be raised about the attainability of each objective for students at this developmental level. Have prerequisite skills been taught? Does the objective fit student needs? Again, the first objective in Figure 7.4 seems developmentally more appropriate for students at the eighth grade level, while the second, possibly prerequisite to the first, would be appropriate at a lower program level.

Each objective should finally be scrutinized in light of its contribution to the long-range goals of the system. Referring again to the objectives in Figure 7.4, the first objective has more impact on the broad goals of a district than does the more discrete second objective.

Evaluation for Completeness

Finally, each objective tentatively selected is examined for its completeness. Are the expected behavior, conditions of performance, and standard of performance all included?

Figure 7.5 shows two objectives to be compared for completeness. The first, familiar from the above discussion, clearly states the expected behavior — list their union or intersection — and the conditions — given two sets. The standard of performance is implicitly "without error." The second objective, however, would need considerable revision before being admissible to a performance curriculum. Neither an observable behavior nor the conditions of performance are included in the second objective.

Objective 1:   Given two sets, the student will list their union and intersection.

Objective 2:   Students will know the union of sets.

Selection of Objectives with Two Levels of Completeness
Figure 7.5

As this process of evaluation is repeated for each objective tentatively sorted into a course content outline, the course and instructional objectives are clarified, instructional planning and management are enhanced, and systematic evaluation activities are made possible. The process can greatly increase the effectiveness of instruction and decision-making.

Selecting Objectives from a System

The second example of objective selection considers the objective bank and supporting selection procedures prepared by Aschbacher and Fitzgerald (1972) under the direction of Dr. Rodney Skager at the Center for the Study of Evaluation (CSE). It is more appropriate at the program and program element levels than the first example. Staff at the CSE have for some time been engaged in a project involving the development of a bank of reading objectives, associated test items, and a field manual for selecting objectives. The bank now makes available some 500 reading objectives (generic in form) to be located within the grade levels of a reading program by the user and later also used to prepare tests by withdrawing related test items from an item bank.

The CSE's SOBAR (System for Objectives Based Assessment — Reading) bank incorporates the following basic operations in the selection procedure:

(1)   Selection through the successive levels of a content outline
(2)   A numbering scheme for uniquely identifying objectives
(3)   A leveling method
(4)   A rough sequencing procedure
(5)   A method for rating importance or emphasis
(6)   Suggested evaluation criteria

The Content Outline

The most general level of the SOBAR content outline is reproduced in Figure 7.6 (Aschbacher & Fitzgerald, 1970, p. 10), which shows the six major categories in which objectives are grouped.

Encoding (10000)	Translating a spoken letter or word into a written letter or word. Student hears a sound and writes its letter(s).
Decoding (20000)	Translating written letters and words into sounds. Student correctly pronounces letter combinations.
Vocabulary (30000)	Includes word-meanings, some "grammar," and technical terms.
Comprehension (40000)	Reading passages of various lengths are given. A distinction is made between literal meanings and interpretations.
Reference, Location, and Study Skills (50000)	Contains objectives dealing with using books to find information and with some study skills related to reading. Reading is here considered a tool that the student would use in the course of his work in subjects other than reading.
Affective (60000)	Deals with feelings and attitudes about reading. This is an important area, but it has many measurement problems.

The Six Major Categories of the SOBAR Content Classification System

Figure 7.6

The user starts the selection process by familiarizing himself with the content outline and by working down through as many as three additional levels of content, as shown in Figure 7.7 (Aschbacher & Fitzgerald, 1972, p. 12). For example, if the user decided the superordinate category, Encoding, as defined in the manual, was appropriate for students at his level of the system, he would eventually be led to the actual objectives at the finest level of content classification. (In the example shown in Figure 7.7, the objective is "The learner will divide given words into syllables.")

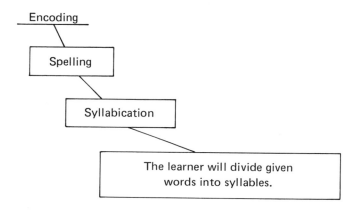

Successive Levels of Content in the SOBAR
Content Classification System

Figure 7.7

The process of working through successive levels of content allows for the elimination of entire segments of a bank without at first examining the objectives themselves. The objectives and levels of classification are further coded numerically with a five-digit number, one digit for each level of classification, with the last two digits identifying a particular objective within the levels of content, as shown in Figure 7.8 (Aschbacher & Fitzgerald, 1972).

Objective 13201

1   Encoding

3   Spelling

2   Syllabication

0   Place Holder

1   The Objective

Numerical Coding Scheme in the
SOBAR System
Figure 7.8

Leveling, Sequencing, and Selecting for Importance

Working first individually and then in groups or teams, the SOBAR users select objectives appropriate for a given grade level, using the labels Essential, Supplemental, and Not Appropriate as defined in Figure 7.9.

When the selection procedure is completed individually (each teacher in each level on a selection team), the selection team comes together to combine their decisions in a single chart incorporating all grade levels as shown in Figure 7.10 (Aschbacher & Fitzgerald, 1972, p. 24). This consensus results in a rough sequencing in terms of the location of objectives in levels. The corresponding indication of E, S, or N on the same objective at different levels serves to identify roughly its point of introduction, the level of greatest emphasis (and, incidentally, its point of mastery), and the points of review or recycling.

Evaluation Criteria

The evaluation criteria presented in the SOBAR system are limited. The user apparently accepts the objectives, once selected, as they stand. Apparently, no extensive rewriting or modification are expected or recommended except for the addition of specific content appropriate to the level(s) for which an objective was selected. A section of the manual, however, does suggest that the character-

---

Essential (E)
Objectives labeled E should:

a. represent reading skills so fundamental and important to the program that 90% of the target students at a given grade level are expected to achieve them,

and

b. be few enough in total number that they are a realistic definition of what most students are expected to learn.

Supplemental (S)
Objectives labeled S should:

a. be profitable for the children to master if there is instructional time after the E objectives have been mastered,

or

b. be geared to a smaller portion of the students than the 90% level of E. The S objectives could either be remedial or enrichment for a given grade level.

Not Appropriate at This Level (N)
Objectives labeled N should:

a. be inappropriate at the level you represent. The N objectives may be appropriate at another level or they may be inappropriate for the entire program.

Criteria for Leveling and Selecting Objectives
on Importance in SOBAR

Figure 7.9

			K	1	2	3	4	5	6
Auditory Discrimination	11101	Pair of speech sounds; identify identical pairs							
	11102	Identify pairs of oral words beginning w/same con sound							
	11103	Identify pairs of oral words containing same medial consonant sound							
	11104	Identify pairs of oral words ending w/same con sound							
	11105	Identify pairs of oral words w/same vowel sound							
	11106	Pairs of oral words; identify rhyming pairs							

Decision Chart for Recording Objectives Selections in the
SOBAR System for the Total Reading Program

Figure 7.10

istics of target students be taken into account and that selection is limited by local availability of reading materials implied by a set of objectives.

Summary

The two examples presented above and the discussion previous to the examples focused on the selection of objectives for a course or content area
through the use of a content outline and a series of tests of inclusion suitability
for each objective.

These methods will be of value to a user not only to insure the selection of
a comprehensive and well-defined set of course or content area objectives, but
also to assist in the explication of program structure.

Objective banks or collections vary in the quality of their material, in the
extent of their explicit contribution to the program structure organization in the
types, levels, and specificity of objectives included, and in the extent to which

the objectives contribute to the derivation of related test items for evaluation. Depending on the structure and content of the objective source, the user will have more or less work to do in specifying the structure of the course or content area in performance terms and in creating conditions for measurement and evaluation. Once the objectives are selected, the next step in specifying the structure is organizing the objectives for instruction and evaluation.

Chapter 8

The Organization of Objectives
for Instruction and Evaluation

The preceding chapters have presented the operations involved in the generation of the overall structure for a program as well as the derivation and content organization of performance-based curricula included therein. The procedures considered to this point result in an internal structure with the following major characteristics and level of organization:

— A tentative content or skills outline exists for developing objectives communication.
— The curriculum may include more than one type or level of objective.
— Objectives have been identified in terms of importance or emphasis.
— Objectives have been roughly sequenced into levels.
— Objectives which may be considered developmental are now clearly apparent by their repetition from level to level in the curriculum structure.

The purpose of this chapter is to illustrate the additional levels of structure needed to create a performance curriculum that directly supports instructional and evaluation activities. The tentative structure resulting from the process of selecting objectives obviously must come before the more complete organization underlying an instructional system. A more complete underlying structure must in turn be developed before the development of instructional materials and methods is undertaken, or the evaluation approach is determined. The discussion in this chapter intends to illustrate the structure and activities needed to organize objectives for instruction and evaluation. This structure is applicable to entire programs as well as to single courses.

In order for instructional planning to proceed realistically, the objectives must be allocated within a time framework. That is, before lessons can be planned the available time for instruction has to be spread out over the objectives in a fashion that reflects their relative importance.

Similarly, administrative decisions regarding the assignment of personnel, space, and materials depend on analysis of the needs of instruction within the system. These needs can be determined only by refining the structure of curricula to the point where the resources needed to teach the system's content to its clientele become clear.

Evaluation activities await the instructional organization also. Until the fully developed instructional system is documented, there is no explicit structure for deriving an evaluation design. In addition, the design of periodic evaluation instruments must be preceded by knowledge of when curricula objectives are to be introduced to students. The organizational scheme presented in this chapter provides examples of this final structuring needed to support the instructional, administrative, and evaluative activities necessary to implement curricula.

A Theoretical Curriculum Structure

The further structuring of objectives into units for instruction is variously known as course design, program design, or course structure. The course or program design implies the evaluation design and the tests and reports needed to support decision-making by the instructor, students, and others. A grade level structure with traditional instructional units will effectively use one particular type of evaluation design; an individualized program with many levels and smaller instructional units will use a basically different type of design.

The design or structure of a course or of a program area with several levels obviously also constrains the organization and pacing of instruction and ultimately its flexibility in relating to individual needs. The point at which instructional staff may appropriately attend to this basic issue of course or program design is during the process of selecting objectives. At that time, additional rules for leveling, organizing, and sequencing objectives may be generated to achieve a given design which will ultimately be consistent with the local education philosophy.

The design used here to provide an example of this final level of organization is called the block design. The block design is generally applicable as a basis for structuring a relatively lengthy program area, such as K-6 reading, or shorter program portions, such as a single course. The principle of blocking may be applied directly to a grade level oriented, group-paced area of instruction, and will eventually provide an adequate structure for an individualized program.

Leveling and Blocking

The initial step in developing a block design for an entire program is to create a set of ordered levels within which blocks of objectives and related instruction will be organized. For most program areas, about ten levels will be sufficient. These levels are roughly analogous to a course or grade level in a program. A major difference between a level and its constituent blocks and a grade level in a program area is that the former includes a single ordinal level of instruction, while the latter may simultaneously include several overlapping levels of instruction. For example, in a blocking system with levels, level 5 represents a unique level of instruction more difficult than level 4 and less difficult than level 6. A grade level, however, may include levels 4, 5, and 6 simultaneously. The levels in a blocking structure thus communicate the developmental levels of a curriculum set in the context of a smooth continuum.

Figure 8.1 shows how blocks of objectives may be organized into levels for the same program area. The first column demonstrates a one-to-one relationship between grade and curriculum levels. The second column shows the objectives blocked into semester-length units. The third column shows how the objectives might be blocked into levels for an adult education program.

In the adult education program, note how the usual notions of time are collapsed into aggregates of former grade levels. The relation of levels and time to learn is a matter of local choice emanating from such considerations as optimal periods for cycling students, the ability to form teams of teachers for instruction, and the availability of required instructional materials. Levels are currently set largely by traditional notions of grade and the availability of textual materials which take about a school year to cover or get through.

Blocks in Levels

Once a system of levels is decided upon, it is then necessary to create the blocking unit for organizing objectives for instruction. Often, a set of 10 blocks for such a level will be found adequate for grouping objectives. This blocking principle and its relation to time to learn are shown in Figure 8.2. A block normally represents a period of learning of 15 to 30 hours, the average being approximately 20 hours. In addition, the block is an administrative and instructional unit to be formed around a related set (or group) of objectives which can be

Levels 200 Hrs.	Levels 100 Hrs.	Levels Adult Ed	Equivalent Grade Levels
14	28	6	
	27		College
13	26	5	
	25		
12	24		12
	23		
11	22	4	11
	21		
10	20		10
	19		
9	18		9
	17	3	
8	16		8
	15		
7	14		7
	13		
6	12		6
	11	2	
5	10		5
	9		
4	8		4
	7		
3	6		3
	5		
2	4	1	2
	3		
1	2		1
	1		

Curriculum Objective Levels for Different Program Organizations
Figure 8.1

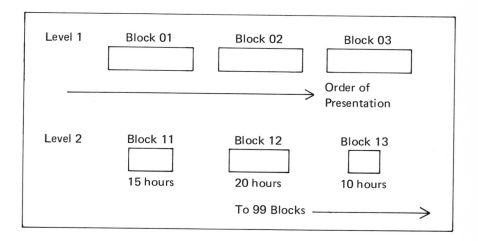

The Blocking Organization Within Levels

Figure 8.2

organized in relation to available staff and material resources. Blocks may be ordered from easy to difficult or presented in random order as determined in the local scheme. A completed system of levels and blocks so ordered represents a structure within which a specific placement device may be developed for isolating students' levels of instruction.

It should be noted that the foregoing leveling and blocking schemes will be overlaid by an administrative scheme for organizing staff and resources to present the instruction on the objectives placed in blocks. This latter scheme may be a traditional graded organization with different students in a grade level involved in different levels and blocks of instruction. More advanced and flexible approaches would eliminate grade levels and utilize certain forms of teaming, continuous regrouping of students, and so on.

Content and Administrative Units in Blocks

The next step in block organization involves the placement and sequencing of objectives into content and administrative units within blocks. This activity will draw heavily on the information locally generated in selecting objectives and organizing them into a tentative curriculum as described in the previous chapter. The content unit will usually incorporate two levels of content drawn from the outline used in the local selection of objectives. Table 8.3 shows excerpts from two such content outlines modified to serve as content units. Such content units represent the labels to be used in reporting performance of a student or of a level of the educational system and should be selected accordingly. For example, a student's report card may communicate his current level of a performance on number systems or whole numbers. It is important to adjust the language of content units so that the type of behavior involved is easily understood by teachers, parents, and students. The content unit is always synonymous with a group of objectives and sometimes with a unit of instruction and a set of lessons.

Mathematics	Reading
Number Systems	Vocabulary
Whole Numbers	Words in Context
Integers	Historical Origins
Rational Numbers	Meaning
Real Numbers	Analyzing New Words
Complex Numbers	
Finite Number Systems	Comprehension
Matrices and Determinants	Main Idea
	Details
	Sequence

Examples of Content Units

Figure 8.3

The administrative units within a block of instruction are the module or instructional unit, followed by the lesson, and the objective. The formation and organization of these administrative units is facilitated by the integration of the content units with the system of levels generated for the local application. Figure 8.4 shows the placement of levels of content units within the levels of blocks.

Topics by Levels	I	II	III	IV
Number Systems	Zero; whole numbers; place value; counting; addition	Numeration systems; factors; primes; operations on integers	Operations on rationals; negative integers	Operations on negative numbers
Algebra			Solutions of open sentences	Solutions of equations; polynomials
Geometry	Common Shapes	Triangles	Informal plane geometry	Characteristics of lines
Measurement	Common Systems	Linear, angular measurement	Linear, angular measurement; area; volume; metrics	Measurement as a system
Statistics		Sets	Graphs and measures of central tendency	Deductive proof

Example of Placement of Topics by Levels

Figure 8.4

The superordinate content unit (Topic) is potentially applicable to every level of the system. The second order of content may be applicable to more than one level of the system or may be modified from level to level. For example, main idea, a second-order content unit in reading, would be applicable to every level of a reading continuum, at differing appropriate levels of difficulty.

Following the placement of the content units into the levels of the curriculum, the second-order content units are ordered into tentative blocks and instructional units. The objectives initially selected for the curriculum are then located in the instructional units. Units of instruction will thus be developed around the conjunction of one or more second-order content units in a block, the associated objectives for those content units, and the actual content of the objectives. The overall organization of administrative units into levels, blocks, and objectives is shown in Figure 8.5.

The final step in creating the curriculum structure for any given block is to specify the end behaviors expected as a result of instruction on the content of the units in blocks. Often, these will consist of the complex sampling objectives defined previously in the discussion of performance objectives. An example is a performance objective which specifies the drawing of a random sample of 20 addition facts, with the conditions that the student must show 95% correct performance in three minutes. At another level in the curriculum, and in another block, this same objective simply presents a more difficult set of problems under the same conditions of speed and accuracy. Finally, there is a true terminal point in that the most difficult content is sampled in the most advanced block dealing with this objective. A summary of the steps in this organizing procedure is shown in Figure 8.6.

The application of the blocking concept to a curriculum generates the kind of definite structure required for rational instructional planning, administrative resource allocation, and the application of an appropriate evaluation design. Instructional planning is facilitated by the clear relationship established among curricular objectives and the available time for instruction on them. Evaluation is enhanced by having the objectives clearly enunciated, sequenced, and organized chronologically.

Coding Rules for the Block Design

As the curriculum structure is developed, its organization in terms of units, content, and objectives is most conveniently represented by numerical coding. What follows here are some brief suggestions for coding this structure where the program area extends over a period of several years. The same coding scheme is

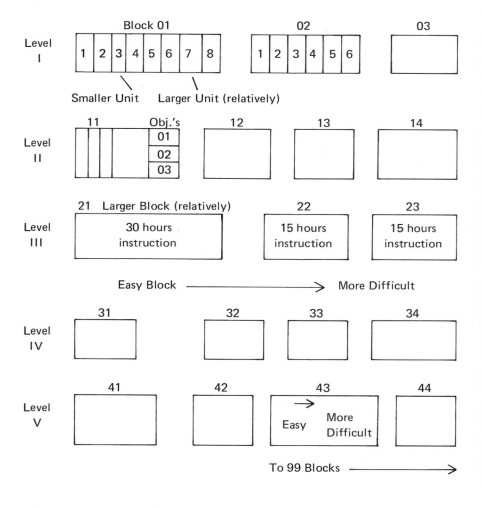

Block Organization for Units and Objectives

Figure 8.5

1. Define the two levels of the content unit (topics and subtopics).
2. Integrate content units and levels.
3. Organize the second-order content units into blocks.
4. Organize the content units in blocks into tentative instructional units.
5. Place the performance objectives derived from the selection process into the tentative instructional units and/or blocks.
6. Locate and organize the course level objectives and content into blocks and units on the basis of the convergence of similar objectives and content; for example,

Course Objective	Content	Level I Content	Level II Content
Given 10 addition problems with up to 8 addends and place value to 1 X 10^6, $\underline{S}$ will solve 9/10 correctly in 5 mins.	All possible addition problems.	332 +406	237492 1056731 + 472310
		490 +124	Etc.
		Etc.	Any Problem

Summary of Steps in the Curriculum Structure Organization

Figure 8.6

easily adapted for shorter programs or single courses.

Figure 8.7 illustrates the coding rules for communicating the administrative units in a program area with 10 levels. A total of four digits is used to carry the information on the organization of the objectives into levels, blocks, units, and objectives. The first two digits communicate both level and block. Level I has the first 10 blocks (1-10), Level II has the next 10 (11-20), Level III the next 10 (21-30), and so on. Objectives are then organized within blocks into groups or units of 20. For example, the numbers 0101 to 0120 are reserved for numbering objectives in the first unit in Block 1, Level I. This numbering scheme thus allows for five units of instruction in every block, up to 99 objectives in a block at any level, and a total of 999 objectives over all levels. The use of a numbering

Levels	Blocks	Unit 1	Unit 2	Unit 5
I	1-10	0101-0120	0121-0140	0181-0199
II	11-20	1101-1120	1121-1140	1181-1199
III	21-30	2101-2120	2121-2140	2181-2199
IV	31-40	3101-3120	3121-3140	3181-3199
V	41-50	4101-4120	4121-4140	4181-4199
VI	51-60	5101-5120	5121-5140	5181-5199
VII	61-70	6101-6120	6121-6140	6181-6199
VIII	71-80	7101-7120	7121-7140	7181-7199
IX	81-90	8101-8120	8121-8140	8181-8199
X	91-99	9101-9120	9121-9140	9181-9199

Coding Structure for Administrative Units in the Block Design

Figure 8.7

scheme such as this will allow ready identification of the components of the program structure in computer-generated reports and in discussions of program and individual student results.

Summary

The leveling and blocking procedure described in this chapter is an illustration of how to proceed to the final level of performance objectives organization needed to establish a workable framework in which a criterion-referenced evaluation model can be applied. Following this last step in the derivation and organization of objectives, the testing instruments and the evaluation designs are ordinarily developed to gather the evaluation data for decision-making.

The application of evaluation design principles will reflect the unique structure of the program or course of interest and the philosophy or model of instruction to be applied therein. Depending on the instructional model to be used, the block structure depicted previously might imply an evaluation design composed of survey tests used to place individuals in levels and thus form instructional groups. Thereafter, a series of pretests and posttests might be used to control the progress of instructional groups in each block. An individualized instructional model, applied to the same program structure, would result in the use of not only more tests, but also additional test types. The convergence of the course design or structure and the instructional model in a particular evaluation design is the subject of the next section.

PART III

Evaluation Design

Evaluation designs in education are usually either implicit or informal affairs applied for classroom purposes or are specially contrived and applied for purposes external to the operations of a school or district. The latter case includes funded research and evaluation studies which use a rich and substantial literature as a source for generating appropriate designs. This literature includes tests, technical research reports, and other materials which focus on the designs and analytical procedures appropriate to a broad variety of research questions and contexts.

By contrast, the contemporary evaluation design literature specifically relevant to the needs of the practicing educator is starkly lacking in quantity, richness, and detail. One gains the impression that the designs generally applied are those identified as least adequate or desirable in the educational research literature. There is thus a great and obvious need for a new literature on evaluation design which will address the unique and various needs of the educational practitioner.

Part III is a limited exploration of the elements and language of the evaluation design literature generated over the course of the development of the CAM concept. This discussion is based on evaluation designs generated in the field to fit the needs of teachers and others in a variety of courses and programs. The discussion begins with the concepts and procedures underlying the derivation of tests for criterion-referenced evaluation. Following the discussion of test derivation, a hypothetical curriculum is outlined and four different evaluation designs are presented to illustrate the relative gains and losses in information implicit in various designs. This initial presentation of evaluation design is relevant to group-paced instructional contexts; a final section shows how evaluation design elements may be applied to individualized instructional contexts.

129

Chapter 9

Deriving Tests for the
Criterion-Referenced Evaluation Model

Initial discussion in this section focuses on the derivation of tests for use in criterion-referenced evaluation. The discussion is first concerned with the types of tests used to generate achievement data for decision-making and the tasks of writing and selecting test items to measure objectives achievement. In the final chapter section, a brief discussion of evaluation design precedes a suggested process for efficiently constructing test forms appropriate for particular evaluations.

The type of test used, the range of content tested, and the points of test administration are all elements of evaluation design. They must be selected to reflect the curriculum structure and the information needs of the decision-maker in relation to this structure.

The Concept of Test Type

The test forms to be included in a given evaluation design can be classified in two dimensions: content and time of administration. The content of a test refers to the behaviors sampled in it. The content may be restricted to a single, narrowly defined behavior such as "addition of pairs of single-digit numbers," or it may include a very broad set of behaviors such as "fifth grade mathematics." The time of test administration is always considered relative to the time of instruction over its content.

Test Form Content

In terms of its content, a test may generally be classified as either a survey test or a mastery test.

A survey test, as its name implies, surveys the content of a curriculum structure in some systematic way. For instance, a survey test may sample from among the major cumulative objectives of several levels of a program. An example of such a test would be a reading test sampling five to ten different comprehension factors, each at ten different levels of readability. A more narrowly conceived survey test may contain one item for each key objective in a course and thus represent a survey of the total course content. The sampling plan for a survey test may be selected on the basis of the relative importance of objectives by choosing objectives according to an arbitrarily set interval, for instance, every sixth objective in a course, or by some other method. The point is that a survey test seeks a broad approximation of student achievement by measuring attainment of a sample of the objectives in one or more levels of a curriculum.

Survey tests are customarily used in one of three ways. First, as a gross placement device, a survey test yields information for determining the appropriate level of a program in which to place a student. Secondly, survey tests are used at the conclusion of a relatively long instructional sequence (a course or a program) to measure achievement of the major objectives of the sequence. Such a use of the survey test is familiar as a final examination when time limitations preclude testing every instructional objective. Finally, a set of survey tests can be used to determine group standing in relation to a sequence of objectives. Such a set might include four tests, each measuring achievement on a different quarter of a course's objectives. The group of test takers would be divided into four heterogeneous subgroups, each taking a different form. When the results are compiled, a picture of the total group's achievement relative to the objectives emerges.

The survey test obviously has no immediate implications for decisions relating to the contemporary progress of a given student's instruction. Therefore, a mastery test is usually employed to get more detailed information about student achievement over a short range of objectives. The concept of the mastery test describes a test in which the content is systematically sampled to aid decision-making for individual students at a given point in time. The content span of such a test is much narrower and thus usually yields an estimate of a given student's performance on one or more discrete behaviors or objectives. For this reason, mastery tests are often used to support individualized instructional programs.

Both survey and mastery type criterion-referenced tests have a place in educational evaluation. Each is a reflection of two points in a continuum, in turn reflecting the organization of the curriculum's behavioral content. Therefore, each offers certain data-gathering advantages for specific decision-making situations.

Time of Administration

Tests may also be classified according to the relationship between administration and time of instruction on objectives included in the content of the test. The shortest time designations made are relative to units of instruction, which typically include at least one and usually several objectives. Four time-related classifications are generally used: pretest, curriculum-embedded test, posttest, and retention test.

Pretest is the well-known term for a test given before instruction. A pretest is designed to discover what prior information or skills students bring to the instructional environment before instruction begins. This information may be sought for placement purposes, for decisions regarding the amount of instruction a student or an objective may need, for curriculum validation, or for assessment of the impact of instruction or instructional materials.

A curriculum-embedded test is given during the course of instruction. Such a test may even be a part of the instructional process itself, as in the programmed learning mode where immediate feedback to the learner is heavily utilized. Curriculum-embedded tests relate to the immediate time frame of the unit only, whereas the pretest, posttest, and retention test may be relative to courses, levels, or whole programs.

A posttest is given at the conclusion of an instructional sequence, usually before instruction on new content has begun. A posttest may be used to measure student achievement of the objectives in a unit (or course or program) immediately following instruction without regard for the student's prior knowledge. Or a posttest may be used in conjunction with a pretest to assess the effectiveness of instruction or resources, or for curriculum validation.

A retention test is given after instruction has occurred and new content has intervened. A retention test measures how well students have integrated skills or knowledge after the immediate impact of instruction has been affected by the passage of time and the introduction of different content. In practice, a test is often classified as seeking retention information if it is given more than 20 (instructional) days after the conclusion of instruction. The purpose of a retention test includes measuring student achievement after a long instructional sequence (e.g., a course) as well as curriculum validation and assessing the long-range impact of instructional activities and materials.

From the discussion above, it is clear that there are several program levels within which a test may be classified according to its time of administration. A pretest may be given prior to a whole program, to a level in a program, to a course, or to a unit. A posttest or retention test may be related to a program in the same way.

Each type of time-classified test serves specific informational purposes. The selection of test types in relation to time in a given evaluation design depends on the needs of the decision-makers who will use the data to be gathered by the tests. The time-related information needs of different decision-makers may be accounted for in the same test type.

A Matrix of Test Types

The criterion-referenced tests used to gather data for evaluation can be classified according to both content and time of administration. A matrix is shown in Figure 9.1 that portrays how the two classification dimensions come together to specify test forms for specific purposes. Some examples drawn from the matrix are discussed more fully below.

Level/survey pretest. This test type samples all the important criterion objectives for a curriculum (or grade) level — for instance, third grade reading. Results of a level or survey pretest would tell a teacher which level of the curriculum was appropriate for a student or which broad groups of objectives or skills were already practiced by a group or class. In the latter case, the test results would give the teacher a general idea as to which areas of the curriculum would need emphasis, which areas might be eliminated altogether, and how pupils might be grouped for instruction.

Unit/mastery pretest. A unit pretest covering all the important objectives for a unit diagnoses student needs by determining which objectives in the unit the students have already mastered and which they have yet to learn. In a totally individualized program, each student would be given instruction only on the objectives which he did not know. If a student showed mastery of all of the objectives in the unit, he would move on to a different unit and would take another pretest.

The pretest data could also be used to bring together students who have similar needs or show the same degree of mastery. That is, pupils could be grouped on the basis of the objectives they have or have not achieved prior to instruction.

In a group-paced program where the majority of students had mastered the objectives, the teacher would go on to another unit, making special provision for students who did not know the objectives.

A pretest might also include items on prerequisite objectives. It would thus indicate whether the pupils were ready to learn the objectives in the new unit.

| | **Content** | |
	Survey	Mastery
Pretest	Find approximate entry level for a student	Find precise entry point for a student
	Determine topics needing special emphasis	Find objectives to be learned or needing special emphasis
	Curriculum validation	Instructional or materials effectiveness
	Instructional or materials effectiveness	Provide periodic feedback to learner
Curriculum-Embedded Test		Monitor progress through objectives
		Provide ongoing feedback to learner
Posttest	Determine achievement over lengthy content span	Determine achievement over short content span
	Certify completion of longer instructional sequences, a level or range of levels	Certify completion of shorter instructional sequences
	Assess instructional effectiveness	Assess instructional effectiveness
	Exit achievement level on wide range of content	Exit achievement level on narrow range of content
Retention Test	Determine retained knowledge over long instructional sequences	Determine retained knowledge over short instructional sequences
	Assess course or program effectiveness	Assess course or program effectiveness
	Validate curriculum	Validate curriculum

*(left margin label: **Time of Administration**)*

A Matrix of Test Types

Figure 9.1

Curriculum-embedded test. The curriculum-embedded test (CET) tells how the student is progressing through the unit — whether he is learning from the instruction received. The CET could be a quick quiz on material just taught, it could be a single item or measure given informally by the teacher, or it could be a precise exercise that the pupil scores himself. If a student did not pass the short curriculum-embedded tests, the teacher would want to give him more detailed diagnostic tests. These might lead to instruction on prerequisites or to another mode of instruction for the same objective. Poor group results on CET's might affect the pace of instruction or prompt the teacher to use alternate methods or materials for the entire group.

Unit/mastery posttest. The unit posttest measures all the important objectives in a unit and is used in part to determine whether or not students have mastered or met the performance standards for the unit objectives. The posttest results would indicate whether there are students who need to repeat the unit or particular objectives in it before going on to the next. Repetition with an individualized approach would not mean doing the same things over again but rather working on the same objectives with alternate methods and/or materials.

In a situation where instruction is adapted to meet student needs as shown by pretests and curriculum-embedded tests, there should be few or no failures on posttests. This assumes that the student would be given enough time to master skills at his own pace and that, if he were unsuccessful with one mode of instruction, alternative methods would be available to him.

When there are failures on posttests, a number of questions can be asked. Some of these concern the tests used, some refer to the instruction itself. Here are some examples of questions the teacher and others might ask:

(1) Were students who received very low pretest scores or who failed to show progress on the CET's given tests on prerequisite objectives?

(2) Was attention given to individual scores on CET's, and was action taken on negative results?

(3) Was instruction on the objectives broken down into steps small enough to facilitate mastery?

(4) Was there flexibility so that students learned the objectives in any order which seemed logical to them, and was there recognition that the child's learning style will influence his concept of what is logical order?

(5) Was sufficient practice provided, and was the practice relevant to the behavior called for in the objective?

(6)   Were the learning opportunities provided appropriate to the
interests, developmental levels, and experience of the learners?

(7)   Did students receive feedback on test results, and were they reinforced by recognition of their success in achieving objectives?

(8)   Did the items developed to test for mastery on the pretest,
CET's, and posttest really measure the behavior called for in
the objectives?

(9)   Was instruction varied or intensified on the basis of the CET's
that showed some students were failing to achieve mastery?

Level/survey retention test. A level or survey retention test covers the
most important objectives in which a student has been instructed during the
school year. Its purpose is to check on the maintenance of skills, to find out
how well the student has retained what he had once learned.

Test scores showing loss of achievement on objectives once attained would
be reason for providing review on previously learned material. This might be giv-
en to selected individuals or to an entire group, depending on the extent of need
and the instructional model.

When a survey retention test is given to a group, objective and item sampling may be used to broaden the content sampled and shorten the individual
test forms.

Course/survey posttest. A course or survey posttest covers all of the important objectives for the course. Results tell which units students mastered and
which they did not. Results of a survey posttest might be used to determine
whether a student will progress to the next level of the curriculum or be recycled
through parts of the same level before advancing.

Test Types and Evaluation Design

Depending on needs and resources, an evaluation design appropriate to a
course or program will incorporate a number of test types to sample student performance through the content. The conjunction of a test type and a plan for
sampling content usually takes the form of a table of specifications, which is a
precise documentation of how the content is to be sampled in a given test form
or set of test forms. The evaluation designs presented in Chapters 11 through 14
demonstrate the variety and flexibility of sampling plans that can be applied to
specific situations.

Deriving Test Items for Performance Objectives

When the specifications for each test form in an evaluation design have been generated, the information is used to develop or select the required test items and produce the test forms. This section deals with the issues involved in developing or selecting test items appropriate for effecting the evaluation.

There are many types of specific test item formats available for measuring achievement. They all have two elements in common. First, there is always a stimulus designed to elicit a behavior from the test taker. This stimulus may be in the form of a question, a request, an incomplete statement, or a situation, to name a few. Regardless of its form, the stimulus is presented to elicit a behavior that indicates the test taker's accomplishment of an objective. Secondly, all test items seek a response, which is whatever action is taken as a result of the presentation of the stimulus. If the test taker performs the intended response(s), accomplishment of the objective is evidenced. Performance of any response other than that intended demonstrates a lack of achievement of the objective. Through careful design and analysis of incorrect responses, it is often possible to diagnose the cause of failure to master objectives.

Types of Test Items

Obviously, there are many possible ways to present a stimulus to a test taker, and many possible responses the test taker can give to a stimulus. Generally, however, the types of items fall into one of two categories: supply items and choice items.

Supply items ask the test taker to create an original response to the stimulus. The stimulus is presented as a direct question, an incomplete statement, a request, or a direction. In some cases, the stimulus may simply be the situation or environment. The test taker must respond to this stimulus on the basis of his or her interpretation of the stimulus with no other clues. Examples of supply items include questionnaires aimed at affective information, essay questions, incomplete sentences in need of completion, questions asking for short (e.g., a paragraph) answers, and items dealing with physical or athletic capabilities. While there is some feeling that supply type test items are better than choice items because clues are not given in the form of a set of possible answers, the sophistication of some choice type items makes them equally reliable for most situations. It is true, however, that supply items are more suited to some applications. For instance, an essay question that seeks to determine a student's ability to write an original theme could not be replaced by a choice item, nor could a physical education assessment be accomplished very well with choice type items.

Choice items, as has been indicated, provide various possible responses to a given stimulus to the test taker, who must choose the most appropriate. Within the choice type item classification there are, again, two different varieties. The first is the alternate choice item. In the alternate choice item, the test taker selects one of two alternate responses as the best answer. Examples are true/false, right/wrong, and yes/no items. While alternate choice items are adequate to measure some learning outcomes, they tend to be somewhat unreliable because of the high probability that a guess will be correct. The restriction of having to couch the stimulus in either/or terms sometimes also leads to awkwardness of phrasing or convoluted stimulus structure.

The second choice type item is the multiple choice item. Both single-stimulus/multiple-response and matching items are included in this choice type variety. The stimulus of a multiple choice test item is called the stem. The possible responses are called options or alternatives. The intended option is, of course, the answer, while the others are known as distractors or foils.

Multiple choice test items are the most familiar to American education. They offer at least three advantages over other test items. Multiple choice items can measure a wide range of learning outcomes very efficiently. Secondly, the ease of results tabulation allows very efficient data scoring and analysis for multiple choice items. This leads to a capability for electronic data processing of multiple choice tests, relieving the teachers or other classroom personnel of the scoring burden. Third, the presence of a set of possible answers restricts and directs the test taker's responses to a relevant field of behavior, without including a high probability of guessing correctly. As do other evaluation modes, criterion-referenced evaluation often relies heavily on multiple choice test items for data collection.

The evaluator's choice of one of the test item types above depends largely on the kind of behavior defined in the table of specifications. Very generally, behavior in the psychomotor and affective domains must be measured by supply type test items or direct observation. In the psychomotor domain, observation of a test taker's response by a trained, competent observer is used to judge achievement. Outcomes in the affective domain are often so personal and unique in nature that construction of choice type test items is unlikely to provide adequate response alternatives. In addition, the notion of a "correct" answer in affective terms is highly subjective and very suspect. Open-ended, written, or verbal responses or observation of behavior by trained personnel will give the best indication of achievement of affective objectives. It is in the cognitive domain that choice type items are most useful and least controversial.

To sum up this discussion of test item types, it is sufficient to note that the choice of a particular type of item to measure behavior is a function of a combination of considerations. Among the considerations are the purposes of the test item, the importance of scoring ease, and the type of behavior which is meant to be measured. Each of these considerations, as well as the preferences of the evaluator, must be taken into account in the decision as to which test item format should be used in measuring a particular behavior.

Test Item Development

The selection of the types and categories of items that best fit the needs of a particular evaluation is followed by the actual item development. The most important concern of the item developer is the extent to which the test item reflects the objective it is designed to measure. This must remain the standard by which the item's validity is assessed. Consequently, the item developer must be sure that, from the beginning, he understands the objective. A good policy is to be sure an item developer has at least competence, if not expertise, in the content area of the objective.

For supply type items, the stimulus is the only portion of the item over which the developer has any control. It must be stated precisely so the expectations of the item (and of the evaluation) are clear to the test taker. To illustrate this point, the following essay item is presented. In the final examination in a course on American history, the stimulus was presented as:

> Discuss the Civil War's impact on American life in the last
> half of the 19th Century.

Clearly this "essay question" carries the potential for generating a complete library of voluminous answers, any one of which could be entirely appropriate. The student has little chance of providing a complete answer. The request is for much too broad a sample of behavior. A test item that would provide reasonable guidelines for an answer and still measure the student's understanding of the Civil War's importance might be:

> Discuss three primary economic consequences of the Civil
> War.

Such an item would not limit student responses to too specialized a field of knowledge while creating a referential framework in which students could demonstrate their understanding of the impact of the War Between the States.

In writing choice type items, the test developer has control over both the stimulus and the responses. In the stimulus, the developer must be as careful as in supply type items to provide a clear request of the test taker. At the same time, the alternative responses must also be precise and clear. All possible responses must also appear plausible or reasonable, but the answer must be obvious to one who does know the objective. That is, the item must discriminate between those who are competent at the objective and those who are not. An item with an obscure or ambiguous stimulus or with unclear alternatives is unlikely to discriminate well. Likewise, an item with absurd or irrelevant foils will not separate those who know the objective from those who do not, for the likelihood of guessing the answer is increased by the presence of only one reasonable option.

In addition to these concerns, there are some generally applicable rules for item development. There are other sets of rules, too, equally valid; for instance, see Gronlund (1971). The rules follow:

(1)   The level of difficulty of directions or items should be appropriate to the developmental growth of a student. The stimulus and the directions of the item should be written at a level below that at which a student can read and understand to insure the test is of the objective content and not of direction reading capability.

(2)   The stimulus and response portions of any test item should be as concise as possible. The inclusion of superfluous information clouds the purpose of the item and creates an unnecessary and unfair obstacle for the test taker. There are cases, of course, where the purpose of the item is to measure a student's ability to pick out or use relevant material in a passage, but unless it has a purpose in the item, irrelevant and extraneous information should be eliminated.

(3)   A test item should be straightforward. The stimulus should make the request or directions to the test taker directly and simply. Like irrelevant material, ambiguity has no place in a test item. An ambiguous test item may be measuring more the ability to interpret the item than the skill involved in the objective.

(4)   Grammatical or syntactical clues that point to the correct response must be avoided. This is an obvious point, but one that nevertheless is overlooked by inexperienced test developers. Such a clue might be given by an article in the stimulus, as in

this example:

> To protect themselves against scurvy, sailors used
> to eat an _____ every day.
>
> (A) orange   (B) banana   (C) pear

The article <u>an</u> before the missing word gives the answer away.
This kind of simple error goes easily undiscovered unless the
item writer is sensitive to it from experience or training. A
good test item can be negated by such minor oversights.

(5)   The structure of the stimulus and responses should be simple.
An item that is presented in an awkward or unclear grammatical construction can be as ambiguous as one with irrelevant or
unclear content. The item then becomes a test of the test
taker's ability to interpret the item rather than of his ability
to perform the behavior called for by the objective.

These test development rules briefly illustrate some of the considerations
underlying the creation of effective test items. Other lists of rules may be more
exhaustive or comprehensive, but will contain basically the same guidelines to
item development. Attention to relevance to the objective, to clarity and precision, and to the five rules above will aid the development of effective tests.

Item Validation

Once test items are developed, they should be validated before being used.
Several methods for validating items are suggested.

<u>Editorial validation</u>. Every test item should be edited by someone other
than the writer. The editing should be done in two ways. To check that the
item measures the objectives precisely, a set of uncorrelated items and objectives
should be given to a third party to match. An experienced item writer or editor
should be able to match an item to its objective if it is clearly written and to the
point. An item that cannot be matched to its objective should be reconsidered.
Secondly, the test items should be taken by another person with competence or
expertise in the field of the objectives' content. If that person cannot answer
the items, they should be examined again and reworked.

<u>Developmental validation</u>. Another recommended procedure for validat-
ing test items is to review items conversationally with several examinees working
individually or in pairs. This kind of discussion about the items with students
representative of the population for whom the items are being developed will

reveal a great majority of the problems with any inappropriate test items. The responses to items obtained in such an interview situation will allow the item developer to eliminate or revise items before they are used with a general testing population.

Pilot testing. A third method of validation is pilot testing. Before any commercial test publisher releases test items for general use, the items are extensively pilot tested as a validity check. Although a program of pilot testing may be too esoteric an enterprise for a local educational system to want to undertake, keeping a historical record of student performance on items as they are used is an effective way to provide revision information for the evaluation system. The criterion-referenced evaluation model in this monograph maintains historical information on each test item within its reporting component.

Ideally, a pilot test of an item would show an almost equal distribution of response selections for the item prior to instruction. A response that attracts no or few choices prior to instruction should be reviewed for its reasonableness or plausibility. Similarly, an item showing fairly equal distribution of response choices after instruction reveals something about either the effectiveness of instruction or the validity of the item. If other items on the same objective share this kind of distribution, then it is probable that the instruction is not leading to achievement of the objective. On the other hand, if other items show that students are achieving the objective the item having even distribution should be reviewed. In either case, the item should be analyzed.

Dynamic revision. Finally, the history of responses to an item as it is used in the field provides a highly useful data base for dynamic revision of test items. As items are used in evaluation, item analyses should be cumulatively maintained. On the basis of an item analysis, inappropriate or ineffective test items can be identified and culled or revised. Obviously, this process is very close to a pilot test program, but can be undertaken without the expense and time lag between development and use that extensive pilot testing in the field necessitates.

A careful editing procedure involving third party item-to-objective correlation and blind editorial test taking, discussion of items with potential examines, and a pilot testing or response selection history will provide adequate information by which to judge the clarity and appropriateness of test items. These procedures should be included in the implementation of an evaluation system for reliable data generation.

Item Banks

As was mentioned regarding objectives, many sources have made available banks of ready-to-use test items. These banks usually include test items developed by experienced item writers which have sometimes been subjected to stringent validation efforts. In the case where an educational system is selecting objectives from a bank, an item bank related to the objective bank is the easiest way to generate test items. In the case where the system is developing its own objectives, item banks may still provide appropriate test items. The selection committee should review the banked items for validity in the same way as if the items were developed locally.

Test item development is a lengthy and arduous task, for to be useful, items must conform to the rigid specifications of the objectives they are meant to measure. Theoretically, each teacher or curriculum planner would develop test items for use in the course he teaches or plans. The process of item development and validation is very instructive to those establishing a performance-based curriculum and evaluation system. It tends to generate both test items that are most appropriate to the local situation in which they will be used and a sense of involvement and commitment that increases the potential for creative use of the curriculum and evaluation system. However, practical considerations of time and money often mandate selection of prepared items from an existing bank. In either case, items should be developed or chosen within careful guidelines for preparation and review to insure their adequacy for the purpose of gathering data useful for relevant and accurate decision-making. The precision, clarity, and straightforwardness of the items used are of paramount importance in the creation of a viable evaluation system.

Summary

The kinds of information the decision-maker requires dictate the types, numbers, and administration points of tests in an evaluation design. From the types and numbers of tests required in a design, tables of specifications are drawn, showing precisely the content of each test form to be used in the evaluation. In turn, the test items are generated or selected from an item bank, or are written to conform to specifications.

Each table of specifications is an exact "recipe" for one or more test forms. Prior to pilot testing or actual data collection, these test forms must, of course, be assembled from the individual items that have been selected or derived for each objective to be sampled. Using the tables of specifications, the actual testing documents are produced, followed by a series of editorial procedures designed to eliminate some common sources of invalidity in the construction of test items. The test forms, once produced, are dynamically pilot tested through use in the implementation of an evaluation design and are gradually refined in the application context.

Chapter 10

A Hypothetical Curriculum Structure

In the discussion of some of the elements of evaluation design, it was indicated that the structure of a particular evaluation design reflects the structure of the curriculum in the light of the decision-maker's need for specific kinds and quantities of information at certain intervals. The use of a pretest form, for example, is a reflection of the decision-maker's need for performance data prior to instruction. The process of generating an appropriate evaluation design usually begins by making explicit the underlying curriculum structure in terms of its organizational or administrative units (e.g., modules of instruction) and the distribution of objectives in the units. As the curriculum structure becomes apparent, it indicates the attendant instructional decision-making activities. This information in turn reveals the extent and frequency to which the various test types may be applied in an appropriate evaluation design.

To facilitate understanding of this process of generating an evaluation design, Chapter 10 presents a hypothetical curriculum. The following four chapters then apply four evaluation designs to this hypothetical curriculum evolving from experience in applying the Comprehensive Achievement Monitoring system.

The hypothetical curriculum is a conventional one-semester course in which the content is organized into eight consecutive instructional units numbered 11, 12, 13, 14, 21, 22, 23, and 24. The units define the course content and are taught in numerical sequence. Two weeks of instruction are planned for each unit. Thus, Units 11 through 14 are taught during the first half of the semester, Units 21 through 24 during the second half. The arrangement of the course into sequential units implies the need for both survey and mastery tests administered before, immediately after, and long after instruction. For instance, for an overall estimate of student performance over the entire course content prior to instruction, a survey pretest is needed. Or, for precise achievement data immediately following instruction on each unit, a unit mastery posttest is indicated.

Each of the eight units has six course level objectives. Individual objectives are identified by a four-digit number. The first two digits of the number are the unit number, while the last two digits refer to the objective sequence within the unit. Thus, the first objective in Unit 11 is designated as 1101, the second 1102, and so forth. All objectives beginning with 11 belong to Unit 11; similarly, Objectives 2301 through 2306 are in Unit 23. The objective numbers themselves thus also reflect the course structure and provide easy identification of an objective position within the course.

A pool of six test items is available for each objective. Each test item is identified by a six-digit number, consisting of the objective number as its first four digits and a unique sequential item number as its last two digits. For example, Items 210202 and 210206 are both related to Objective 2102. Each test item is related to one and only one objective, as each objective is related to one and only one unit. Figure 10.1 shows this hierarchical relationship among units, objectives, and test items. (Note: It is not the intent of this illustrative hypothetical curriculum to suggest that a given semester course should contain exactly 48 objectives or that each objective should have six test items.)

This system for numbering units, objectives, and test items is consistent with the requirements of the CAM data processing system as documented by Pinsky (1972).

The hypothetical course has an enrollment of 240 students distributed among eight classes of 30 students each. There are three instructors for the course: Mr. Johnson, Ms. Hanson, and Mr. Smith. In the CAM data processing system, each teacher has an identification number unique within the course. This number is called the Teacher Number and is abbreviated TNB on some of the computer reports. Mr. Johnson's Teacher Number is 13, Ms. Hanson's 48, and Mr. Smith's 72.

The term "section" is used to denote physical groupings of students. A section may be a period or module in a school. SECTN and SECTION are used to denote sections on the computer reports. Mr. Johnson teaches Sections 2 and 4, Ms. Hanson Sections 1, 5, and 6, and Mr. Smith Sections 3, 7, and 8. Thus Ms. Hanson and Mr. Smith each instruct 90 students, while Mr. Johnson instructs 60.

Unit	Objective	Test Item
11		
12		
13	1401	140401
	1402	140402
	1403	140403
14	1404	140404
	1405	140405
21	1406	140406
22		
23		
24		

A Hypothetical Curriculum Structure
Figure 10.1

Summary

A decision-maker must determine what information is needed before an evaluation design can be formulated. When this determination is made, the types of tests, the range of content for each, the sampling plan, the number of different types of test forms, and the frequency of administration of each test form are selected to apply to the course structure to gather the appropriate decision-making data. In the chapters to follow, four different evaluation designs are applied to this curriculum to support four different decision-making strategies.

Chapter 11

The Unit CAM Design

In this and the three following chapters, discussion focuses on the application of four different evaluation designs to the hypothetical curriculum presented in Chapter 10. The four designs, known as the unit CAM design, the sliding unit CAM design, the standard CAM design, and the standard/unit CAM design, have grown out of extensive experience with the Comprehensive Achievement Monitoring system. Each of the designs reflects a slightly different decision-making strategy and, therefore, a need for slightly different data. The discussion includes examples of some of the appropriate computer output generated by the CAM data processing system.

Common Design Elements

Prior to the specific discussion of the unit CAM evaluation design, it is necessary to present some design elements common to all four examples so they need not be repeated in the text.

First, three concepts which have been vaguely mentioned previously must be more exactly defined. They are test form, test set, and test administration.

test form:	a set of test items arranged in some order.
test set:	a collection of more than one test form related to the same curricular content.
test administration:	the point in time when a test is given.

Test Administration	Week of Course	Day of Course	Date	Objective Instructed
1		0	2/04/74	
		1		1101
		2		1101
	1	3		1102
		4		1103
		5	2/11/74	1103
		6		1104
		7		1104
	2	8		1104
		9		1105
2		10	2/18/74	1106
		11		1201
		12		1202
	3	13		1202
		14		1202
		15	2/25/74	1203
		16		1203
		17		1204
	4	18		1205
		19		1206
3		20	3/03/74	1206
		21		1301
		22		1301
	5	23		1302
		24		1302
		25	3/10/74	1303
		26		1304
		27		1304
	6	28		1305
		29		1305
4		30	3/17/74	1306
		31		1401
		32		1402
	7	33		1403
		34		1403
		35	3/24/74	1403
		36		1403
		37		1404
	8	38		1405
		39		1406
5		40	3/31/74	1406
		41		2101
		42		2101

Test Administration	Week of Course	Day of Course	Date	Objective Instructed
	9	43		2102
		44		2102
		45	4/07/74	2103
		46		2103
		47		2104
	10	48		2105
		49		2105
6		50	4/14/74	2106
		51		2201
		52		2201
	11	53		2202
		54		2202
		55	4/21/74	2203
		56		2204
		57		2204
	12	58		2205
		59		2206
7		60	4/28/74	2206
		61		2301
		62		2301
	13	63		2302
		64		2303
		65	5/05/74	2304
		66		2305
		67		2306
	14	68		2306
		69		2306
8		70	5/12/74	2306
		71		2401
		72		2401
	15	73		2402
		74		2402
		75	5/19/74	2403
		76		2403
		77		2404
	16	78		2404
9		79		2405
10		80	5/26/74	2406

The Relation of Instruction, Test Administrations, and
Days and Weeks of the Hypothetical Course

Figure 11.1

In all four evaluation designs presented, there are 10 test administrations during the hypothetical 16-week course. A test is administered at the beginning of the course, at the end of Weeks 2, 4, 6, 8, 10, 12, and 14, and two tests are given at the end of the course. The test administrations are numbered consecutively from 1 through 10. Figure 11.1 displays the relationship between test administration dates and instruction on the course objectives.

The number and types of test forms given at each test administration in each design presented in subsequent chapters differ, but each form in all the designs contains 24 test items. However, the number of test items per test form and the biweekly test administration period used in the examples are illustrative only. The exact details of a particular evaluation design must be worked out in each specific situation to provide the most efficient method of gathering the needed decision-making information.

The Unit CAM Design

The unit CAM design consists of a survey pretest of the hypothetical course at Test Administration 1, unit mastery posttests at Test Administrations 2 through 9, and a course or survey post/retention test at the last administration. Figure 11.2 portrays this design.

Survey Test Component

The survey tests given at the beginning and end of the hypothetical course are known as standard CAM tests in the CAM evaluation system. A standard CAM test systematically samples the entire course content to obtain a performance estimate that indicates strengths and weaknesses among students across the content of the whole course. This information gathered before instruction gives the teacher guidance in areas which may need more or less attention during the course and provides a baseline for measuring achievement gains at the end of the course. The standard CAM test given at the course conclusion indicates overall student growth and provides the teacher with data relative to revising the course in the future.

Chapter 13, which discusses the standard CAM evaluation design, provides more detail about the composition of the standard CAM test Forms 1 and 2, shown in Figure 11.2. It is sufficient to note at this point that each form contains one test item related to every other course objective and is administered to half the students in the course at Test Administration 1 and to the other half at Test Administration 10. In this way a very rough estimate of individual achieve-

Test Administration	Test Form	Test Type	Units Tested
1	1, 2	Survey Pretest	11—24
2	115	Mastery Posttest	11
3	125	Mastery Posttest	12
4	135	Mastery Posttest	13
.	.	.	.
.	.	.	.
.	.	.	.
9	245	Mastery Posttest	24
10	1, 2	Survey Post/Retention	11—24

Tests Given in Unit CAM Design

Figure 11.2

ment and a more reliable indication of group achievement are generated at the beginning and at the end of the course.

Unit Mastery Posttest Component

During each of Test Administrations 2 through 9, a mastery posttest covering the content of the unit instructed the previous two weeks is given. Each unit posttest contains four items related to each of the six objectives in the unit. Figure 11.3 shows the mastery test composition for Unit 22. The test for Unit 22 is Form 225 and is given at Test Administration 7, just after instruction on the unit.

By including four test items for each objective in a unit, each unit mastery posttest generates reliable performance data for each student, while the aggregated data for all students provides reliable information for group achievement.

Note here that since the unit mastery posttest gathers data about only the unit just concluded, no performance data are yielded about instruction previously

Question Position	Items Assigned to Test Form 225
1	$22^a01^b01^c$
2	220102
3	220104
4	220106
5	220202
6	220203
7	220204
8	220206
9	220301
10	220303
11	220305
12	220306
13	220401
14	220403
15	220404
16	220405
17	220501
18	220502
19	220503
20	220505
21	220602
22	220603
23	220605
24^d	220606

Items Assigned to Each Question Position on the
Unit Test for Unit 22 (Test Form 225)

Figure 11.3

[a] Unit identification number: Unit 22
[b] Objective identification number: Objective 1 in Unit 22
[c] Test item identification number: Test Item 1 for the
first objective in Unit 22
[d] Total number of items on test

given (retention) or about upcoming units (preinstruction).

CAM Reports

Of the more than 30 different reports available in the CAM system, three are discussed in this section. Other reports are presented in later chapters.

<u>Individual Student Report</u>

Figure 11.4 displays an <u>individual student report</u> generated by the CAM data processing system. A student report is generated for each student after each test administration. The report in Figure 11.4 represents the results of Anna Paulson on Test Form 225 (covering Unit 22), which was given at Test Administration 7 on April 28, 1974.

The following abbreviations are used on the student report:

FORM	Test form number: Anna took Test Form 225.
FRN COR ALL	Fraction of correct responses on all test items on a test form: On Test Administration 7, Anna correctly answered 22 of the 24 test items on the test.
FRN COR YES	Fraction of correct responses on those test items for which instruction has been completed (INS = YES): On Test Administration 7, Anna did not correctly answer 2 of the 24 items on which she had been instructed.
INS	Instruction completed data column: A "yes" means instruction has been given, a blank means it has not. In this case, instruction has been given on all six objectives.
OBJ	Objective
QP	Question position: This simply means the order of each item on the test form.
RP	Response that the student chose for the test item: A "+" indicates a correct response, a "-" indicates

an incorrect response. The number before the + or - is the answer the student chose.

SECTN   Section number: Anna is in Section 6.

TEST ADM   Test administration number: This is the seventh test administration.

CUM TOT   Cumulative total score: This figure is newly added each time a test is given. So far, Anna has correctly answered 122 of the 168 test items to which she has responded, and 116 of the 144 on which she has been instructed.

PAULSON ANNA M   MS. HANSON
                                                                               HC102
            TEST ADM 7 - 4/28/74
FRACTION CORRECT ON ALL ITEMS IS 22/24   FORM 225
FRACTION CORRECT ON YES ITEMS IS 22/24

QP	OBJ	RP	INS	QP	OBJ	RP	INS	TEST ADM	FORM	FRN COR ALL	FRN COR YES
1	2201	3+	YES	13	2204	3+	YES	1	1	6/24	0/0
2	2201	3+	YES	14	2204	3+	YES	2	115	18/24	18/24
3	2201	3+	YES	15	2204	1+	YES	3	125	20/24	20/24
4	2201	2-	YES	16	2204	2+	YES	4	135	14/24	14/24
5	2202	2+	YES	17	2205	3+	YES	5	145	22/24	22/24
6	2202	3+	YES	18	2205	1+	YES	6	215	20/24	20/24
7	2202	2+	YES	19	2205	1-	YES	7	225	22/24	22/24
8	2202	3+	YES	20	2205	2+	YES				
9	2203	4+	YES	21	2206	1+	YES				
10	2203	2+	YES	22	2206	4+	YES				
11	2203	2+	YES	23	2206	3+	YES				
12	2203	1+	YES	24	2206	2+	YES				

                                                             CUM TOT   122/168 116/144

An Individual Student Report for the Unit CAM Design
Generated by the CAM Data Processing System
Figure 11.4

The student report in Figure 11.4 enables the user to make decisions concerning the individual student's mastery of objectives. For example, has Anna Paulson learned Objective 2202? It would seem so, since she answered all four of the test items related to that objective. Are there objectives she needs review work on? She missed an item relating to Objective 2205; perhaps she should review that objective. With such data, a teacher would know how well a student has learned a particular set of objectives and could make instructional decisions about the student based on such data — e.g., review, reteach.

The report in Figure 11.4 does not provide information for making decisions relative to preinstruction and retention achievement. For example, it is not known if Anna had prior knowledge related to Objective 2301, or how well she has retained her knowledge of Objectives 1301-1306. Such data are gathered by other CAM evaluation designs.

Note also in Test Administrations 2-7 on Figure 11.4 that the FRN COR/ALL and the FRN COR/YES scores are identical. This reflects the unit mastery tests containing no items on objectives not yet taught (the difference between these two scores in test administration 1 is explained in a later chapter).

Figure 11.5 shows a CAM group summary report. The group summary report can be generated for any group of students. The group can be a teacher section, all a teacher's students, all students in the course, all minority students, all students in a given achievement level, or any other group the decision-maker designates. Chapters 14 and 15 contain more information on the use of the CAM group summary report. Figure 11.5 is a report for Ms. Hanson's sixth section. The following abbreviations are used in the group summary report:

CGN	Content summary group number (used mainly for data processing purposes).
CONTENT GROUP	Content summary group label representing a set of objectives or units.
NUM	Number of student responses for all students in the student summary group to all test items contained in the relevant content summary group.
NUMBER OF STUDENTS	Number of students in the relevant student summary group who responded to any test form during a test administration.
PCT	Percentage of the NUM responses that are correct.

STUDENT	Student summary group number (used mainly by
GROUP	data processing) followed by the student summary
	group label.

```
COMPREHENSIVE ACHIEVEMENT MONITORING - GROUP SUMMARY REPORT
HYPOTHETICAL COURSE - UNIT CAM DESIGN                          HC102
          STUDENT GROUP   486    MS. HANSON      SECTION   6
```

				TEST ADMINISTRATION						
CGN	CONTENT GROUP		1	2	3	4	5	6	7
	NUMBER OF STUDENTS		28	29	28	30	27	26	30
22	UNIT 22	PCT	37	***	***	***	***	***	80
		NUM	84	0	0	0	0	0	120
2201	OBJECTIVE 2201	PCT	30	***	***	***	***	***	84
		NUM	14	0	0	0	0	0	120
2202	OBJECTIVE 2202	PCT	29	***	***	***	***	***	89
		NUM	14	0	0	0	0	0	120
2203	OBJECTIVE 2203	PCT	29	***	***	***	***	***	69
		NUM	14	0	0	0	0	0	120
2204	OBJECTIVE 2204	PCT	41	***	***	***	***	***	62
		NUM	14	0	0	0	0	0	120
2205	OBJECTIVE 2205	PCT	19	***	***	***	***	***	82
		NUM	14	0	0	0	0	0	120
2206	OBJECTIVE 2206	PCT	51	***	***	***	***	***	89
		NUM	14	0	0	0	0	0	120

A Group Summary Report for the Unit CAM Design
Generated by the CAM Data Processing System
Figure 11.5

Figure 11.5 shows that in Test Administrations 2-6, there are no test items related to Unit 22 objectives in the unit CAM evaluation design. Thus there is no periodic preinstruction information generated on Unit 22 objectives (except for the pretest in Test Administration 1). Similarly, when data for Test Administrations 8 and 9 are generated by the unit CAM design, there will be no retention information relative to the Unit 22 objectives.

The group summary report represents the compilation of results from all the students in the group on all questions relating to specified content. For instance, Objective 2202 was sampled twice during the course through Test Administration 7, once in the course survey pretest, and once in the Unit 22 mastery posttest. On the survey pretest, given at Test Administration 1, 14 student responses were collected on Objective 2202, and 30 percent of the responses were correct. On the unit mastery posttest, 120 responses were gathered and 80 percent were correct. This gain in achievement suggests that instruction may have been successful in teaching Objective 2202 for a great majority of the students. However, suppose the percentage had remained at 30 or risen only slightly. The teacher would then know that instruction had not been successful and would have to consider alternate teaching strategies or materials, or might even question whether the objective was appropriate at this point of the curriculum.

Form Analysis Report

Figure 11.6 shows a CAM form analysis report. For each test administration, there is a form analysis report for each test form that is used. Thus during Test Administrations 2-9, there is only one form analysis generated, while during Test Administrations 1 and 10, there are two form analyses generated — one each for Forms 1 and 2 (refer to Figure 11.2). The form analysis report in Figure 11.6 is commonly called an "item analysis." However, there are many different "item analyses" reports available in the CAM system, and each of these has been given a unique name. Figure 11.6 is called a form analysis because it contains data pertaining to individual items that appear on a particular test form.

Using the form analysis report, a teacher is able to analyze the appropriateness of the test items in a form to the objectives they test. Thus, a further measure of quality control is introduced into the test development process by providing feedback on the results of each test item. For instance, if the percent correct on item number 10 (Question Position) in Form 225 were 38 rather than 70 and the percent correct for other items related to Objective 2203 remained high, it would be an indication that the item may not measure the objective. The feedback in the form analysis report assists in maintaining high test relevance standards with respect to the objectives of a curriculum. This feedback also assists in verifying that student scores on tests are valid indicators of achievement.

Summary

The unit CAM evaluation design primarily uses unit mastery posttests to provide decision-makers with detailed information about student achievement

COMPREHENSIVE ACHIEVEMENT MONITORING - FORM ANALYSIS REPORT
HYPOTHETICAL COURSE - UNIT CAM DESIGN   HC102

FORM 225 QUESTION POSITION	OBJECTIVE	ANSWER	219 FORMS PROCESSED PCT CORRECT	NR	TEST ADMINISTRATION 7 RESPONSES (%) 1	2	3	4	5
1	2201	3	76	4	6	6	76	6	0
2	2201	3	73	5	4	6	73	10	0
3	2201	3	79	9	6	0	79	3	0
4	2201	1	65	9	65	14	4	6	0
5	2202	2	72	11	10	72	4	0	0
6	2202	3	80	4	4	10	80	0	0
7	2202	2	70	16	2	70	10	0	0
8	2202	3	69	18	2	0	69	0	0
9	2203	4	91	3	0	4	0	91	0
10	2203	2	70	19	0	70	0	9	0
11	2203	2	63	9	20	63	6	0	0
12	2203	1	68	14	68	10	3	3	0
13	2204	3	73	7	3	6	73	10	0
14	2204	3	65	0	10	10	65	13	0
15	2204	1	80	6	80	11	0	0	0
16	2204	2	69	9	10	69	0	9	0
17	2205	3	70	5	4	9	70	9	0
18	2205	1	68	2	68	9	11	6	0
19	2205	3	76	4	5	2	76	10	0
20	2205	2	79	1	1	79	16	2	0
21	2206	4	72	6	9	2	11	72	0
22	2206	4	70	0	5	22	2	70	0
23	2206	3	91	2	2	1	91	2	0
24	2206	2	63	1	6	63	10	20	0

SUMMARY DATA FOR FORM 225:   TOTAL PERCENTAGE CORRECT=73

A Form Analysis Report for the Unit CAM Design
Generated by the CAM Data Processing System
Figure 11.6

on a unit-by-unit basis as a course or program progresses. It allows the teacher, student, parent, or other user to see, following instruction, how well a given student has mastered a set of material. By so doing, it enables systematic instructional decision-making relative to each student.

The unit CAM design does not generate much preinstruction or retention achievement data for either individual students or groups. Some preinstruction and retention data are generated by the survey test forms administered at the beginning and end of the course, but this is of very limited scope, because the focus of the unit CAM design is largely on postinstructional data obtained at the conclusion of each unit.

Chapter 12
The Sliding Unit CAM Design

The unit CAM evaluation design presented in the last chapter primarily employs only one test form at each test administration. With the exception of the first and last, the tests are meant to obtain detailed performance data on only the unit just taught. In contrast, the sliding unit CAM evaluation design, the focus of the present chapter, incorporates multiple test forms (thereby comprising a test set) during each test administration to gather preinstructional and retention data in addition to postinstructional information about students and the curriculum. The construction of multiple test forms is made possible by the technique of objective and item sampling. The principles involved are discussed to illustrate the method by which the tests are constructed which support the sliding unit CAM design. Finally, the discussion turns to two CAM reports associated with the sliding unit design and introduces the concept of objective completion in that context.

The Sliding Unit CAM Design

The sliding unit CAM evaluation design combines the two survey test forms in the unit CAM design (composed of Forms 1 and 2 and technically known as standard CAM components) with two test forms given at the conclusion of each unit in the hypothetical course. As in the unit CAM design, the survey test Forms 1 and 2, given during Test Administrations 1 and 10, sample all the course objectives and represent a pretest/posttest component for the entire course. In contrast to the unit CAM design, however, the test given at the end of each unit samples objectives from three course units: the one just completed, the prior unit taught, and the next unit. Thus, rather than obtaining only

postinstructional mastery data, the sliding unit design gathers retention, postinstructional, and preinstructional data during Test Administrations 2 through 9.
This information represents a great increase in the amount of data available for
certain types of instructional decision-making.

Figure 12.1 shows the relationship of test forms to test administrations in
the sliding unit CAM design.

Test Administration	Test Form	Test Type	Units Tested
1	1, 2	Survey Pretest	11—24
2	111, 112	Post, Pre	11, 12
3	121, 122	Retention, Post, Pre	11, 12, 13
4	131, 132	Retention, Post, Pre	12, 13, 14
.	.	.	.
.	.	.	.
.	.	.	.
8	231, 232	Retention, Post, Pre	22, 23, 24
9	241, 242	Retention, Post	23, 24
10	1, 2	Survey Post/Retention	11—24

Test Forms and Test Administrations in the
Sliding Unit CAM Evaluation Design

Figure 12.1

Survey Test Component

As in the unit CAM design, the survey test forms used during Test Adminis-

trations 1 and 10 in the sliding unit CAM design generate limited preinstructional, postinstructional, and retention data. The information generated by this component of the design would establish a preinstructional baseline for measuring
achievement gains, provide guidance for instructional emphasis during the course,
and contribute to course revisions.

Sliding Unit Component

The sliding unit tests given at the conclusion of each unit generate retention (except at Test Administration 2), postinstructional, and preinstructional
(except at Test Administration 9) data. Thus the teacher is able to check on how
well students are retaining previously learned material (retention), how thoroughly they have achieved the content just taught (postinstruction), and how well
they can perform on the next unit's material before it is taught (preinstruction).

To illustrate the sliding unit component, Figure 12.2 presents the test set
of two forms given after Unit 22. Each form has items relating to three of the
objectives in Unit 21 to check retention, three items for each objective in Unit
22 to check mastery of the unit just completed, and items related to three of the
objectives in Unit 23 to determine preinstructional performance.

The sliding unit component generates slightly less detailed data on mastery
of the unit just completed (because the sample of responses to each objective is
smaller), but supplies data not provided in the unit design about retained and
preinstructional performance. During a given test administration, half the students would take one test form and half the other, thus generating group retention and preinstructional information on all the objectives in the units covered
while limiting the length of the test forms. The individual teacher must decide
whether the consequent loss in detail of the mastery data is not too great a price
to pay for the gain of the retention and preinstructional information.

Objective and Item Sampling

Figure 12.2 represents a test set related to Units 21, 22, and 23. This test
set contains two test forms, 221 and 222, each with 24 test items. The test set
thus has 48 test items: six items related to Unit 21, 36 items related to Unit 22,
and six items related to Unit 23.

The six items related to Unit 21 represent each of the Unit 21 objectives,
2101 through 2106, once only. Similarly, the six test items related to Unit 23
represent each of the objectives in that unit, 2301 through 2306, once only.
These items are assigned to the test forms so that each form has three items relating to each of Units 21 and 23. This is an application of objective sampling,

Question Position	Items Assigned to Each Form 221	222	Content
1	210103	210202	
2	210305	210404	Unit 21
3	210601	210506	
4	220101	220102	
5	220103	220104	
6	220105	220106	
7	220202	220201	
8	220204	220203	
9	220206	220205	
10	220301	220302	
11	220303	220304	
12	220305	220306	Unit 22
13	220402	220401	
14	220404	220403	
15	220406	220405	
16	220501	220502	
17	220503	220504	
18	220505	220506	
19	220602	220601	
20	220604	220603	
21	220606	220605	
22	230103	230206	
23	230405	230304	Unit 23
24	230501	230602	

Items Assigned to Each Question Position of the
Sliding Unit CAM Test Forms Used for Unit 22

Figure 12.2

in that not all of the objectives related to each unit are tested on a given test form. Rather, a sample of the objectives is tested in each form. If only some objectives related to a unit appear on one test form and some on another in a test set, the principle involved is objective sampling.

In regard to the objectives from Unit 22, all are tested in both Forms 221 and 222. The objectives are not sampled. However, not all of the items related to each objective are included on each test form. The term item sampling is therefore applicable for Unit 22, meaning in this case that items, not objectives, are sampled in the test forms of the set. If only some of the items related to an objective are included on one test form in a test set, and other items on one or more other test forms, the principle involved is item sampling.

To extend this discussion of sampling further, recall the content of the survey tests given at the beginning and end of the course. The two forms of the survey test set cover all of the course objectives. But only half of the objectives are tested in each test form. Therefore, objective sampling is involved. Furthermore, of the six test items available for each objective, only one is used. Thus, the survey test forms represent a case of objective and item sampling.

The techniques involved in sampling discussed above are also known as stratified random sampling techniques. Further details concerning these and other sampling techniques can be found in Gorth (1971).

CAM Reports

The reports generated for the sliding unit CAM evaluation design are known by the same names as those for the unit CAM design. However, the data they display are slightly different, reflecting the difference in the test content.

Individual Student Report

Figure 12.3 contains a CAM student report for Sam Smith following Test Administration 7. The reader can verify that Form 222 contains the objectives listed in Figure 12.3 by referring to Figure 12.2. Note that question positions 22, 23, and 24 do not have a YES under the instruction completed column (INS). Test Administration 7 occurs after instruction on Unit 22 but before instruction on Unit 23 (see Figure 11.2).

The CAM data processing system keeps a record for each student of the date of completion of instructional activities related to each objective in the course. Note that the FRN COR/YES column is not identical to the FRN COR/ ALL column. This reflects the sliding unit CAM design's containing preinstructional testing on all test forms during Test Administrations 2 through 9. Thus,

SMITH SAM   765432 SECTN 5   MS. HANSON
                                                                                  HC102
            TEST ADM 7 - 4/28/74
FRACTION CORRECT ON ALL ITEMS IS 18/24   FORM 222
FRACTION CORRECT ON YES ITEMS IS 17/21

QP	OBJ	RP	INS	QP	OBJ	RP	INS	TEST ADM	FORM	FRN COR ALL	FRN COR YES
1	2102	2+	YES	13	2204	3+	YES	1	2	6/24	0/0
2	2104	1+	YES	14	2204	3+	YES	2	112	17/24	15/18
3	2105	2+	YES	15	2204	2+	YES	3	122	18/24	17/21
4	2201	3+	YES	16	2205	1+	YES	4	132	17/24	15/21
5	2201	3+	YES	17	2205	3+	YES	5	142	16/24	15/21
6	2201	1+	YES	18	2205	3+	YES	6	212	20/24	18/21
7	2202	0	YES	19	2206	1+	YES	7	222	18/24	17/21
8	2202	2-	YES	20	2206	2-	YES				
9	2202	1+	YES	21	2206	1-	YES				
10	2203	2+	YES	22	2302	2-					
11	2203	3+	YES	23	2302	1+					
12	2203	1+	YES	24	2306	1-					

                                                         CUM TOT   112/168   97/123

An Individual Student Report for the Sliding Unit CAM Design
Generated by the CAM Data Processing System
Figure 12.3

the data on objective completion is important in determining achievement on objectives taught.

The report in Figure 12.3 enables the user to make mastery decisions concerning Sam Smith on each of the objectives in Unit 22. Has he learned Objective 2201? He correctly answered all three test items related to Objective 2201. The conclusion can tentatively be made that Sam has mastered the content of 2201. For Objective 2202, he skipped one of the three items and answered a second one incorrectly. It would seem that Sam needs additional work here. Note that there are only three items related to Objectives 2201-2206 in Figure 12.3, while the unit CAM student report (Figure 11.4) contains four test items per objective. Figure 12.3 also provides some information relative to Units 21 and 23. Has Sam mastered Objective 2102? Objective 2104? Objective 2302? Clearly, one item per objective is not sufficient information to determine mastery by itself, but there is some indication of retained and preinstructional achievement.

Thus far, only the Unit 22 test has been examined. The tests related to the other seven units are similarly constructed. The tests related to each unit contain 48 items (two forms with 24 items each). Six of the 48 items are used to measure the previous unit taught. This would provide retention data on how well the students had remembered the objectives of the previous unit as a group. There are 36 items used to measure the unit just completed (postinstructional data), and six items used to measure the unit to be taught next (preinstructional data). The actual construction of each of the forms is similar to the specification of Forms 221 and 222 shown in Figure 12.2.

Group Summary Report

Figure 12.4 contains a CAM group summary report for all of Ms. Hanson's students (i.e., Sections 1, 5, and 6) following Test Administration 7. Group summary data give information about the achievement level of groups of students on objectives and units. The group summary report consists of two main components: the student summary group and the content summary group. Examples of student summary groups are a teacher section, all sections for a teacher (as in Figure 12.4), and all students in a course. As noted previously, other student summary groups might be created by ethnic origin, socioeconomic status, ability level, treatment group, etc. (Each student summary group has a four-digit student summary group number which is primarily used for data processing purposes.)

The content summary group is a set of objectives for which data are combined. Examples of content summary groups are an objective, the objectives in a unit, and all objectives in a course. (Each content summary group has a four-digit content summary group number also used primarily for data processing purposes.)

Because of space limitations, Figure 12.4 represents only a sample of a group summary report. Note that each of the units and objectives contains some preinstruction data (refer to Figure 11.2 for the relationship of instruction to test administrations). At the end of the course (i.e., after Test Administration 10) all units and objectives will be represented by retention information. For example, look at content summary group 1401, Objective 1401. The entry level of Ms. Hanson's students at the beginning of the course (Test Administration 1) was 16 percent, while the achievement level at Test Administration 4 (still prior to instruction) was 40 percent. The immediate postinstructional level was 82 percent, while the short-term retention level was 90 percent. Thus the sliding unit CAM design generates some preinstruction and retention data on the objectives in the

COMPREHENSIVE ACHIEVEMENT MONITORING - GROUP SUMMARY REPORT
HYPOTHETICAL COURSE - SLIDING/UNIT CAM DESIGN   HC102
          STUDENT GROUP   4800   ALL MS. HANSON'S STUDENTS

					TEST ADMINISTRATION			
CGN	CONTENT GROUP		1	2	3	4	5	6	7
	NUMBER OF STUDENTS		85	87	84	89	83	90	88
14	UNIT 14	PCT	30	***	***	35	71	75	***
		NUM	255	0	0	267	1602	270	0
21	UNIT 21	PCT	35	***	***	***	52	88	86
		NUM	255	0	0	0	249	1620	264
22	UNIT 22	PCT	20	***	***	***	***	30	68
		NUM	255	0	0	0	0	270	1584
23	UNIT 23	PCT	63	***	***	***	***	***	70
		NUM	255	0	0	0	0	0	264
1401	OBJECTIVE 1401	PCT	16	***	***	40	82	90	***
		NUM	42	0	0	45	249	45	0
2101	OBJECTIVE 2101	PCT	15	***	***	***	30	80	72
		NUM	43	0	0	0	41	270	44
2102	OBJECTIVE 2102	PCT	18	***	***	***	40	88	92
		NUM	42	0	0	0	42	270	44
2201	OBJECTIVE 2201	PCT	25	***	***	***	***	40	90
		NUM	43	0	0	0	0	45	264
2203	OBJECTIVE 2203	PCT	32	***	***	***	***	36	80
		NUM	43	0	0	0	0	45	264
2205	OBJECTIVE 2205	PCT	27	***	***	***	***	28	60
		NUM	42	0	0	0	0	45	264
2302	OBJECTIVE 2302	PCT	48	***	***	***	***	***	52
		NUM	43	0	0	0	0	0	44
2304	OBJECTIVE 2304	PCT	36	***	***	***	***	***	34
		NUM	42	0	0	0	0	0	44

A Group Summary Report for the Sliding Unit CAM Design
Generated by the CAM Data Processing System

Figure 12.4

course. (The reader may wish to compare Figure 12.4 to Figure 11.6, the group summary report for the unit CAM design, and note the differences between the two types of reports for the two different CAM designs.)

When there is more than one form being used in a test, there arises a need to schedule the administration of the test forms carefully. Objectives 2101 and 2103 appear on different test forms within the Unit 22 sliding unit CAM test. The results shown in Figure 12.4 show that 44 of the 48 students in Ms. Hanson's three periods responded to each of Forms 221 and 222. Whenever item or objective sampling is used, careful test scheduling procedures must be used to equate the student groups receiving each test form at a test administration. Chapter 13 contains more information about the scheduling of tests in an item or objective sampling environment.

Summary

The sliding unit CAM evaluation design generates detailed individual student information on a postinstructional basis, but the information is not as detailed as that generated by the unit CAM design: three items per objective for the sliding unit CAM design as opposed to four items per objective for the unit CAM design. In addition, the sliding unit CAM design uses item and objective sampling with multiple test forms to generate some preinstructional and retention information for the individual student and groups of students. There is a trade-off of individual student information for group and curriculum validation information. The next chapter presents the standard CAM design, which more heavily emphasizes group and curriculum validation information.

Chapter 13

The Standard CAM Design

The third evaluation design to be considered is known as the standard CAM design. The standard CAM design has many variations, but its distinguishing feature is the incorporation of objective and/or item sampling in a test set of multiple forms. The two survey test forms used in Test Administrations 1 and 10 in the previous designs are examples of standard CAM tests. The standard CAM design extends the use of such survey tests throughout the hypothetical course.

The standard CAM design is most useful for evaluating the developmental components of a curriculum. Developmental objectives receive continual or recurring focus, change slowly over time, and are important long-range instructional outcomes. Comprehension and study skills are good examples of such developmental objectives. The standard CAM design is also applicable in situations where there are a very large number of possible test items per objective, such as vocabulary and spelling. Instructional decision-making information for group-paced programs is provided, while relatively little useful data for individual instructional decisions are provided by any given single test form or test administration.

The Standard CAM Design

The standard CAM design for the hypothetical course consists of 10 comprehensive, interchangeable test forms containing 24 items each. These forms are comprehensive in the sense that each one uniformly covers objectives in all eight instructional units. They are interchangeable in that they each test a randomly assigned half of the total course content.

171

Question Position	1	2	3	4	5	6	7	8	9	10
				Items Assigned to Each Form						
1	110106	110201	110102	110205	110204	110103	110104	110203	110206	110105
2	110403	110306	110302	110406	110301	110405	110305	110401	110304	110402
3	110506	110605	110604	110501	110603	110504	110502	110602	110503	110601
4	120202	120101	120203	120105	120104	120204	120201	120103	120206	120102
5	120303	120406	120306	120402	120401	120305	120405	120301	120404	120302
6	120505	120605	120501	120604	120506	120603	120602	120503	120606	120504
7	130106	130202	130103	130201	130205	130104	130204	130105	130206	130101
8	130404	130306	130405	130303	130302	130401	130402	130301	130403	130305
9	130501	130601	130502	130606	130503	130604	130504	130603	130602	130505
10	140103	140203	140104	140206	140201	140105	140205	140106	140204	140102
11	140405	140305	140401	140304	140303	140402	140302	140406	140301	140404
12	140502	140602	140503	140601	140506	140606	140505	140604	140501	140603
13	210104	210203	210203	210106	210101	210202	210102	210201	210103	210205
14	210301	210401	210405	210302	210404	210303	210306	210406	210403	210304
15	210603	210503	210604	210502	210605	210501	210606	210505	210602	210504
16	220105	220205	220106	220204	220203	220102	220103	220206	220104	220201
17	220302	220402	220306	220401	220304	220405	220406	220305	220403	220301
18	220604	220504	220503	220605	220601	220502	220602	220501	220506	220603
19	230201	230106	230202	230104	230203	230103	230206	230102	230205	230101
20	230302	230402	230401	230303	230304	230405	230305	230404	230301	230406
21	230504	230604	230505	230603	230501	230602	230606	230506	230605	230503
22	240101	240201	240102	240205	240106	240206	240203	240104	240202	240105
23	240403	240303	240302	240404	240301	240405	240306	240401	240304	240402
24	240505	240605	240506	240604	240502	240603	240503	240606	240601	240504

Items Assigned to Each Question Position of Each of the Standard CAM Test Forms

Figure 13.1

The items on each of the test forms are presented in Figure 13.1. Note that the forms, numbered 1 to 10, comprise a test set. Each of these forms contains three items related to each of the eight units, and every item on a form is related to a different objective. Every pair of forms (1 and 2; 3 and 4; etc.) contains one item related to all 48 objectives in the course.

Objective sampling is used first to assign the objectives to the question positions in each form. Item sampling is then used to select the actual test items to be assigned to each question position.

At the beginning of the course (Week 0 = Test Administration 1), 24 (or one-tenth) of the 240 students in the course respond to each of these 10 forms. Furthermore, three students in each of the eight sections respond to each of the forms. Two weeks later, at Test Administration 2, the process is repeated except that each student takes a different test form. For example, if a student took Form 6 during Test Administration 1, he would take Form 5 during Test Administration 2. This process occurs 10 times during the course. The last two test administrations occur on the same day, creating, in essence, a 48-item final examination at the end of the course, one item related to each objective. During the semester, every student responds once to each test form. No student gets the same test form twice. (Details concerning the specification of standard CAM test forms are presented in Gorth, 1971.)

Test Administration	Test Form	Test Type	Units Tested
1	1–10	Survey	11–24
2	1–10	Survey	11–24
3	1–10	Survey	11–24
.	.	.	.
.	.	.	.
.	.	.	.
9	1–10	Survey	11–24
10	1–10	Survey	11–24

The Relationship of Test Forms to Test Administrations in the Standard CAM Design

Figure 13.2

Notice that the standard CAM is the only design presented to this point that repeats a test form in Test Administrations 2-9. The relationship of test forms to test administrations for the standard CAM design is presented in Figure 13.2. A formal definition of a standard CAM test includes the specification that it is a test set composed of more than one form and used in more than one test administration.

As the course progresses, the part of the test which represents preinstructional data shrinks while the part that represents retention grows, as shown in Figure 13.3. The small portion of each test form that gathers postinstructional data remains the same size and is present in each administration. The standard CAM test set thus generates contemporary preinstructional, postinstructional and retention data for a group each time it is administered.

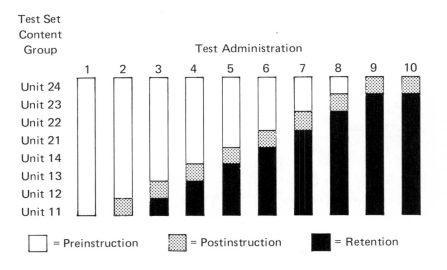

The Changing Nature of the Standard CAM Test Set:
A Longitudinal Design

Figure 13.3

Scheduling Test Forms

The scheduling of test forms for students is complex and must be carefully done to insure both that each student responds only once to each test form during the semester and that each form is responded to by an equal number of students in each section (in the case of the hypothetical course, three students). The scheduling of the form given during the first test administration can generally be done by the classroom teacher in a manner such that all 10 test forms are used an equal number of times in each section. Thereafter, during Test Administrations 2 through 10, it is most convenient for the data processing operation to schedule the test forms for each student and to precode this form number on the student's answer sheet, using a latin square technique to facilitate the process. In the latin square shown in Figure 13.4, note that each column and each row contains the numbers 1-10. Each row gives the order in which the test forms are administered to a student. (Numbers in the body of the figure represent test form numbers.)

Student(s)	Test Administration									
	1	2	3	4	5	6	7	8	9	10
A	1	2	7	8	5	6	9	10	3	4
B	2	1	8	7	6	5	10	9	4	3
C	3	4	1	2	7	8	5	6	9	10
D	4	3	2	1	8	7	6	5	10	9
E	5	6	9	10	3	4	1	2	7	8
F	6	5	10	9	4	3	2	1	8	7
G	7	8	5	6	9	10	3	4	1	2
H	8	7	6	5	10	9	4	3	2	1
I	9	10	3	4	1	2	7	8	5	6
J	10	9	4	3	2	1	8	7	6	5

A 10-by-10 Latin Square for Test Form Scheduling

Figure 13.4

Consider a student who is given Form 1 by the teacher during Test Administration 1. Data processing uses Figure 13.4 and assigns the student Form 2 during Test Administration 2, Form 7 during Test Administration 3, Form 8 during Test Administration 4, and so on. A student assigned Form 6 during Test Administration 1 is scheduled Form 5 during Test Administration 2, Form 10 during Test Administration 3, to Test Administration 10. Neither the teacher nor the student knows in advance what form the student will take during a test administration. This technique of scheduling insures that all students will respond to any given test form (for instance, Form 8) only once during Test Administrations 2-9.

The latin square technique is also used to insure that an equal number of students per section get the same form (e.g., Form 8) during a given test administration. This is accomplished by creating student schedule groups to be assigned the same test forms. Therefore, the teacher might take care during Test Administration 1 not to assign the same form to students who often sit next to each other. The CAM data processing system provides for the use of student schedule groups to facilitate the scheduling and the precoding of test form numbers on the student answer sheets. (Details concerning the latin square scheduling technique are presented in Gorth, 1971.)

The latin square scheduling procedure guarantees that stratified random sampling of students to test forms will also occur for all 10 test administrations. If one looks at a fixed test form, say Form 3, during a test administration, then the above scheduling procedure will randomly select 24 students from the population of 240 students in the course. Moreover, this random selection is done on a stratified basis by sections of the course (three students per section X eight sections = 24 students). In certain applications of the standard CAM design, there may be the need to consider two characteristics of the student population: say physical groupings such as sections and treatment groups. In this instance the scheduling problem becomes more complex, because double stratified random sampling must be used. (The interested reader is referred to Pinsky, 1971.)

Reporting

Figure 13.5 contains an individual student report for Tom Robinson following Test Administration 7 in the standard CAM design. Notice that instruction has been completed for Units 11, 12, 13, 14, 21, and 22 (i.e., INS = YES), but not for Units 23 and 24.

The actual student response is not printed on the report. This is done for test security, since these standard CAM test forms are used 10 times during the semester. The CAM data processing system allows the user the option of masking

ROBINSON   TOM   MS. HANSON
                                                                                           HC102
          TEST ADM   7 -   4/28/74
FRACTION CORRECT ON ALL ITEMS IS   16/24   FORM   9
FRACTION CORRECT ON YES ITEMS IS   15/18

QP	OBJ	RP	INS	QP	OBJ	RP	INS	TEST ADM	FORM	FRN COR ALL	FRN COR YES
1	1102	+	YES	13	2101	+	YES	1	1	6/24	0/0
2	1103	+	YES	14	2104	+	YES	2	2	8/24	2/3
3	1105	+	YES	15	2106	+	YES	3	7	12/24	6/6
4	1202	−	YES	16	2201	+	YES	4	8	12/24	8/9
5	1204	+	YES	17	2204	+	YES	5	5	13/24	9/12
6	1206	+	YES	18	2205	+	YES	6	6	15/24	12/15
7	1302	+	YES	19	2302	−		7	9	16/24	15/18
8	1304	+	YES	20	2303	−					
9	1306	+	YES	21	2306	+					
10	1402	−	YES	22	2402	−					
11	1403	−	YES	23	2403	−					
12	1405	+	YES	24	2406	−					

CUM TOT   76/168   52/63

An Individual Student Report for the Standard CAM Design
Generated by the CAM Data Processing System
Figure 13.5

the student responses on the report.

Consider the type of information provided by the report in Figure 13.5. Tom responded correctly to all three items related to Unit 11, but does this mean that he knows all six objectives in Unit 11? Clearly not, as there is only one response each for Objectives 1102, 1103 and 1105, and none related to Objectives 1101, 1104 and 1106. Thus, the administration of a simple standard CAM test form provides little information for deciding if a student has learned a specific objective at a certain point in time. As will be discussed in Chapter 15, however, over time the standard CAM design does provide information regarding the mastery of objectives on a retention basis.

Note that the report in Figure 13.5 contains some testing of objectives taught several weeks ago (Objectives 1102, 1103, 1105, 1202, etc.). In this case, the standard CAM is testing for retention. There are also some test items related to objectives not yet taught (Objectives 2302, 2303, 2306, 2402, etc.). Thus, the standard CAM design is also collecting some preinstructional material.

The FORM column in Figure 13.5 shows that Tom Robinson's testing schedule has been determined by the first row in the latin square (Figure 13.4). The FRN COR/ALL column contains an estimate of Tom's overall progress in the course. Remember that each of the 10 standard CAM forms contains a sample of all the objectives in the course. Therefore, the score on any one test form is an estimate of the student's overall achievement in the course. Tom's report indicates that he has made satisfactory progress thus far in the course: from 6/24 or 25 percent at Test Administration 1 to 16/24 or 67 percent at Test Administration 7.[3]

The FRN COR/YES column contains the fraction of correct responses to test items for which instruction has been completed. Notice that the denominator of these fractions increases during each test administration. The FRN COR/YES column provides a measure of the student's retention of the material already taught. Tom's retention level at Test Administration 7 is 15/18 or 83 percent.

Finally, notice that the difference between the FRN COR/ALL and the FRN COR/YES columns is a measure of the student's preinstruction achievement level. Tom's preinstruction achievement level at Test Administration 1 was (6-0)/(24-0) = 6/24 or 25 percent; at Test Administration 5 it was (13-9)/(24-12) = 4/12 or 33 percent. The CAM system also allows the user the option of printing out a preinstruction score on the reports.

Figure 13.6 contains a group summary report for all of Mr. Smith's students following Test Administration 7. All the unit data and a sample of the objective data are displayed in this report for explanatory reasons. The full report contains data for all 48 objectives. Notice that in the standard CAM design, estimates of the students' achievement levels on each of the eight units and each of the 48 objectives (in the full report) are provided by each of the seven test administrations. Compare Figure 13.6 with the group summary data for the sliding unit CAM design in Figure 12.4 and the unit CAM design in Figure 11.6. The standard CAM design generates much more complete group summary data than the other two designs. That is, the standard CAM design generates estimates of performance on every objective at every test administration.

Notice in Figure 13.6 that the number of responses (NUM) is evenly distributed among units and among objectives. This even distribution of responses

---

[3] The CAM system allows the user the option of reporting results in fractions or percentages.

```
COMPREHENSIVE ACHIEVEMENT MONITORING - GROUP SUMMARY REPORT
HYPOTHETICAL COURSE - STANDARD CAM MODEL                              HC102
        STUDENT GROUP   7200      ALL MR. SMITH'S STUDENTS
```

			\multicolumn{7}{c}{TEST ADMINISTRATION}						
CGN	CONTENT GROUP		1	2	3	4	5	6	7
	NUMBER OF STUDENTS		85	88	86	89	90	86	88
0	ALL OBJECTIVES	PCT	35	42	46	52	60	64	68
		NUM	2040	2112	2064	2136	2160	2064	2112
12	UNIT 12	PCT	36	80	75	76	72	74	73
		NUM	255	264	258	267	270	258	264
13	UNIT 13	PCT	37	36	42	73	80	82	78
		NUM	255	264	258	267	270	258	264
14	UNIT 14	PCT	28	29	41	46	60	62	75
		NUM	255	264	258	267	270	258	264
22	UNIT 22	PCT	37	38	32	37	34	40	76
		NUM	255	264	258	267	270	258	264
23	UNIT 23	PCT	36	37	38	41	40	39	41
		NUM	255	264	258	267	270	258	264
24	UNIT 24	PCT	40	38	39	40	50	52	56
		NUM	255	264	258	267	270	258	264
1301	OBJECTIVE 1301	PCT	36	41	43	80	79	82	76
		NUM	42	44	43	45	45	43	44
1401	OBJECTIVE 1401	PCT	38	45	39	38	46	51	48
		NUM	43	44	43	44	45	43	44
2201	OBJECTIVE 2201	PCT	20	18	26	25	20	26	79
		NUM	43	44	43	45	45	43	44
2301	OBJECTIVE 2301	PCT	27	29	32	35	38	42	43
		NUM	42	44	43	44	45	43	44
2401	OBJECTIVE 2401	PCT	31	28	33	36	39	41	38
		NUM	43	44	43	44	45	43	44

A Group Summary Report for the Standard CAM Design
Generated by the CAM Data Processing System

Figure 13.6

can only be achieved in an item or objective sampling environment such as the
standard CAM design when the proper scheduling techniques mentioned in this
chapter are observed.

Summary

The standard CAM test forms provide a continuous measure of the students' overall progress in the course. The main advantage of the standard CAM design is the continuous or longitudinal information generated for student group and curriculum validation decisions on each unit and each objective during each test administration.

The standard CAM evaluation design does not, like the two previous models described, provide individual student information that can be used to make decisions such as the mastery or non-mastery of an objective on the basis of a single test administration. The design is especially applicable to the measurement of student growth on a set of developmental objectives, such as reading comprehension.

Chapter 14

The Standard/Unit CAM Design

To this point, three evaluation designs have been discussed: the unit CAM design, the sliding unit CAM design, and the standard CAM design. Chapter 14 introduces the standard/unit CAM design, which combines some desirable elements of the previous designs. Also provided are additional examples useful for understanding some definitions of new concepts presented later.

The standard/unit CAM evaluation design is applicable to a situation that calls for both regular survey testing over the entire course content and mastery testing of the course units. By gathering both course survey and unit mastery performance data, the standard/unit design supports the evaluation of achievement of developmental objectives and decision-making for a group instructional setting as well as decisions regarding individual student mastery. Thus, the standard/unit CAM design introduces a measure of flexibility for planning and decision-making beyond that provided by the earlier designs.

The Standard/Unit CAM Design

The standard/unit design consists of a standard CAM component and a unit CAM component. The standard CAM component is a test set of six standard CAM survey test forms. The unit CAM component is made up of test sets of two forms each. Each unit mastery test set covers the content of two units.

Standard CAM Survey Test Component

The standard CAM component of the standard/unit design contains six standard CAM survey test forms covering the content of the entire course. The test set is constructed through item and objective sampling in the same way as the test set of 10 forms in the standard CAM design, except that fewer items are needed from the item pool. Thus, each pair of standard CAM test forms (1 and 2; 3 and 4; 5 and 6) includes one item for each course objective, three from each unit in each form. The use of the standard CAM survey test provides a continuous monitoring of course retention data and preinstructional group diagnosis.

The scheduling for the six standard CAM test administrations is done with a six-by-six latin square. Forty students spread as evenly as possible among the six course sections take each form at each test administration, allowing group data for each section to be based on a broad sample of test items. Each student thus responds to each of the six standard CAM test forms once during the course. Figure 14.1 shows the test administrations at which the standard CAM survey tests are given.

Test Administration	Test Forms	Test Type	Units Tested
1	1–6	Survey	11–24
2	1–6	Survey	11–24
3	128, 129	Mastery	11, 12
4	1–6	Survey	11–24
5	148, 149	Mastery	13, 14
6	1–6	Survey	11–24
7	228, 229	Mastery	21, 22
8	1–6	Survey	11–24
9	248, 249	Mastery	23, 24
10	1–6	Survey	11–24

The Testing Sequence in the Standard/Unit CAM Design

Figure 14.1

Unit CAM Mastery Test Component

Unit CAM mastery tests are derived to cover the content of consecutive pairs of course units. Each unit test set has two forms, as Figure 14.1 shows. Two items are sampled for each objective in the pair of units on each form. Figure 14.2 displays the content of the test forms for Units 21 and 22, thus illustrating the distribution of items and objectives over any pair of mastery test forms.

Question Position	Items Assigned to Each Form 228	229
1	210104	210105
2	210101	210104
3	210205	210206
4	210202	210205
5	210306	210303
6	210303	210304
7	210401	210404
8	210404	210403
9	210502	210503
10	210505	210502
11	210603	210606
12	210606	210605
13	220104	220105
14	220101	220104
15	220205	220202
16	220202	220201
17	220306	220303
18	220303	220302
19	220401	220402
20	220404	220401
21	220506	220504
22	220504	220505
23	220602	220603
24	220605	220602

Items Assigned to Each Question Position of a Pair of
Unit Test Forms in the Standard/Unit CAM Design

Figure 14.2

Half the students in each course section respond to each form at the conclusion of instruction in the second of the two units tested. Thus group performance data are generated from a sample of three test items per objective. An additional, but secondary, advantage of using two forms of a mastery test is the availability of an alternate test form for students recycled in any of the units of instruction. Although this would necessitate a student's taking one item twice for the objectives through which he recycled, Schriber (1973) has shown that this does not offset the validity of the item the second time it appears.

Reporting

The individual student report and the group summary report are generated in the standard/unit design. Their content reflects the unique features of this design.

JONES   SALLY   MR. JOHNSON
                                                                                    HC102

FRACTION CORRECT ON ALL ITEMS IS 20/24   FORM 229
FRACTION CORRECT ON YES ITEMS IS 20/24

QP	OBJ	RP	INS	QP	OBJ	RP	INS	TEST ADM	FORM	FRN COR ALL	FRN COR YES
1	2101	2+	YES	13	2201	4+	YES	1	1	6/24	0/0
2	2101	1+	YES	14	2201	1+	YES	2	6	8/24	2/3
3	2102	3+	YES	15	2202	3+	YES	3	129	19/24	19/24
4	2102	4+	YES	16	2202	1+	YES	4	2	12/24	8/9
5	2103	4+	YES	17	2203	4+	YES	5	149	16/24	16/24
6	2103	1+	YES	18	2203	2+	YES	6	3	15/24	12/15
7	2104	2+	YES	19	2204	2−	YES	7	229	20/24	20/24
8	2104	2+	YES	20	2204	4−	YES				
9	2105	1+	YES	21	2205	3+	YES				
10	2105	3+	YES	22	2205	2+	YES				
11	2106	4+	YES	23	2206	1−	YES				
12	2106	4+	YES	24	2206	5−	YES				

CUM TOT   96/168   77/99

An Individual Student Report for the Standard/Unit CAM Design
Generated by the CAM Data Processing System

Figure 14.3

Individual Student Report

Figure 14.3 shows the student report for Sally Jones following Test Administration 7 in the standard/unit CAM design. As the report points out, Sally took Form 229, a unit mastery test on which each of the objectives in Units 21 and 22 is represented by two items. Instruction therefore has been completed (YES) for all objectives on Form 229. This is reflected in the coincidence of the ALL and YES fraction correct scores.

The pattern of standard and unit CAM tests is shown clearly in the FRN COR/YES column of the summary information on the right side of the report. At Test Administrations 3 and 5, unit test Forms 129 and 149 were administered so all items were related there also to instruction-completed objectives. In contrast, the standard CAM survey test was given at Test Administrations 1, 2, 4, and 6, in association with a gradual increase in the number of objectives to which the student was exposed. This interspersion of individual unit mastery data with retention and preinstructional information makes the standard/unit CAM design an attractive evaluation option.

Group Summary Report

Figure 14.4 contains a portion of a group summary report for the standard/unit CAM design for one of Ms. Hanson's sections. Notice how the standard component in Test Administrations 1, 2, 4, and 6 generates an estimate of achievement level for each unit and objective in the course, while the unit component generates an estimate of achievement level only for the 12 relevant objectives during Test Administrations 3, 5, and 7. From the group data generated by the standard survey component, general retention and preinstructional data support ongoing course planning and revisions and provide feedback for curriculum validation. On the other hand, the unit tests make more detailed individual and group information available about performance of recently taught objectives. The latter data are useful for the management of group progress on or about the point of instruction.

Summary

The standard/unit CAM design combines components of two evaluation designs in order to generate data for a wide range of decision-making concerning the student's knowledge on individual objectives on a postinstructional basis within no more than a month of instruction on each objective. The student responds to at least two test items related to that objective. And, if the student

```
COMPREHENSIVE ACHIEVEMENT MONITORING — GROUP SUMMARY REPORT
HYPOTHETICAL COURSE — STANDARD/UNIT CAM DESIGN
          STUDENT GROUP   4805      MS. HANSON      SECTION 5
```

CGN	CONTENT GROUP		TEST ADMINISTRATION 1	2	3	4	5	6	7
	NUMBER OF STUDENTS		28	29	28	30	27	26	30
0	ALL OBJECTIVES	PCT	27	29	28	30	27	26	30
		NUM	672	696	672	720	648	624	720
11	UNIT 11	PCT	30	75	80	74	***	76	***
		NUM	84	87	336	90	0	78	0
13	UNIT 13	PCT	28	27	***	81	84	80	***
		NUM	84	87	0	90	324	78	0
21	UNIT 21	PCT	30	32	***	40	***	41	85
		NUM	84	87	0	90	0	78	360
23	UNIT 23	PCT	20	25	***	23	***	26	***
		NUM	84	87	0	90	0	78	0
1101	OBJECTIVE 1101	PCT	32	85	89	86	***	85	***
		NUM	14	14	56	15	0	13	0
1301	OBJECTIVE 1301	PCT	25	28	***	56	59	55	***
		NUM	14	15	0	15	54	13	0
2105	OBJECTIVE 2105	PCT	56	62	***	63	***	60	95
		NUM	14	14	0	15	0	13	60
2301	OBJECTIVE 2301	PCT	20	21	***	60	***	70	***
		NUM	14	15	0	15	0	13	0

A Group Summary Report for the Standard/Unit CAM Design
Generated by the CAM Data Processing System

Figure 14.4

performs poorly on a form of the unit test, he can retake the other form of the test after completing the necessary review activities. The standard CAM component of the design monitors each student's and the group's overall progress in the course by measuring retention and preinstructional achievement levels.

Chapter 15
Generalized Evaluation Designs

This chapter identifies, in the technical language associated with the Comprehensive Achievement Monitoring system, some additional concepts and notation used to describe a wide variety of criterion-referenced evaluation designs and expands upon some terminology introduced earlier. The evaluation designs presented previously are described in terms of this notation. Finally, the concluding section compares the four evaluation designs presented earlier in terms of the information generated for decision-making relative to individual students, to groups of students, and for curriculum validation. The comparison is meant to aid the reader in evaluating the usefulness of the data generated by the different designs.

Evaluation Design Elements

The terminology presented here represents the major elements of the concept of evaluation design developed over the course of implementing the Comprehensive Achievement Monitoring project. These terms are used to represent the structure of the program or course in terms of its administrative units (units or modules of instruction), the related ordering of its content (topics and objectives), its divisions of time, and its structure in the testing components. These terms form an integrated whole technically describing a given evaluation design and are partially illustrated in Figure 15.1.

Set

A set is considered one or more. For example, a set of objectives is one or

Objectives for Q1	Test Administration 1		Test Administration 2		Test Administration 3	
	Test Form 11	Test Form 12	Test Form 21	Test Form 22	Test Form 31	Test Form 32
0101	010101	010102				
	010104	010103				
0102	010202	010201				
	010203	010204				
0103	010301	010302				
	010303	010304				
0104	010402	010401				
	010404	010403				
0201			020102	020101		
			020103	020104		
0202			020201	020202		
			020204	020203		
0203			020302	020301		
			020304	020303		
0301					030101	030102
					030103	030104
0302					030202	030201
					030204	030203
0303					030301	030302
					030304	030303
0304					030401	030402
					030403	030404
0305					030502	030501
					030503	030504

Item Numbers for Each Test Form — Quarter One

Figure 15.1

more objectives; a set of test forms is one or more forms; a set of tests is one or more tests.

Content Span

Content span is defined as a collection of ordered objectives specified in terms of the first and last objectives in the collection. In most instances, the ordering of objectives is defined by the order in which they are taught. The name given the collection is related to that portion of the curriculum covered by the objectives in terms of content in text or time. For example, in the leftmost column of Figure 15.1 the objectives for Quarter 1 are listed in the order they are taught. The two leftmost digits of the objective number refer to a unit in the textbook. The content span from Objective 0101 to Objective 0104 is Unit 1; the content span from Objective 0201 to Objective 0203 is Unit 2; the content span from Objective 0301 to Objective 0305 is Unit 3. The content span from Objective 0101 to Objective 0305 is Quarter 1.

The content span of Quarter 1 and the related numerical coding incorporate information on a reporting period (Quarter 1), an administrative unit of instruction (e.g., Unit 2), and content units (unit, topic, objective). The numerical objective coding scheme is designed to reflect the content span in its order of presentation in a course or program.

Test Form

A test form is defined as a collection of test items. The numerical representation of the collection of items is characterized in one of two ways. First, the item numbers may be ordered in the sequence in which the items are presented to a student. This order is called a question position order. Second, since each item is associated with an objective, the item numbers may be ordered to correspond with a content span. A list of item numbers in either of these orders represents a test form. The item listings for six different test forms are shown in Figure 15.1. The term "form" is an acceptable short version of the term "test form" and is defined equivalently.

Test Set

This is a set of test forms that all contain the same content span. For example, in the course shown in Figure 15.1, there are three test sets: one on Unit 1 — Forms 11 and 12; one on Unit 2 — Forms 21 and 22; and one on Unit 3 — Forms 31 and 32. The term "test" is often used synonymously with "test set."

Objective Density

This is the proportion of items related to a given objective on a test set or test form to the total number of items on the test set or form. For example, the objective density for Objective 0101 on Test Form 11 in Figure 15.1 is 2/8; the objective density for Objective 0101 for the test set on Unit 1 is 4/16. The denominator of the objective density is the total number of items on the test or test form; the numerator is the number of items related to the specific objective on the test or test form.

Evaluation Period

This is a set of test administrations.

Standard Evaluation Component

This is a test consisting of more than one form used for more than one test administration during the evaluation period.

Sliding Unit Evaluation Component

This is a set of tests such that the content span of each test contains one or more objectives from the content span of the test used in the immediately preceding and/or the immediately following test administration. Each test is used only once in an evaluation period.

Unit Evaluation Component

This is a set of tests such that the content span of each test contains no objectives from the content of any other test in the set. Each test is used only once in an evaluation period.

Evaluation Design

This is a set of all the evaluation components defined for an evaluation period.

Design Characteristics

The unit CAM design presented in Chapter 11 is an evaluation design with two components: a standard component during Test Administrations 1 and 10, and a unit component during Test Administrations 2-9. The standard component consists of Test Forms 1 and 2 in Figure 13.1. Half the students take Form 1 and the other half take Form 2 during Test Administration 1. This process is repeated during Test Administration 10, with the students taking the other form (i.e., if a student took Form 1 during Test Administration 1, he will take Form 2 during Test Administration 10). This standard CAM test (Forms 1 and 2) is based upon the semester content span — i.e., Objective 1101 through Objective 2406. Each of these objectives appears once on the test, and the objective density in the test is 1/48 for each of the 48 objectives.

The unit component of the unit design consists of eight tests, each related to one of the eight units in the curriculum. Consider the Unit 22 test shown in Figure 11.3. The content span of the test is Unit 22 — i.e., Objectives 2201 through 2206. The one form of the test contains 24 items and each objective appears four times, giving an objective density of 4/24 for each of the six objectives in Unit 22. Within the unit component the content span for the Unit 21 test is Objectives 2101 through 2106, while the content span for the Unit 23 test is Objectives 2301 through 2306. Note that the content spans of these tests do not overlap — i.e., they do not contain the same objectives.

The sliding unit CAM design is an evaluation design consisting of two components: a standard component in Test Administrations 1 and 10, and a sliding unit component in Test Administrations 2-9.

The sliding unit component consists of eight tests, one test related to each of the eight units. The test for Unit 22 has a content span of Objectives 2101-2306 (refer to Figure 12.2). This test contains 48 items, 24 items per form. Objectives 2101-2106 each appear only once on the test and have an objective density of 1/48; Objectives 2201-2206 each appear six times on the test and have an objective density of 6/48; Objectives 2301-2306 each appear once on the test and have an objective density of 1/48. Likewise, the test for Unit 21 has a content span of Objectives 1401-2206. Objectives 1401-1406 each appear only once on the test and have an objective density of 1/48; Objectives 2101-2106 each appear six times on the test and have an objective density of 6/48; Objectives 2201-2206 each appear once on the test and have an objective density of 1/48 on the test.

The standard CAM design is an evaluation design consisting of a single standard evaluation component. The standard test (refer to Figure 13.1) consists of 10 test forms defined over the semester content span (Objectives 1101 through 2406). The content span contains 48 objectives, and each objective appears five times on the test. Thus the objective density of 5/240 for each objective in the curriculum.

The standard/unit CAM design is an evaluation design consisting of a standard evaluation component for Test Administrations 1, 2, 4, 6, 8, and 10 and a unit evaluation component for Test Administrations 3, 5, 7, and 9. The standard test has a content span containing Objectives 1101 through 2406 and contains Forms 1 to 6. The objective density for each of the 48 objectives in this test is 3/144, as each objective appears three times in the test set.

The unit component consists of four tests, one each for the content spans consisting of Units 11 and 12, Units 13 and 14, Units 21 and 22, and Units 23 and 24. Figure 14.1 displays the two forms of the Unit 22 test. The objective density for the 12 objectives in Units 21 and 22 is 4/48 each, as there are 48 items on the test and each objective appears four times. The objective density for Objective 2103 on Test Form 228 is 2/24.

Student Achievement Data and Test Types

The various evaluation components include both survey and mastery type tests used for collecting preinstructional, postinstructional, and retention information about student achievement. The data may be collected to support decisions about individual students or groups of students in various aggregations.

Individual Student Information

Both survey and mastery tests may gather data relative to individual student achievement. However, mastery tests are the most useful for indicating individual performance on the objectives of a unit or other content span at one particular point in time. Survey tests do not typically elicit a broad enough sample of relevant behavior to judge achievement of a specific objective. Over the period of an entire course or program, a set of survey test forms can demonstrate student achievement, but one such form has not enough items per objective to generate reliable data useful for individual decisions on objectives. The main requirement for information about a particular student's learning is that the data have a high degree of reliability in relation to relatively small units of performance.

Group Information

Survey tests generally provide the most useful information for managing groups of students and for making decisions about programs and the curriculum. If data are sought about the general level of performance in a group of students, a set of survey tests can provide a large enough sample of responses from the whole group to make reliable estimates of performances on which to base decisions about review, enrichment, skipping topics and other concerns in a group-paced instruction environment. A survey test given periodically over the entire content span of a course or program provides preinstructional, postinstructional, and retention information.

Curriculum Validation Information

The data generated by either survey or mastery testing can be used for making decisions relative to the effectiveness of instruction and the validity of the curriculum itself. These decisions are usually made following the completion of the instructional program. Relevant decisions include the inclusion, exclusion, and sequencing of objectives and resources, and the evaluation of test items.

A Comparison of the Four Designs

Each of the four evaluation designs discussed serves a slightly different data gathering purpose. One concentrates on student mastery of course units, another on a combination of achievement data over a month's time. The third design focuses on the long-term pattern of achievement, and the last attempts to combine the advantages of having both short-term mastery and course survey performance data.

Individual Student Information

Of the four designs described in this monograph, the unit CAM design provides the most useful information for making decisions concerning an individual student's mastery of objectives on an immediate postinstruction basis. Every two weeks the unit design generates four responses to each of the last six objectives completed. However, the unit CAM design does not provide any information concerning the student's preinstruction or retention achievement levels on the objectives in the course, which is the purpose of the sliding unit CAM design.

The sliding unit CAM design provides very good information for mastery decision-making relative to the individual student. This model generates three responses to each of the last six objectives completed. In addition, the sliding unit design provides a sampling of preinstruction and retention achievement levels for the individual student. In comparison with the unit design, the sliding unit design sacrifices some reliability concerning the immediate postinstruction mastery decisions (three items per objective rather than four) in order to gain some information concerning the student's preinstruction and retention achievement levels.

The standard/unit CAM design provides less information for individual student mastery decision-making. The unit component of the model generates data only once a month (as opposed to every two weeks for the above models), and generates only two responses per objective for the last 12 objectives instructed. On the other hand, the standard component generates information concerning the student's preinstruction and retention achievement levels on all objectives in the course.

The standard CAM design provides very little information concerning the student's mastery of objectives at isolated moments in time. During each test administration, the illustrated standard CAM design generates only one response to half of the objectives in the course for any student. However, this design does provide an estimate of each student's preinstruction and retention achievement levels across all objectives every two weeks.

Group Information

The unit CAM design provides very little student group information across all objectives at one time. During Test Administrations 2-9, the model only provides the class achievement level on the last unit covered each time. There is no information concerning student preinstruction and retention achievement levels on the other objectives in the curriculum and therefore no data for preplanning. The teacher is given no information to decide what objectives already covered should be reviewed or what objectives should be emphasized during the next two weeks of instruction.

The sliding unit CAM design provides more group student information than the unit design. In addition to the group achievement level on the six objectives just covered, the design generates estimates of group achievement on the six objectives completed two weeks previously, and on the six objectives to be covered during the next two weeks. No information is provided concerning objectives taught more than two weeks previously, nor objectives to be taught more than two weeks in the future. For example, following Test Administration 7, the design generates 720 student responses on each of the six objectives in Unit 22 (240 students times three items per objective) and 120 student responses for each of the six objectives in Units 21 and 23. There is no information generated for the students' achievement levels on the objectives in Units 11, 12, 13, 14, and 24 during Test Administration 7.

The standard/unit CAM design provides more data for group student decision-making than the above models. During Test Administrations 1, 2, 4, 6, 8, and 10, the standard component of the design generates information relative to all 48 objectives. There are 120 student responses for each of these objectives during the above test administrations. These 120 responses are evenly divided among three items related to each objective. During Test Administrations 3, 5, 7, and 9, the unit component of the design produces group information relative to the 12 most recently instructed objectives. The 480 student responses per objective (240 students times two items per objective) are evenly divided among the four items per objective (two items per objective per form times two forms).

The standard CAM design provides information concerning the students' achievement on all 48 objectives following each test administration. There are 120 student responses per objective, evenly divided among five items per objective.

The information for groups of students generated by the four designs is summarized in Figures 15.2, 15.3, and 15.4. Figure 15.2 contains an analysis of the information about Objective 2201 generated by the four designs in each test administration. Number of Responses refers to the number of possible student responses in each test administration to items related to Objective 2201. The hypothetical curriculum structure and evaluation designs were planned so that each objective is responded to 1200 times by students during the course. It is the distribution of these 1200 responses over the test administrations that differs from one design to another. This distribution is given by the row Percentage of Total Responses. Number of Items Used refers to the degree of item sampling that is used in each design. For instance, in Test Administration 1, all designs produce 120 student responses to Objective 2201. However, the standard design uses five items (10 forms are used), the standard/unit uses three items (six forms are used), while the sliding unit and unit designs use only one item each (only two forms are used). Remember that an objective only appears on every other form in the standard evaluation component. This figure illustrates the unit and sliding unit designs' generating more postinstruction information, while the standard/unit and standard designs generate more preinstruction and retention information. Remember that instruction on Objective 2201 occurs immediately prior to Test Administration 7.

Figure 15.3 contains an analysis by time reference of the information about Objective 2201 generated by the designs. The student responses are broken down into PREINSTRUCTION (a response before instruction on the objective); POSTINSTRUCTION (a response from 0 to 28 days since instruction on the objective); and RETENTION (a response at least 29 days since instruction on the objective). Note that as in Figure 15.2, each design generates 1200 student responses during the semester. It is the distribution of responses over the time references (Percentage of Total Responses) that changes from design to design. Figure 15.4 contains an analysis by time reference of the information

Design	Statistic	Test Administration									
		1	2	3	4	5	6	7	8	9	10
Standard	Number of Responses	120	120	120	120	120	120	120	120	120	120
	Percentage of Total Responses	10%	10%	10%	10%	10%	10%	10%	10%	10%	10%
	Number of Items Used	5	5	5	5	5	5	5	5	5	5
Standard/ Unit	Number of Responses	120	120	0	120	0	120	480	120	0	120
	Percentage of Total Responses	10%	10%	0%	10%	0%	10%	40%	10%	0%	10%
	Number of Items Used	3	3	0	3	0	3	4	5	0	3
Sliding Unit	Number of Responses	120	0	0	0	0	120	720	120	0	120
	Percentage of Total Responses	10%	0%	0%	0%	0%	10%	60%	10%	0%	10%
	Number of Items Used	1	0	0	0	0	1	6	1	0	1
Unit	Number of Responses	120	0	0	0	0	0	960	0	0	120
	Percentage of Total Responses	10%	0%	0%	0%	0%	0%	80%	0%	0%	10%
	Number of Items Used	1	0	0	0	0	0	4	0	0	1

Analysis of Responses to Questions Measuring Achievement on Objective 2201 by Test Administration

Figure 15.2

Design	Statistic	Preinstruction	Postinstruction	Retention
Standard	Number of Responses	720	240	240
	Percentage of Total Responses	60%	20%	20%
Standard/Unit	Number of Responses	480	600	120
	Percentage of Total Responses	40%	50%	10%
Sliding Unit	Number of Responses	240	840	120
	Percentage of Total Responses	20%	70%	10%
Unit	Number of Responses	120	960	120
	Percentage of Total Responses	10%	80%	10%

Analysis of Response to Questions Measuring Achievement on Objective 2201 by Time Reference

Figure 15.3

PREINSTRUCTION = Student response before instruction on Objective 2201.
POSTINSTRUCTION = Student response from 0 to 28 days since instruction on Objective 2201.
RETENTION = Student response at least 29 days since instruction on Objective 2201.

Design	Statistic	Preinstruction	Postinstruction	Retention
Standard	Number of Responses	360	240	600
	Percentage of Total Responses	30%	20%	50%
Standard/Unit	Number of Responses	240	600	360
	Percentage of Total Responses	20%	50%	30%
Sliding Unit	Number of Responses	240	840	120
	Percentage of Total Responses	20%	70%	10%
Unit	Number of Responses	120	960	120
	Percentage of Total Responses	10%	80%	10%

Analysis of Responses to Questions Measuring Achievement on Objective 1304 by Time Reference

Figure 15.4

PREINSTRUCTION = Student response before instruction on Objective 1304.
POSTINSTRUCTION = Student response from 0 to 28 days since instruction on Objective 1304.
RETENTION = Student response at least 29 days since instruction on Objective 1304.

about Objective 1304 generated by the four designs. Notice that Figures 15.3 and 15.4 are identical for the sliding unit and unit designs, but differ for the standard and standard/unit designs. This shows that the standard design (and the standard component of the standard/unit design) comprehensively measures all objectives in the course. Since Objective 1304 was taught a month prior to Objective 2201, the standard design generates more retention data (and correspondingly less preinstruction data) for Objective 1304 than for Objective 2201. Figures 15.3 and 15.4 also display that the unit and sliding unit designs generate more postinstruction information, while the standard/unit and standard designs generate more preinstruction and retention information.

Figure 15.5 presents a visual summation of the discussion of the types of data the different evaluation designs provide for decision-making.

Design	Preinstruction		Postinstruction		Retention	
	Individual Student	Group	Individual Student	Group	Individual Student	Group
Unit	—	—	X detailed data	X	—	—
Sliding Unit	Some	(only for 2 weeks)	X	X	Some	(only for prior 2 weeks)
Standard/ Unit	X	X	X	X	X	X
Standard	—	X	—	X	—	X

Types of Information Generated by the CAM Design

Figure 15.5

Curriculum Validation Information

The standard CAM design provides information that is most useful for instruction and curriculum validation decisions and for the measurement of growth.
The standard/unit CAM design provides some information for curriculum validation decisions through the standard component. The sliding unit and unit designs
provide substantially less information for instruction and curriculum validation
decisions.

Consider the question as to the proper sequencing of objectives in the curriculum structure. By providing estimates of the class achievement level 10 times
during the course (i.e., a longitudinal achievement measure), the standard design
enables the teacher to recognize interactive instructional effects. Suppose that
the instructional activities related to Objective 1203 also affect the achievement
level on Objective 2201. Instruction on Objective 1203 occurs between Test Administrations 2 and 3. The standard design not only provides an estimate of the
students' achievement on Objective 1203 during Test Administrations 2 and 3,
but also provides an estimate of the students' achievement on Objective 2201
during these test administrations (see Figure 15.2). If there is significant change
in the achievement level on Objective 2201 from Test Administration 2 to Test
Administration 3, the course structure might be resequenced the following year
to teach Objectives 1203 and 2201 at the same time. An analysis of Figure 15.2
shows that the standard/unit design generates less frequent longitudinal data,
while the sliding unit and unit designs generate virtually no longitudinal data.

Consider an input-output analysis of the effectiveness of the hypothetical
course structure. Input is taken to mean the students' entering achievement level, and output is taken to mean the students' retention achievement level. Retention is being used as the output measure because postinstruction achievement
levels sometimes contain transient achievement such as rote memory. An analysis of Figures 15.3 and 15.4 indicates that the standard design generates 80 percent of the student responses on a preinstruction and retention basis. The stan-
dard/unit design generates 50 percent; the sliding unit design, 30 percent; and
the unit design, 20 percent on a preinstruction and retention basis. Thus, the
standard design generates data that are more useful for an input-output analysis
of a course or program.

Summary

Four generally-used Comprehensive Achievement Monitoring evaluation
designs have been examined in terms of a specific technical jargon. Comparisons
of the designs show that each fulfills a unique performance reporting function

reflective of different decision-making concerns. The unit CAM design supports decision-making about individual student mastery of short content spans. The sliding unit CAM design provides data on objectives in three content spans and supports preinstructional decisions for the next instructional unit. The standard CAM design, although it generates little individual student mastery information at any one time, provides reliable group data for instructional planning and curriculum validation. Finally, the standard/unit CAM design intersperses the use of survey and mastery tests to generate both kinds of decision-making data.

Chapter 16

Examples of Group-Paced
Evaluation Designs

The previous chapters in this part of the monograph have presented a hypothetical curriculum structure so that the basic concepts of criterion-referenced evaluation designs could be illustrated. Actual curriculum structures are rarely as simple and neat as the hypothetical curriculum structure presented earlier. Moreover, the implementation of the concepts discussed thus far must account for boundary effects — that is, the beginning and ending of courses and program levels or divisions. At the start of a course or program level, there is usually no testing of retention achievement levels, while at the conclusion there is generally no preinstruction testing. The four examples that follow are based upon actual evaluation designs developed in group-paced instructional environments. Modifications of these designs are also presented to fit the requirements of individually paced programs of instruction.

A Design for Earth Sciences

The earth sciences curriculum used here as an example is divided into four one-quarter courses, one each on astronomy, geology, oceanography, and meteorology. The program contains much laboratory work and individualized study within the quarter courses. All students work on the same quarter course; that is, the program is not individualized across the courses. The astronomy course contains five learning activity packages (LAPS) with 20 objectives; the geology course contains five LAPS with 20 objectives; the oceanography course contains six LAPS with 21 objectives; and the meteorology course contains three LAPS with 18 objectives. This structure is summarized in Figure 16.1.

The evaluation span for the entire earth sciences program contains 16 test

Quarter	Number of LAPS	Number of Objectives
Astronomy	5	20
Geology	5	20
Oceanography	6	21
Meteorology	3	18

Earth Sciences Curriculum

Figure 16.1

administrations during the year, or four test administrations during each quarter course. The evaluation design consists of four standard CAM components, one component related to each quarter course. Each standard component contains four forms and is used during four test administrations. The evaluation design for the year-long course consists of 16 test forms used over 16 test administrations, and each student responds only once to each test form during the year. Figure 16.2 demonstrates this evaluation design.

The astronomy CAM test contains four forms of 25 items each. Therefore, the astronomy test contains 100 items. The content span of the standard CAM test is the objectives in the astronomy and geology courses. The 20 objectives in the astronomy course appear once on each of the four forms and therefore have an objective density of 4/100. The 20 objectives in the geology course appear only once on the test, and each objective has a density of 1/100. Note that these geology objectives will be measuring preinstruction achievement during the astronomy quarter course.

The geology CAM test contains three forms of 30 items each, and one form of 31 items. Thus, the geology test contains 121 items. The content span of this CAM test is the objectives in the astronomy, geology, and oceanography courses. Each objective in the astronomy and oceanography courses appears once on the test and has an objective density of 1/121. Each objective in the geology LAP appears once on all four forms, and therefore has an objective density of 4/121.

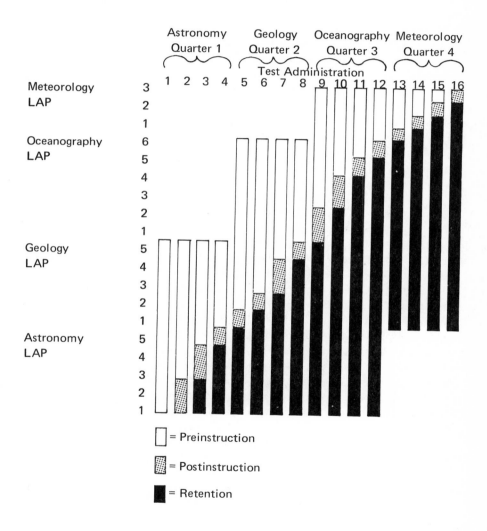

Standard CAM Evaluation Design for Earth Sciences

Figure 16.2

The geology CAM measures the astronomy objectives on a retention basis, and the oceanography objectives on a preinstruction, postinstruction, or retention basis depending upon the instructional activities of each of the students during the second quarter of the program.

The oceanography CAM test contains two forms of 36 items each, and two forms of 35 items each. There are 142 items on the test. The content span of the oceanography test contains the objectives in all four quarters' courses. The objectives in the astronomy and geology courses each appear once on the test and have a density of 1/142. These objectives are measured on a retention basis by the oceanography CAM. The objectives in the oceanography course each appear on all four forms, and have a density of 4/142. These objectives are measured on a preinstruction, postinstruction, or retention basis depending upon the instructional activities of the students. The objectives in the meteorology course appear once on the test, having an objective density of 1/142, and are measured on a preinstruction basis.

The meteorology CAM contains three forms of 28 items and one form of 29 items. The test contains 113 items. The content span of the meteorology test is the geology, oceanography, and meteorology courses. The geology and oceanography objectives each appear once on the test, have an objective density of 1/113, and are measured on a retention basis by the meteorology CAM. Each of the meteorology objectives is contained on all four forms, has a density of 4/113 on the test, and is measured on a preinstruction, postinstruction, or retention basis during the meteorology course.

The earth sciences evaluation design provides a balance of information for individual student, group student, and curriculum validation decision-making. Within each quarter's course, the design provides a measure of each student's achievement on all the objectives in the quarter's course during each test administration. Thus, the design facilitates the individualization of instruction within the quarter's courses. Notice that the design generates more information on a retention basis than on a preinstruction basis. This retention information can be used to evaluate the long-term achievement effects of the program for each student. Each objective in all four quarter courses is measured on a preinstruction, postinstruction, and retention basis by the above design. This information can be used to rewrite the curriculum materials for the following year.

A Design for Chemistry

The curriculum for the semester-long chemistry course consists of eight units. The first unit covers fundamental laboratory skills such as mathematics, graphing, and using laboratory equipment. Unit 1 contains 14 objectives. The other seven units cover various topics of chemistry and contain eight objectives each. There are a total of 70 objectives in the course. The chemistry course is presented in a flexibly scheduled school with each student attending a large group lecture, a medium group discussion session, and two labs a week. The teachers pace the instructional activities by the weekly lectures. However, there is much individualized study, particularly in the laboratory work. This individualization is necessitated to some degree because of the relative scarcity of laboratory equipment.

The evaluation period contains 10 test administrations. The evaluation design consists of both a standard and a sliding unit component. The standard component is used during Test Administrations 1 and 10 — i.e., at the beginning and end of the course. The sliding unit component is used during Test Administrations 2 through 9. Figure 16.3 presents the sliding unit CAM evaluation design used for the chemistry course.

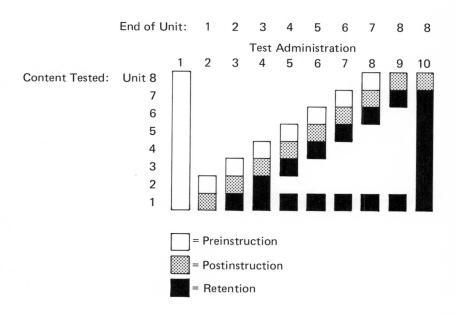

Sliding Unit CAM Evaluation Design for a Chemistry Course

Figure 16.3

The standard CAM test contains 70 items with two forms each containing 35 items. The content span of this test is all objectives in the course. Each objective appears once on the test and has a density of 1/70.

The sliding unit tests are identified by the unit to which they are related. Thus, the Unit 1 test is given during Test Administration 2, which occurs following the completion of instruction on Unit 1.

The Unit 1 test has a content span of Units 1 and 2, and contains two forms of 22 items each. The objective density for all 22 objectives in the content span is 2/44. Thus, each objective appears on both forms.

The Unit 2 test has a content span of Units 1, 2, and 3, and contains two forms of 30 items each. The 30 objectives in the content span appear on both forms, and have an objective density of 2/60.

The tests related to each of Units 3-7 have a content span which includes Unit 1 and the previous, present, and next units. Thus, the Unit X test has a content span of Units 1, X-1, X, and X+1, where X=3, 4, 5, 6, and 7. The teachers included Unit 1 in these content spans because they felt that the laboratory skills were extremely important for the students to learn. Therefore, the teachers wanted to monitor these skills continually. The tests contain two forms of 31 items each. The objective density of the previous, present, and next units is 2/62 (i.e., these objectives appear on both forms). The objective density of the objectives in Unit 1 is 1/62 on these tests. Thus, each of the 14 objectives in Unit 1 appears once on the test, seven objectives per form.

The Unit 8 test has a content span of Units 1, 7, and 8, and contains two forms of 23 items each. The objectives in Units 7 and 8 each appear once on both forms (the density is 2/46), while the objectives in Unit 1 appear only once on the test (the density is 1/46).

The standard CAM component of this evaluation design provides data for curriculum validation decisions and for measuring overall student growth. The sliding unit CAM component provides data for individual student and group student decision-making. The continuous monitoring of the laboratory skills enables the teachers to review certain skills during the lecture session if the data indicate such a need. The sliding unit tests have a uniform objective density over the previous, present, and next units. This uniform density means that the sliding unit tests are relevant for students who deviate from the normal instructional program. The two forms of each sliding unit test enable a student to retake a test on which he has done poorly, yet respond to a different set of items.

A Design for Vocabulary

One part of a remedial reading program deals with vocabulary. Each week the students are expected to master 10 new vocabulary words. Each vocabulary word is treated as an objective. The students enter with a wide spectrum of vocabulary skills, and the vocabulary work is group-paced. Other aspects of the reading program, such as comprehension, are individually paced. The focus of the vocabulary evaluation design is two-fold: the teachers want to monitor each student to help him master all 160 words by the end of the course, and they want to monitor the overall progress of the program, which is being used for the first year. Seventeen test administrations are used during the 16-week course.

There are two evaluation components: a standard CAM and a sliding unit CAM. The standard CAM test is administered during the first and eighteenth test administrations — i.e., at the beginning and end of the program. The standard CAM test consists of four forms, each form containing 40 test items. Thus, each objective appears only once on the test. Note that in this application of a standard CAM evaluation component, each student will only respond to two of the four test forms. There is no prior need to have each student respond to all forms of a standard CAM test during a course. The first administration of the standard CAM test provides information concerning each student's entry level on the set of 160 vocabulary items (remember that each of the forms contains a stratified random sample of 40 words).

The sliding unit component consists of 16 tests, each test being identified by the unit after which it is administered (a unit consists of 10 vocabulary words). The teachers want the forms to reinforce mastery of the vocabulary words, and are not interested in preinstruction testing on the sliding unit test forms. All unit tests consist of two forms so that a student may retake a test with independent items.

The Unit 1 test has a content span of Unit 1, and contains 10 items on each form. The objective density of the 10 objectives in the content span on the test is 2/20. Each objective appears once on both forms. The Unit 2 test has a content span of Units 1 and 2; each form contains 20 items, one for each of the 20 objectives in the content span. The Unit 3 test has a content span of Units 1, 2, and 3; each form contains 30 items, one for each of the 30 objectives in the content span. The tests related to Units 4-16 contain four units in their content span. The content span for the Unit 4 test is Units 1-4; the content span for the Unit 5 test is Units 2-5; the content span for the Unit 6 test is Units 3-6, etc. These tests have two forms of 40 items each, one item for each of the last 40 objectives covered. Thus, the students are tested four times on each vocabulary word by the end of the course (with the exception of the words in Units 14, 15, and 16). Figure 16.4 summarizes the design.

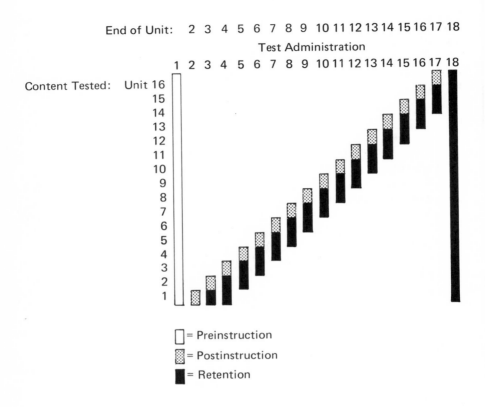

Evaluation Design for Remedial Reading Vocabulary

Figure 16.4

A Design for Geography

The first semester of a world geography course consists of four units. The themes of the units are cities, manufacturing and agriculture, cultural geography, and political geography. Each of these units has 16 objectives, six of which are considered core objectives, and 10 enrichment objectives. The teachers expect all students to learn the core objectives. The students can study as many of the enrichment objectives as they want. Each student attends one lecture and two discussion sections each week.

The goals of the evaluation design are to monitor the effectiveness of the curriculum materials and to provide guidance for the teachers in the lecture and discussion sessions. The monitoring of individual student mastery of objectives in the core area is a first priority, whereas the monitoring of mastery of the enrichment objectives is considered to be less important.

The evaluation design consists of one standard CAM component over an evaluation period of five test administrations. The CAM test is administered at the beginning of the course and at the completion of instruction on each of the four units. There are five forms of the test, and the content span of the test is all four units. Each form contains 40 items; the test contains 200 items. The 24 core objectives appear on each form and have a density of 5/200 in the test. The 40 enrichment objectives each appear twice and have a density of 2/200 in the test. The evaluation design is portrayed in Figure 16.5.

This standard CAM design measures the students' achievement on all core objectives during each test administration. While each student only responds to a sample of the enrichment objectives during a test administration, the group data provide an estimate of the class achievement on all enrichment objectives during

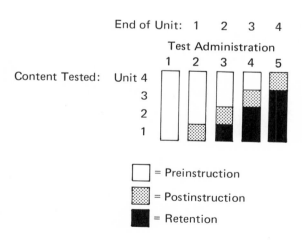

Geography Evaluation Design

Figure 16.5

each test administration. During the course, a student will respond to each enrichment objective twice and to each core objective five times.

Summary

This chapter has shown examples of how different criterion-referenced evaluation designs have actually been implemented. The CAM designs are very flexible and allow an extremely wide range of adjustability and flexibility in order to meet the decision-making needs of an individual teacher, a class, or a course of instruction. CAM evaluation components are designed to meet the specific decision-making needs of educators. They are meant to facilitate decision-making. Therefore, in implementing evaluation designs, it is necessary first for the individuals concerned to determine the kinds of data they need for the educational decisions they must make. In this chapter, the focus has been on various aspects of data needed relative to groups. The next chapter examines some different data needs relative to individual students.

Chapter 17

Examples of Individually Paced
Evaluation Designs

The previous chapters in Part III have been concerned with criterion-referenced evaluation primarily for a group-paced mode of instruction. This chapter uses the same designs and concepts to illustrate evaluation designs for an individually paced program of instruction. The individually paced program used in the chapter consists of a hierarchical set of units, modules, learning activity packages (LAPS), or teaching/learning units (TLU's) which each student is to learn. The term "unit" is used in the chapter to refer to any of the above curriculum structures. The student must complete the units in a predetermined order. The units contain approximately five objectives each, and there are five test items available per objective.

The sequential individually paced instructional design illustrated here is certainly not the only model for individualized instruction. The purpose of this chapter is to show how the models and concepts in this monograph may be used to develop evaluation designs for a wide variety of instructional programs — in this instance, a sequential individually paced curriculum. In general, the user must spend considerable time in formulating an evaluation design to fit his own needs. There are no cookbook techniques for developing an evaluation design.

Chapter 15 presented three types of decisions that are supported by criterion-referenced evaluation data: individual student, group student, and curriculum validation decisions. Chapter 16 analyzed evaluation designs for group-paced instruction in terms of these three decision categories.

Individual student decision-making obviously plays a much larger role in an individualized program. In general, an individualized instructional program requires more criterion-referenced testing than a group-paced program in order to support all the decisions that need to be made concerning the instructional activities of each student. This does not mean that group-based decisions are never made or are never important. In fact, decisions regarding instruction revision, materials evaluation, curriculum validation, and revision of the evaluation all depend on information gathered from groups.

The most common mechanism for managing the instructional activities of students is through a pretest-posttest design. In this design, the student takes a criterion-referenced test on a unit before he has formally studied the material. If he shows mastery on the test (for instance, by correctly answering at least 80 percent of the test items), he goes on to the pretest for the next unit. If he fails to master the test, he studies material in the unit, his activities hopefully being directed by the results of the pretest. When the student feels he has learned the material in the unit, he takes the posttest. All forms of the pretest and posttest measure the same content materials; i.e., they are parallel forms of the same test. If the student masters the posttest, he goes on to the pretest of the next unit in the program; if he fails to master the posttest, he continues to study the material in the unit with the posttest results guiding his activities.

The pretest-posttest management mechanism, however, does have certain disadvantages. For example, the amount of clerical work necessary to support such a testing program is substantial. Programs using the above testing procedures should have several forms of each unit posttest, and the instructor must provide the correct form for each student. Further, the pretests and posttests are usually processed by members of the instructional staff. Several projects throughout the country are using computer technology to help alleviate this clerical problem. The initial findings, however, indicate that even with a computer system, the cost of operating such a testing program is high.

Another problem with the pretest-posttest design is the types and quality of information generated. Administering criterion-referenced tests immediately after instruction on a curriculum unit does not provide information about the retention of achievement levels a month after instruction has occurred. The processing of these tests usually does not provide any estimates of group achievement levels on the specific objectives in the units. Such estimates could be useful for planning group activities to concentrate on areas of common need, as mentioned above. Systematic information related to curriculum validation decisions is not usually provided by a pretest-posttest design.

Two evaluation designs for individually paced instruction based upon the CAM experience are presented in this chapter. The first deals mainly with the monitoring of achievement levels. This design does not provide daily information for student decision-making. In the monitoring design, all students are tested at the same time every two or three weeks.

The second design deals with the actual management of instruction. In the management design, the students respond to mastery tests whenever they have completed a certain amount of work. The management design measures immediate postinstruction achievement as well as preinstruction and retention achievement. The advantages and disadvantages of the above designs are discussed at the end of this chapter.

Consider an individually paced program which has two distinct evaluation systems operating concurrently. The first is used to manage or control the instructional activities of each student. The design of this system would be similar to the pretest-posttest design discussed above. However, the students might process their own tests and make their own instructional decisions. Fellow classmates might make the decisions; aides might process the tests and teachers make the decisions. The point is that there is a mechanism for managing the activities of the students independent of the CAM evaluation design. In fact, this management mechanism need not involve paper and pencil testing. Every third week, all students are administered a CAM test. The purpose of this test is to monitor the progress of individual students on a preinstruction, postinstruction, and retention basis, to provide information concerning the progress of all students in the course, and to generate information for curriculum validation.

The instructional program referred to at the beginning of this chapter consists of a series of units. The CAM evaluation design contains three test forms for each unit. The students respond to a form of the CAM test for the unit they are working on when the tests are administered. For example, if Sally is studying Unit 7 when the tests are given, she responds to a form of the Unit 7 CAM test, while if Ronald is studying Unit 10, he responds to a form of the Unit 10 test. The three forms of each test mean that a student can stay in a unit for nine weeks and not repeat a CAM test form (three-week testing interval times three forms per test equals nine weeks). Each of the 30-item test forms contains the distribution of test items over a set of units adjacent to Unit 10. The distribution of items over Unit 10 and adjacent units is shown in Figure 17.1.

The 14 items related to Units 5, 6, 7, and 8 are retention items; the 10 items related to Units 9 and 10 are postinstruction items; and the six items related to Units 11, 12, and 13 are preinstruction items. The set of three forms for each of the units constitutes the equivalent of a sliding unit CAM design as presented in Chapter 12. Note that all forms of the tests need to be constructed before the students start in the program. A scheduling technique should be used so that the three forms of each unit CAM test are evenly distributed among the students working on a unit. For example, if 18 students are in Unit 10, then six students should respond to each of the three forms of the Unit 10 test. Thus the advantages of item and objective sampling can be used by properly scheduling the test forms. However, the scheduling program in an individualized program can become

Unit	Number of Items on a Unit 10 CAM Test Form
1–4	0
5	2
6	3
7	4
8	5
9	5
10	5
11	5
12	5
13	2
14	0

Distribution of Test Items on a Unit 10 CAM Test Form:
A Modified Sliding Unit CAM Design

Figure 17.1

more complex than in a group-paced program. A modified latin square scheduling technique can be used in this environment.

Now consider an evaluation design that both monitors achievement levels and provides information for the management of instruction. In this model, the student responds to a test form whenever he feels that he has completed a unit. Thus, a few students are taking tests every day, as opposed to the sliding unit design above in which all students take a test once every three weeks. There are two types of tests in the management CAM evaluation design: management tests and standard CAM tests. The management test for each unit consists of two 20-item forms. Fifteen of these items measure postinstruction achievement on the unit, while five of the items measure preinstruction achievement on the next unit. The distribution of test items over objectives for the Unit 7 management test is presented in Figure 17.2.

The management tests are a combination pretest-posttest. The applicable

Objectives	Unit	Number of Items on a Unit 7 Management Test Form
0601–0605	6	0
0701–0705	7	3 items per objective
0801–0805	8	1 item per objective
0901–0905	9	0

Distribution of Test Items Over Objectives on a
Unit 7 Management Test Form

Figure 17.2

decision rule may be that if a student answers correctly at least 12 of the 15 items (80 percent) on a unit, he has completed the unit. If he answers less than 12 items correctly, he must review the material in the unit, guided to certain objectives based upon the test results, and must then take the second form of the management test when he or his instructor feels he is ready. Having completed the unit, his activities in the following unit should be guided by his responses to the preinstruction items on the management test. A decision rule may be that if he answers correctly at least four of the five (80 percent) preinstruction items on the test, he can immediately "challenge" the next unit test.

The above management testing system does not provide any measures of retention achievement levels, nor does it provide preinstruction achievement for more than one unit ahead. The standard CAM testing component of the management CAM design is used to provide the above data as well as information for curriculum validation decisions. At the completion of every fifth unit, the student responds to a modified standard CAM test. The standard CAM tests consist of two 35-item forms. The distribution of test items over units on a Unit 10 standard CAM form is displayed in Figure 17.3.

An example of a decision rule that might be applied to the standard CAM test results is that a student must answer correctly 70 percent of the items related to units already completed (or 14 of the 20 items related to Units 1-10 on the

Units	Number of Items on a Unit 10 Monitoring Test Form
1–5	1 item per unit
6–10	3 items per unit
11–15	2 items per unit
16–20	1 item per unit
21+	0 items per unit

Distribution of Test Items Over Units on a
Unit 10 Monitoring Test Form

Figure 17.3

Unit 10 monitoring test). Failure to achieve this criterion would result in a review of Units 1-10 (using the results of the test), followed by the administration of the second form of the test.

The proper scheduling of the two forms of both the management and standard CAM tests will result in each form being responded to by an equal number of students during the length of the course. This scheduling is important to gain the benefits made possible by the use of objective and item sampling that would be used in constructing the actual test forms.

The management evaluation system obviously provides more individual information relevant to a particular point in time than the standard CAM component. In fact, the management system essentially includes the standard component as a part of the evaluation system. However, there are at least two potential disadvantages to the management system: cost and the rigid program structure required. The management tests in the management system require rapid processing turn-around time. Immediate processing is desirable, overnight processing barely acceptable, and 48-hour processing unacceptable. On the other hand, one- or two-day processing turn-around is acceptable for the standard CAM component. Moreover, the management system has several students responding to forms every day, while the standard CAM system requires that all students respond to tests on the same day every three weeks. The data processing aspects of the management system can be five times more expensive than the standard evaluation component.

The second potential problem with the management system is that it requires a more rigid program structure. A student must proceed through each unit in sequence. Any variations from the plan (e.g., the substitution of an alternative unit) causes problems in the overall testing program. The standard component, on the other hand, is much more flexible. The students can jump out of sequence, select activities not contained in the predetermined unit sequence, stop working on the subject area for weeks at a time, etc. The standard CAM component merely continuously monitors achievement on a predetermined set of objectives; the periodic results of this component of the evaluation system may be flexibly integrated with instructional activities as needed.

Summary

The two-component evaluation design postulated for supporting an individually paced instructional program illustrates the general applicability of the CAM evaluation designs. The flexibility they allow in formulating decision-making strategies for educational programs is a necessity in view of the multitude of instructional program structures currently extant.

The concept of evaluation design includes several components which affect the kinds of data gathered for educational decision-making. The types of tests, frequency of test administrations, and sampling plans must be determined by each decision-maker in light of the decisions needed before a specific evaluation design can be developed. The four model evaluation designs and the standardized technical vocabulary in which they are described represent an attempt to provide some generally applicable concepts to guide the derivation of particular designs suited to specific situations and decision-making options.

The close monitoring of unit mastery data facilitated by the unit CAM design is a model for keeping in close touch with student achievement over shorter content spans. The sliding unit CAM design maintains the reporting of detailed postinstructional achievement data and adds retention and preinstructional information as well. In contrast, the standard CAM design enables the monitoring of long-term growth on a systematic basis and also generates useful data for planning and management in a group instructional environment. Finally, the standard/unit CAM evaluation design incorporates components from other designs to provide both individual student mastery data of short content spans and group information for evaluating retention and preinstructional planning.

The application of various elements of the model CAM evaluation designs to both group and individualized instructional programs in previous chapters is drawn from several years of operational experience in which a wide variety of educational decision-making strategies have been successfully supported. Part IV discusses several issues other than evaluation design which also concern the implementation of criterion-referenced evaluation in a school system.

PART IV

Implementation

Part IV concludes the discussion of criterion-referenced evaluation by drawing together the components and considerations previously discussed for the establishment and maintenance of an evaluation system.

Experience with the installation of the criterion-referenced evaluation model has made apparent the complementary changes needed in the administrative organization of a school district to support the evaluation system. Some level of reorganization is necessary to create the technical capability to operate the system. A more far-reaching restructuring is needed at every level of the educational system management to insure the effective operation of the model. Chapter 18 provides examples of both the technical and the managerial structures needed for the successful operation of evaluation activities. A considerable variety of approaches to the problem exist in actual practice, ranging from ad hoc team units which meet after school to more formalized management structures, such as the IGE concept in the Wisconsin Design (Otto & Askov, 1970). The organizational examples of Chapter 18 represent an approximate synthesis of the experience of applying the evaluation model in many different school situations.

The use of criterion-referenced evaluation in the management of instructional activities also depends to a great extent on the existence of an efficient data processing capability. In the application of the model, a variety of data processing systems have been established. In general, the less extensive and least efficient applications have relied more on outside procurement of data processing services, while the larger, more effective applications have included the creation of dedicated data processing shops. Chapter 19 considers the issues involved in providing for efficient data processing.

Another area which must concern the initiator of criterion-referenced evaluation is that of orienting and training personnel to its use. Upon the success of the preservice and inservice training program rests the ultimate success of the evaluation system. Many strategies and techniques exist for imparting new skills to school personnel. In Chapter 20, several of these are discussed and a suggested content outline for a training program is presented.

Finally, to conclude the monograph, Chapter 21 makes some general recommendations regarding the planning, development, implementation, and maintenance of a criterion-referenced evaluation system. These recommendations serve to highlight the overriding importance of careful planning in all aspects of evaluation.

Chapter 18

Management and Organization for Criterion-Referenced Evaluation

This chapter illustrates the technical units and the organizational structures needed to support the development and maintenance of a criterion-referenced evaluation system. The term "technical units" refers to the technicians, professionals, equipment, and materials which are combined for the major necessary support functions. Without some support functions, such as electronic data processing, the broad operation of a criterion-referenced evaluation system would be infeasible. The present discussion identifies and discusses such major technical units as would contribute to the effective and economical operation of a criterion-referenced evaluation system in a school district.

Organizational Structure

The discussion first presents an example of the technical and managerial structures needed to support a criterion-referenced evaluation system integrated into the operations of a district with some 5,000 to 30,000 students. The required restructuring may initially be very minor in terms of new or pilot projects. Technical needs may be handled externally and reorganization of management functions may be informal or voluntary. Eventually, however, the educational system must recognize the need for permanent technical support units and a level of reorganization that requires considerable change in operations and some staff retraining.

A broad structure within which all technical and professional staff might be organized to support the maintenance and utilization of evaluation functions and

223

activities is shown in Figure 18.1. The Evaluation Service Center in this illustration includes the primary technical systems upon which the evaluation system will depend for its operation. The remaining units constitute examples of the internal structural changes to be made in the existing district organization to provide an effective basis for developing and utilizing a criterion-referenced evaluation program.

Program Management Group

Implementation activities in each subject matter area are channelled through a central district organization, here designated the Program Management Group (PMG). The PMG is usually developed out of central staff members who have been concerned with curriculum development and instruction in particular areas, as well as with testing. The major activities of the PMG are to:

— supervise all curriculum development activities (e.g., the selection and organization of performance objectives in each content area).

— develop an overall performance-based curriculum in each program area.

— coordinate all data-based decision-making activities among program units and levels (e.g., integrate performance information on the instructional program in all units and determine appropriate courses of action for the district).

— allocate resources to levels in a program area based on criterion-referenced and other data.

— make decisions at the program element level based on group performance data across all educational units.

Building Management Group

The Building Management Group (BMG) is the local counterpart of the PMG in each program element or building. The BMG is composed of the building principal, a teacher representative from each level (grade) of the program unit, and a parent advisory group. The BMG functions are similar to those listed for the PMG, but operate at the building level. That is, the BMG provides the mechanism for integrating data-based decision-making activities among all units and levels in a

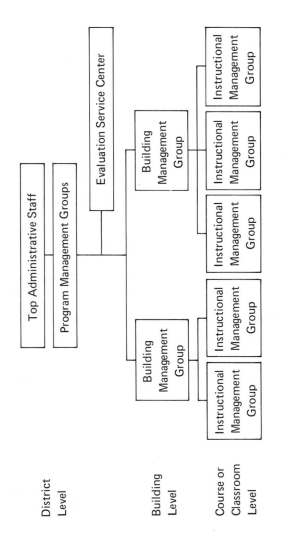

Organizational Structure Encompassing Internal Units to Support
Implementation of a Criterion-Referenced Evaluation System

Figure 18.1

given building. For example, the BMG may move a curriculum objective from one level to another based on performance data across levels in the building program. This represents an adjustment to the program structure for the school and a potential adjustment to the overall district program. The BMG, based on the criterion-referenced and other data available in the program, will further integrate information in planning the curriculum and instructional resources. The Building Management Group:

— coordinates local curriculum development.

— monitors data-based decision-making activities within the building.

— makes decisions at the program subelement level based on performance data across all instructional groups.

Instructional Management Group

Instructional Management Groups (IMG's) are formed to build a stable management structure within the building level to support the direct operations of the project. Within each participating building and at each grade level, a teacher team with a manager is formed from existing staff. The teacher-manager should be given some release time or extra compensation for performing this function. The IMG further embodies the organization and procedures needed to support appropriate instructional management functions among important user groups — students and parents. The functions of the IMG's are to:

— provide a stable management structure within which major decision-making activities may be realized with students and the instructional program.

— utilize criterion-referenced test data and other computer-generated data to support decision-making relating to instructional management for individual students, groups of students, local program refinement, and refinement of the curriculum (e.g., in the last case, adjustments to the developmental placement and sequencing of instructional objectives).

— allocate instructional resources to individuals and maintain interfaces with external systems, such as psychological services, social services, etc.

— support parent-student instructional management functions
   through a parent interface using criterion-referenced evaluation
   reports.

— develop a performance-based curriculum at a particular level for
   each content area.

— provide feedback on the curriculum and the instructional program
   to the BMG, based on the criterion-referenced testing system.

The foregoing structure for internal organization may be adjusted and varied
as local needs dictate. Since there may be little or no cost for the PMG, BMG, and
IMG type units, the implementation plan may easily incorporate them as needed
at each phase of implementation. Early phases of implementation may, for example, utilize only an organization like the PMG, with some representation from particular school buildings. Such would be appropriate in the early stages of developing a performance curriculum. As the system develops and expands into activities
involving test administration and computer processing of reports on student performance, there will be a need to create and activate internal organizations at the
level of the building and grade, eventually extending management and data reporting activities to the individual student and his parents. The extent to which the
various levels and types of organization will apply in a district will, of course, depend on the content areas and number of program units affected.

Technical Support Systems

Technical support systems for criterion-referenced evaluation may be conveniently considered as a total administrative entity called the Evaluation Service
Center (ESC), referred to previously in the overall organizational structure in Figure 18.1. Each service may be organized as a subsystem which can be managed
and physically located either separate from other subsystems, as in an individual
entity, or together with other subsystems, as an integrated total system. The services performed by the Evaluation Service Center are required by all levels in any
criterion-referenced evaluation program. There are four primary services provided
by the ESC as shown in Figure 18.2. Each of these services is briefly elaborated in
the following discussion. The data processing and training components are treated
only briefly here due to the detailed discussions on these topics in later chapters.

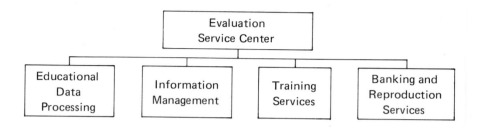

Components of the Evaluation Service Center

Figure 18.2

Data Processing

The data processing component of the ESC provides the capability for processing the raw evaluation data gathered in the schools and converting these data into evaluation reports transmitted to several levels of the organizational structure. Often, the data processing component will not be an integral part of the ESC, but will be a service obtained from an external data processing center. For this reason, a carefully planned human interface must be maintained with the data processing center. This interface may be one person who ensures adequate computer support by scheduling runs at the data processing center, by arranging for data reduction, by maintaining quality control over data collection in the schools, and by transmitting raw and refined data to and from the center. This interface may extend to the actual data reduction operation, so that the ESC would convert the raw data to a form acceptable for processing by the computer.

The interface with the external data processing center may represent one phase of a total service, including all those services represented by the ESC. Most likely, the school district will offer or provide for the other service components of the ESC separate from the data processing service. In another approach, involving the use of a mini-computer located directly in the school district, the data processing function becomes integrated more closely with the other ESC functions.

Information Management

Information management refers to a series of controls, checks, forms, and procedures in the flow of information which begins with the generation of data files and the administration of criterion-referenced tests and terminates in the delivery of processed data to each decision-maker. The activities conducted in this service account for roughly half of the costs of delivering an evaluation report, exclusive of processing costs, and are critical to the effective operation of the evaluation process in the schools. There are three basic components of the information management service: data preparation, data reduction, and data transmission. One of the components, data reduction, is often a function of the data processing service. The flow of raw and processed data and the various major check points involved are shown in Figure 18.3.

Data preparation. Data preparation involves three major phases of activity: coding for the development of the data files, generation and quality control of student response data from the administration of criterion-referenced tests, and monitoring and aggregation of data prior to its transmission to the computer center.

(1)   File generation involves several hours of work in coding for each classroom or course which will participate in the evaluation system. Typically the coding results in the following files:

- a file which identifies the program or course and its member sections or classes.
- a student file identifying each student by name within a section and any subgroups of interest to which the student belongs (e.g., an I.Q. group, a level, or a special program designation).
- a file on the course or program structure identifying objectives by number, and groupings of objectives into administrative and content units.
- a file identifying test items within test forms.
- other information involving the scheduling of test forms (test scheduling) to students and the time periods within which objectives are completed in instruction.

(2)   Student response data refers to the regular collection of test data from students via the administration of the appropriate test forms. The problems in this area relate to:

- insuring that the student has the appropriate test form and response materials (from the test schedule).
- training students to use the appropriate response medium (e.g.,

230

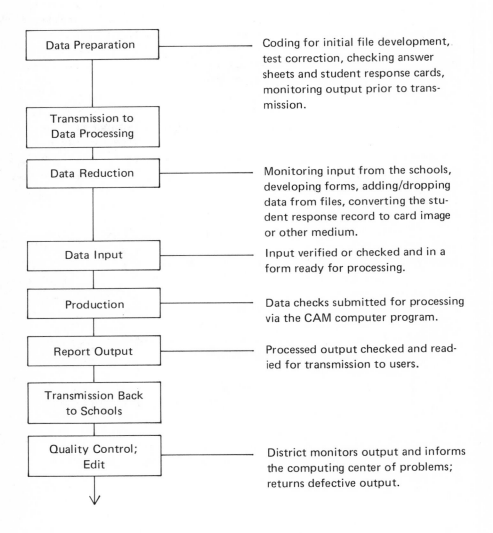

Data Preparation	Coding for initial file development, test correction, checking answer sheets and student response cards, monitoring output prior to transmission.
Transmission to Data Processing	
Data Reduction	Monitoring input from the schools, developing forms, adding/dropping data from files, converting the student response record to card image or other medium.
Data Input	Input verified or checked and in a form ready for processing.
Production	Data checks submitted for processing via the CAM computer program.
Report Output	Processed output checked and readied for transmission to users.
Transmission Back to Schools	
Quality Control; Edit	District monitors output and informs the computing center of problems; returns defective output.

Flowchart of Data

Figure 18.3

marksense cards).
— maintaining quality control over the student response medium (e.g., checking for double marks on IBM marksense cards).
— providing optional response forms for new students and change forms for students added to or dropped from the course.

(3)   The aggregation of data refers to that component of data preparation where the raw data are collected from the participating classrooms, checked, and packaged for delivery to the computing center, along with appropriate transmittal forms. Usually involved here are:

— spot checks of student response forms.
— determination that all units have been collected.
— packaging of the data into appropriate units with a form for transmittal.

Data reduction. This is another preparation phase wherein the data are received in one mode by the data processing service (coding forms, answer sheets, IBM mark-sense cards, etc.) and converted to another form which can be submitted to the computer for processing. The major operations in this phase are:

(1)   Keypunching and verifying the coding forms submitted to set up or update course files.
(2)   Monitoring and quality controlling the student response forms for each test administration.
(3)   Preparing student response forms with precoded information locating the student in a course file.
(4)   Developing and maintaining a cycle for quality control of all input data.
(5)   Reporting problems with the input data.
(6)   Reporting failures to process due to problems in the input data.
(7)   Monitoring output prior to transmission.
(8)   Preparing data decks for transmission to data processing.

Data transmission. This phase refers to procedures for insuring that data are transmitted from point to point on schedule, logged, and finally delivered to the appropriate decision-maker. Figure 18.4 illustrates the various decision-making units and logging points involved in the cycle beginning with the transmission of raw data and ending in receipt of the processed data at the school building or

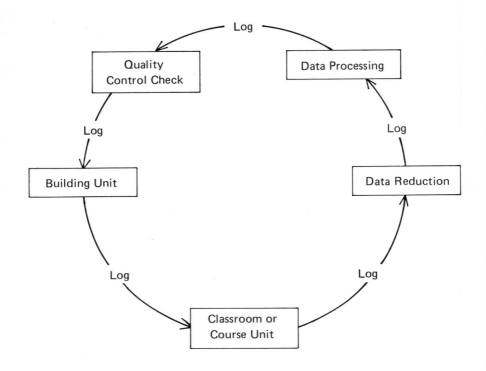

Data Transmission Cycle

Figure 18.4

other unit. The data transmission cycle involves the following functions:

(1)   Logging and directing the flow of input data from course or classroom units through a schedule of test administrations for each unit.

(2)   Logging and directing the flow of processed output to appropriate decision-makers.

(3)   Setting up a mechanism for transmission; monitoring the transmission mechanism.

(4)   Transmitting all information required for processing, including

the test schedule for each unit, coding forms, and student response forms.

Other planning considerations. The failure to plan a system for controlling information management can add days and even weeks to turn-around time in processing. Each factor and function or event is to be identified in relation to the evaluation design and related information developed for each course and program unit. The operations in the information management system are made sufficiently explicit to enable rapid and accurate identification of any problem in data flow.

Training

Aside from the actual provision of specific training experiences for involved staff, the effective implementation of the evaluation system requires consideration of how to organize a system with which training will occur effectively and be maintained. The structure of a system for training may range from a fairly elaborate center, incorporating one or more new personnel in the structure of the ESC, to an extension of present inservice programs. The nature of the system to be developed and installed depends on the extent of the evaluation system plan, the feasibility of cost sharing and the long-term intent of the plan. In any event, planning the development of an organization or system for training should occupy as much attention as that given to data processing or any other supportive service for the evaluation system. The failure to train adequately can be as detrimental to operations as the failure to process the data from a test administration.

The training center: a system. The training center is a self-contained training resource, developed as either an autonomous subsystem or an integral part of the ESC. It incorporates a staff possessing expertise in criterion-referenced evaluation and assumes technical as well as professional training functions. The major functions of the training center are to:

— maintain a centralized training resource for the accession and distribution of training materials.

— operate a centralized training service for all professional and technical or support personnel.

— maintain a decentralized training operation offering appropriate services and materials.

— determine new training needs as they occur and provide for appropriate materials and/or services.

The functions through which the training center provides services and materials in a centralized or decentralized mode are shown in Figure 18.5. One aspect of the decentralized mode would be the ability of local personnel to access certain training materials through the local school building libraries.

The Functions of the Training Center

Figure 18.5

The broad classes of training materials to be selected and maintained in the centralized and decentralized modes are presented in Figure 18.6. Technical documentation, for example, would be obtained or developed for the operation of some project systems, such as information management or banking. Guidance material, consisting of step-by-step operations, would be developed for such processes as showing a clerk how to construct a test form master from a matrix of numbers and a centralized test item bank.

District training organization. An alternative to the training center is a scaled-down version of essentially the same structure developed within the district. Beginning with the central administrative staff and extending to the selected teachers, certain district personnel take on the various training and coordination functions required by project operations. This mode of organization requires the use of a consultant group to conduct the initial training, provide the necessary materials, and show district personnel how to train others. This model involves some added costs for training and for paying district personnel to conduct tasks beyond

Type of Primary Material or Instructional Mode	Content of Material	Primary Center
Technical Documentation	Objective/Item Banking	ESC
Simulation	Using CAM Data	ESC
Programmed Instruction	Writing Objectives	ESC/Local
Adjunct (Textual)	Mastery Learning	ESC/Local
Guidance	Information Management	ESC/Local
Workshops/Demonstration	Evaluation Design	ESC
Consultations	Computer Operations	ESC
Site Visits	Project Operations	ESC

Type of Training Center with Type of Materials

Figure 18.6

their normal responsibilities. A teacher team leader, for example, may show other teachers how to do the coding to develop the course files and may check the output for each course and section.

External training. An alternative to developing a local training system is to hire a consultant group or contract for all required services and materials. It should be noted that, in such a case, the project may forgo the possibilities of developing any lasting local training capability unless otherwise incorporated in the plan.

Banking and Reproduction Services

The final system to be discussed as a component of the ESC, banking and reproduction services, is a basic requirement at some level for a criterion-referenced evaluation system. Essentially, banking involves the process by which test forms are produced based on input data in the form of objectives and related test items. The input information reflects the course or program structure and the evaluation design developed in consultation with the teacher. The gross elements of the banking process are diagrammed in Figure 18.7.

236

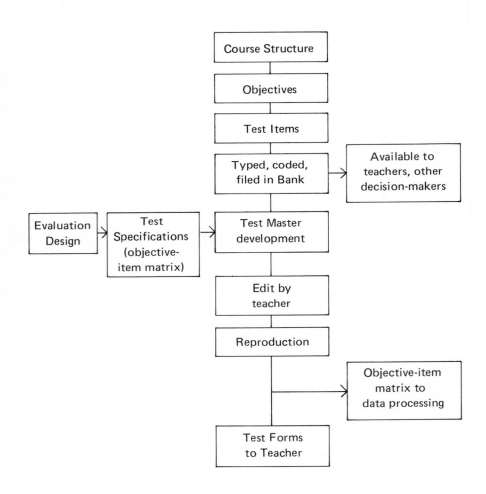

Flow of Basic Elements Through the Banking Process

Figure 18.7

Curriculum development. In the first part of the flowchart, the professional staff develops the program or course structure (defines levels, units, modules, lessons), writes or selects objectives, and prepares or selects test items for each objective. This information is then coded, using a prescribed set of procedures compatible with the computer processing program and submitted as input to banking.

Banking. In the banking component, objectives and test items are checked, typed onto forms, and filed in a manner compatible with efficient reproduction in the form of test masters and master copies of the objectives and test items for each course or program. At this point, the teacher may obtain a complete organized copy of his objectives. The structure of the course or program has, through this process, been made a permanent record.

Evaluation design. Once the files have been created, the teacher can access them for test development purposes in accord with an evaluation design developed in consultation with an evaluation expert. The input data to banking for test development is a matrix specifying the test items to be included on each test form by objective number.

Test development. The objective-item matrix and other information set test development in motion. The appropriate item file is accessed and a test master(s) is produced and sent to the teacher, who checks and returns it.

Test reproduction. The appropriate number of test forms are then reproduced from the master. The objective-item matrix now becomes part of the information needed by data processing to score and process the test forms delivered to the teacher.

The advantages of a banking and reproduction service unit include:

(1)   The structure of each course or program becomes a permanent record.

(2)   Consistency in coding and compatibility with computer services may be more easily maintained.

(3)   Test forms appropriate to a variety of evaluation designs may be produced efficiently on a large scale.

(4)   Objectives and other data are easily accessible to teachers and others and are not lost when a particular teacher leaves the system.

(5)   Quality control over file development is more easily maintained.

(6)   A basis is created for continued development of file contents (e.g., the item file may incorporate item analysis data).

(7)   A basis is created for supporting more advanced evaluation design stages which periodically require new sets of test forms.

Various levels of the process of banking and test reproduction may be considered for the project plan. The most effective operation is a formal system developed within the ESC structure. A plan projecting this type of operation would require a set of detailed, written specifications defining operations, staff, equipment, forms, supplies, and materials needed. Such a formal banking operation might be considered when the number of tests reproduced in a year is expected to run over 100 forms. Scaled-down versions of the banking system could incorporate existing filing and reproduction services, provided the volume is low and existing services are not being used fully.

Effective banking operations have also been developed by particular groups of teachers involved in CAM processing. At that level, the teachers maintain their own files, develop their own test masters and submit them for reproduction through regular channels.

Other considerations. Obviously, the extent to which the plan incorporates banking and reproduction services as an ongoing entity depends on the breadth of the project and the volume of test reproduction needed during a given phase. An adequate plan will, however, incorporate the basic features defined for banking in the previous flowchart. Such a plan may anticipate the separate existence of a banking and reproduction services component at some future point. Early stages of planning would thus include the same rules for coding and indexing the course or program structure, objectives, and test items as would be used in a more formalized system. The plan at this stage would anticipate the need for part-time clerical help and the necessary equipment, supplies, and materials. The location of particular files and materials at this stage may be decentralized to each school, with local teachers providing the manpower for test form development. In later phases, the plan may anticipate a centralized banking operation with the required secretarial and clerical staff, facilities, equipment, and a budget for supplies and materials. At this point, the plan may also include an evaluation design consultant to direct operations and provide assistance.

Summary

Chapter 18 has outlined the management and operational functions needed to implement and maintain a criterion-referenced evaluation system. An organizational structure, composed of management groups at different program levels and an Evaluation Service Center, has been suggested. The scenario of project management presented has assumed a rather large and well-articulated evaluation system. Regardless of the size of any particular project, however, each of the functions discussed above must be accounted for to insure a successful operation.

Chapter 19

Data Processing in Evaluation

It is clear from the previous discussion that a great quantity of data is usually processed even in the early stages of operation of a criterion-referenced evaluation system. Modern data processing technology must be brought to bear on this problem, as manual data processing would be a virtual impossibility. Chapter 19 considers four aspects of data processing in evaluation: the data, data entry, computer hardware, and computer software.

The Data

The data to be processed in criterion-referenced evaluation fall into two categories. One set of data is established prior to test administration; the other is generated by the students as they respond to the test items.

The first set of data, as previously noted, consists of administrative information about the structure or design of the curriculum, the students and teachers, the reports desired, and the testing instruments. This information must be compiled prior to the testing so it may be ready to use when the students' responses to the tests are collected. These administrative data are coded onto forms and made ready for entry into the programs before testing is done. Often, they are actually entered into the analysis and reporting program files before the tests are administered so that only the student responses need to be entered after testing.

The student response data are collected during the test administration. Students may respond to the items on test forms, on prepared answer sheets, or through the teacher or an observer in certain instances. The responses must then be rendered into machine-readable form for entry into the analytical processing programs.

Data Entry

There are four techniques available for rendering the administrative information and student responses into a machine-readable form: keypunching, optical scanning, IBM marksensing, and marksense card reading.

Keypunching

In comparison with the other three techniques, keypunching is slow and expensive, but accurate. A good keypunch operator can punch and verify about 100 student responses per hour. This results in a cost of almost 10 cents per student test. While keypunching, however, the operator is automatically performing certain error reduction functions (such as checking for stray marks, double responses, missing identification numbers). Thus, keypunching generates student response entry cards with very few errors. The major disadvantages of keypunching are the cost per student test and the turn-around time. It can take two or three days for one operator to punch 2000 student tests. Moreover, existing keypunching equipment in the usual school data processing environment may not always be immediately available for evaluation purposes, further delaying the data reduction process. (An IBM 029 keypunch can be leased for approximately $80 per month.) Consequently, the administrative information is usually keypunched but not the student responses.

Optical Scanning

Optical scanning of specially designed answer sheets is a flexible, but usually expensive, technique of data reduction. Most optical scanning devices are expensive ($1000 to $3000 per month). However, some inexpensive ($300 per month) optical scanning devices have recently been introduced by several manufacturers which offer great promise for the educational community. An optical scanner can rapidly read a large number of items per test, check for missing or double responses, and edit out stray marks. It is recommended that student answer sheets be precoded with identification number, name, teacher number, section number, and test form number to reduce data entry errors caused by students or staff recording this information incorrectly.

IBM Marksensing

The IBM marksensing technique is being successfully used throughout the country in several criterion-referenced evaluation projects for reducing student response data. The technique has been used in the computer industry for 15 years. It is fast, accurate, and inexpensive. Specifically designed IBM marksense data cards are prepunched and printed with student identification number, name, teacher number, section number, and test form number. Students record their responses on these cards with electrostatic pencils. The cards are run through an IBM marksensing machine which converts the pencil marks to punches on the same card. The cost of the marksensing machine, card interpreter, and card sorter necessary to support the marksensing procedure is approximately $325 per month. With the assistance of two full-time data clerks, a marksensing system can handle over 10,000 student tests per week, at a cost of approximately four cents per student test.

Marksense Card Reading

The IBM marksensing technique should not be confused with the marksense card readers that are sold by Digital Equipment Corporation, Hewlett-Packard, and other computer manufacturers. Marksense card readers are not very effective data entry devices for most criterion-referenced evaluation systems. The marksense card readers read both punches and marks simultaneously. Thus student response marks can be put on the same card with punches that contain the precoded identifying information. However, most of the marksense card readers can only read one side of a card, thereby reducing by one-half the amount of information each card can contain. Moreover, marksense card readers must be used on-line to a computer, making this a very expensive data reduction option for all but the largest of users.

Computer Hardware

There are three acceptable methods for supplying the computer support for processing criterion-referenced tests: renting time from a service bureau, using the school district's business computer, or leasing or purchasing a computer for instructional use.

The following discussion assumes that the processing is done on a batch basis as opposed to a time-sharing basis, even though there are several advantages to processing the tests in a time-sharing mode with a terminal at each school. In such a time-sharing system, no one has to transport the student responses to the computer center and the results back to the school. Fast turn-around time can be guaranteed by the school staff. The school has ready access to the data base generated by the evaluation system.

However, there are serious problems with the use of a time-sharing criterion-referenced test processing system. The major problem is cost. Computer processing in a time-sharing mode is almost 10 times more expensive than in a batch mode. Each terminal would require a data entry device and a high-speed printer. The cost of high-speed telecommunications equipment is very high. Additional on-line disk storage space would also be required. In addition to computer cost, there would be the need to have trained personnel in each school to run the terminal. Therefore, the discussion below assumes that the tests are being processed in a batch mode.

Computer time is readily available on a rental basis from computer service bureaus or universities. Renting time has the advantage of not necessitating the purchase of a computer or the hiring of a staff to run it. The disadvantages are numerous — the turn-around time is slow, the cost per document processed is high, and the logistics of getting the data from the school to the computer may be problematical. In addition, renting computer time from an outside agency involves a cash flow from the district that will always be vulnerable to budget cuts. Renting computer time is a viable alternative during the first year or two of a small criterion-referenced evaluation project.

The second method is to use the school district's business computer (if one exists). This method has the advantage of not requiring the acquisition of a new computer (although additional core memory or disk storage may be required) or of a new computer staff. However, a computer being used to process the administrative tasks of a school district is periodically very busy. When payroll or grade reports are due, student tests may not be processed for several days.

The third method is to lease or purchase a computer for instructional use. The purchase of a computer does require a capital outlay and requires the hiring of a staff. However, recent advances in computer technology have generated powerful mini-computers that are attractive in capability and price to the educational community. Several school districts throughout the country have purchased computers capable of running 16 to 32 terminals in time-shared BASIC during the day for student problem solving and computer-assisted instruction, and then switching to a disk operating system during the evening to process criterion-referenced tests. These computers cost approximately $65,000 for 16-terminal versions and $125,000 for 32-terminal versions (not including the terminals and telecommunications equipment). Digital Equipment, Data General, and Hewlett-Packard sell systems designed specifically for the educational community. In the disk-operating system, these computers are capable of processing from 300 to 500 student tests per hour.

Computer Software

Once the computer hardware has been selected, computer software must be designed to process the student tests. Several problems have arisen in the development of software to support criterion-referenced testing programs in various school districts throughout the country.

In some instances, due to a limited budget, the software that has been developed merely acts as a test scoring device and does not generate data in a useful fashion. For example, student responses are not stored over time to generate an accessible longitudinal historical file.

Secondly, attempts to develop software that meets a variety of needs in a criterion-referenced context have been expensive (in excess of $100,000) and not always successful. In any case, after the software is designed, coded, and operational, it takes from six months to a year to field test the program thoroughly. Processing errors in the computer program are especially annoying during the first year or two of an evaluation project when the teachers are being trained to rely upon the data for daily or weekly instructional decisions.

Finally, in some evaluation projects, the software is designed by computer specialists. Computer people are sometimes more interested in "exercising" their new hardware than in providing for the needs of the educational community. Resources may be spent in developing real-time access to data bases over phone lines, in computerizing an item and objective bank, or in designing a decision-theoretic test construction algorithm. However, the important educational need is to generate reports that are meaningful to students, teachers, administrators, and parents, and to modify these reports based upon the experience and requirements of the educational community. Many projects during the last few years have attempted to "exercise" third and fourth generation computers to provide evaluation information to the educational community. Some of these projects have had limited success because they have failed to realize that the computer is only a tool that is supporting an educational data processing need.

A set of computer programs designed to support a criterion-referenced testing program such as is discussed in this monograph is available. It is called the CAM3 System.[4] It is the product of six years of research and development in primary and secondary schools throughout the United States (Gorth, Allen & Grayson, 1971). Earlier versions of CAM are operational in many schools. The CAM system supports criterion-referenced evaluation at all grade levels in a wide range

---

[4] Information about the availability of the CAM3 System may be obtained from National Evaluation Systems, Inc., P.O. Box 226, Amherst, MA 01002.

of subject areas (e.g., mathematics, reading, language arts, physical sciences, social sciences, physical education, etc.) and instructional strategies (e.g., group-paced instruction, flexibly scheduled classrooms, individualized instruction, etc.).

The CAM system is written in American Standard FORTRAN IV. The six subsystems of CAM contain approximately 10,000 FORTRAN source statements divided into 40 overlay segments. CAM is operational on IBM, CDC, Burroughs, Xerox, and Hewlett-Packard computers. Versions of CAM are available for Digital Equipment, Data General, Honeywell, National Cash Register, and Univac computers. The CAM system requires a card reader, line printer, disk drive, and a modest central memory. Due to differences in operating systems and FORTRAN compilers, its core size requirements vary from computer to computer. For instance, 65-K bytes are needed on an IBM 360 or 370, while only 32-K bytes are required on a Hewlett-Packard 2100A.

Summary

Once the planners of a criterion-referenced evaluation system have entered the world of data processing, they are involved in activities relating to the following:

— researching and evaluating locally available data processing alternatives;
— establishing efficient data reduction and entry methods;
— designing or selecting appropriate computer software;
— monitoring computer operations;
— leasing/purchasing and installing a computer system;
— staffing the computer center.

All of the foregoing involve complex, largely technical activities of which the outcome may be a substantial waste of resources and failure to deliver needed services to the project. To avoid such problems, the plan for operations should incorporate an appropriate consultant in the early decision-making activities related to the development of a data processing component.

Once the decisions concerning the type of processing facility have been made, a consultant or contractor should again be considered for such activities as software development and installation and periodic operations monitoring. Finally, the planning group may decide to contract the entire processing service, if it is desirable to keep investment in systems low. This approach to data processing seems especially appropriate for the first year of a program.

Chapter 20

Training for School-Based Evaluation

Although criterion-referenced evaluation is often initiated and organized with the aid of consultants to school districts, a major emphasis of this monograph has been to describe a locally based system of evaluation. The evaluation is locally based in the sense that the staff within the school system is responsible for designing and organizing the major activities and systems associated with the evaluation process. For highly technical issues or uniquely complex situations, outside consultants would be expected to provide the school system with initial technical expertise; but the main evaluation activities can and should be carried out by district personnel. Therefore, the evaluation system would be totally organized and managed by the school system, with an emphasis on each individual decision-maker (e.g., the teacher) designating data to be gathered.

New skills must be learned by most personnel within the school system to accomplish the required tasks associated with criterion-referenced evaluation. These skills have been developed in the 1960's and 1970's and generally are not in the repertoires of many school personnel. The technical skills necessary to develop goals, objectives, measurement techniques, and data gathering designs are not usually part of the preservice training program for teachers or administrators. Therefore, training programs are required to help school personnel acquire these skills.

The new skills to be learned by school personnel include organizational articulation for management by objective; goal, content, and objective definition; test item development; evaluation design; the logistics of gathering and processing data; a general understanding of the data processing operation; and reading, interpretation, and using computer-generated reports. Not all skills are needed by all personnel, particularly in a highly structured and extensive evaluation system.

Each of these skills is outlined later in this chapter.

As background for this discussion, several issues associated with the modes of presenting training and the resources necessary are first considered. Then, topical outlines of training activities for teachers, administrators, and testing and evaluation specialists are presented.

Modes of Training

There are several different training modes available for imparting criterion-referenced evaluation skills to school personnel. They vary in the amount of trainer time each takes per trainee. Generally, the more highly trainer-intensive the mode, the more costly it is.

Tutorial

The mode of training which takes the most trainer time per trainee is the individual tutorial. In the tutorial mode, a trainer who is knowledgeable about the components of criterion-referenced evaluation interacts with each trainee individually. In this approach, the trainer is able to personally critique all intermediate products developed by the trainee and to provide specifically tailored advice to each trainee in terms of his specific teaching or administrative responsibilities. This approach to training is very costly because the trainer is able to interact with so few trainees, but it may be worth the additional expense for the local project manager to have this kind of individual in-depth exposure to certain aspects of the evaluation process. The tutorial approach is often appropriate for highly technical functions, such as data processing, where only one or a few trainees will be involved.

Apprenticeship

An alternative to the tutorial approach is an apprenticeship, where one member of a team learns the criterion-referenced evaluation concepts and teaches the other members of the team as they plan, develop, and implement an evaluation. The team member who has learned the techniques acts as a "secondary" trainer to the members of the team. The multiplier effect can significantly increase the number of people trained while maintaining a personalized approach to training. The apprenticeship mode of training might be a viable alternative to the tutorial for the project manager or leader, and suits the requirements for team leaders quite well. The apprenticeship mode is also involved when a group of key staff members receive extensive workshop training and then transfer all of their learned skills in a district.

Lecture/Text, Discussion Session

A more traditional approach to imparting new skills is the combination of large group lectures or assigned textual readings with small group discussion sessions. In this mode, familiar to most people from their own school days, an introductory lecture or assigned reading, or both, is followed by discussion in small groups of the topics under consideration. While some people respond well to this traditional instructional mode, the inability to pay close attention to the individual makes it less desirable for some training functions than other, more personalized modes (e.g., apprenticeship). As an overall orientation session for participants in an evaluation, however, an introductory lecture and group discussions may fit well into a complete training program.

Programmed Self-Instruction

In this mode of training, criterion-referenced evaluation would be presented through self-instructional materials with minimum guidance from a trainer. Prepared booklets and programmed instructional texts would be assigned to the trainees to read. The cost of booklets is usually much lower than that of trainers. However, people do not generally learn all skills easily in isolation from one another. For some skills, individuals should interact and be able to ask questions. Programmed self-instructional materials are most useful for technical concepts, such as coding, and for introducing general information. Other modes of instruction may be used when trainees are ready to begin applying skills.

Simulations

Instruction by creating structured vicarious experiences in which new skills must be used in an appropriate context is a relatively new approach. The impact of simulations is strong and leaves a lasting impression on the learner, as the skills to be learned are introduced, practiced, and reinforced in a context like that in which they will be put to actual use. The impact is heightened by the compression of time and content during a simulation, which can sometimes mildly disorient a learner. Simulations, in addition to establishing a context of relevance, provoke valuable discussions among learners, often because of the disorientation they induce.

Workshops

Workshops are more an organizational structure for instruction than an actual instructional technique. A workshop setting is adaptable to many instructional methods. It combines purpose with informality and can therefore provide a relaxed atmosphere for intensive learning experiences. The workshop structure is particularly effective for organizing instruction for large numbers of trainees while maintaining informality and the capability to respond to individual learning styles and paces.

Each of the training modes discussed above has a place in an integrated training program. Generally, the introduction to each topic associated with criterion-referenced evaluation may be given in a large group situation. After the introduction, various other modes may be used for staff to acquire and practice the actual skills involved in the topic in a more individually compatible fashion. The selection of modes for a training program in a given school system rests on a judgment of its unique requirements and traditions.

Resources Needed for Training

The resources needed for training include staff release time, instructional materials, consultants, and facilities. The major out-of-pocket expense will be for trainee time and for trainers (i.e., consultants), with a small amount for materials.

In setting up a training program, it is important to have a clear idea about the requirements of each different major resource need. Instructional materials required for training will include purchasing self-instructional modules or workshop materials. These modules or workshop materials are essentially equivalent to the purchase of textbooks for a college course. The materials will generally cost from $10 to $20 per person.

The consultants or trainers required to support the school training program in educational evaluation usually must be hired from an outside agency. The cost for consultants can range from $75 to $350 per day. Days must also be arranged during which the consultants would design a training program specifically tailored to a particular school system's needs. For many training needs in the criterion-referenced evaluation context, one consultant is often able to work successfully with only 10 to 20 teachers at a time. Therefore, if training is to be provided to 40 teachers, two to four consultants may be required for each training session. In addition, the consultants' travel expenses, including room and board, must be budgeted.

The facilities required for training should be adequate to allow comfortable interaction among the personnel participating in a training session. Therefore, facilities which foster interaction are desirable. A room which is climate-controlled is helpful. It should contain tables around which three to six people can sit and talk easily, with enough space between tables to prevent the discussion at one table from interfering with the discussion at another. Adequate sound attenuation such as carpeting and acoustical tiles is preferred to a cafeteria environment, which usually has hard floors and allows sound to travel. Several pieces of audiovisual equipment are usually required. Using facilities away from the school system affords a maximum separation of the school people from their day-to-day routines, thereby allowing a maximum amount of attention to the training sessions.

Topical Outlines for Training in Evaluation

Sample topical outlines have been prepared for three groups of people. These include classroom teachers, school administrators, and testing and evaluation specialists. The topical outlines are divided according to the three groups because not everyone in the school system is responsible for all facets of testing and evaluation.

The outline for teachers places evaluation in the overall instructional context. This overall context is followed by specific issues of interest to teachers, such as the use of evaluation data in the classroom and the administration of tests.

The topical outline for school administrators is the briefest. It contains an overview of the more pertinent topics for teachers and testing specialists from an informational standpoint, but does not present the mechanics, which would probably be of more interest to field personnel. However, the administrator's outline includes the overall mechanism of management and evaluation implementation not included in the topical outline for the teachers or the testing specialists.

The outline for test and evaluation specialists is not necessarily related to someone in the school system presently with the title of Evaluation Specialist, or even to the guidance counselor or school psychologist. An administrator or department head might perform the function, or one of a group of teachers in a team teaching situation. The topical outline for this test specialist includes all of the topics for the classroom teacher, plus some of the mechanics of test construction.

Topical Outline for Teacher Training

The first section in the topical outline for teachers covers an overview of how instruction should be developed and implemented. This overview is intended to place evaluation in the context of instructional development and management so that teachers can see where evaluation fits into the cycle of events involved with their classroom instructional activities.

I.   Instructional Development Process

    A.   Statement of Purpose
    B.   Needs Analysis
    C.   Task Analysis
    D.   Behavioral Objectives
    E.   Performance Testing
    F.   Student Characteristics
    G.   Instructional Materials
    H.   Learning Environment
    I.   Evaluation and Validation
    J.   Feedback

Evaluation is next placed in a conceptual framework. Many teachers have had little formal instruction in evaluation, and an even smaller percentage have been taught the use of criterion-referenced evaluation. The information process must proceed from an overall, rational definition of evaluation, to the cycle of events in evaluation, to a comparison of norm-referenced and criterion-referenced evaluation, to a rather comprehensive examination of behavioral objectives and criterion-referenced test items in evaluation. Note that behavioral objectives and criterion-referenced test items are part of the instructional development process, as well as of the evaluation process.

II.   Concept of Evaluation

    A.   Purposes of Evaluation
    B.   Decision Types
    C.   Components of the Evaluation Process
    D.   History of Educational Evaluation
    E.   Current Evaluation Models
        1.   Normative
        2.   Criterion-Referenced
    F.   Elements of Criterion-Referenced Evaluation Models
        1.   Goals, Objectives
        2.   Test Development
        3.   Test Administration
        4.   Analysis and Reporting

5.   Interpreting Data
6.   Using Data

The next major segment of a training program for criterion-referenced evaluation deals with the generation of performance curricula.

III.   Performance Curricula

A.   Rationale
B.   Program Structure
C.   Deriving Objectives
    1.   Content Outline
    2.   Course Objectives
    3.   Instructional Objectives
D.   Assessing Objective Appropriateness
E.   Planning Instructional Activities

The curriculum development component of the training process ordinarily results in an exercise in which objectives are written or selected and organized into program or course structure. The next logical component of the training deals with specific evaluation designs, the development of test specifications, item writing, and test production.

IV.   Evaluation Designs

A.   Purposes of Specific Designs
B.   Design Components
    1.   Test Types
    2.   Test Administration Frequency
C.   Test Specifications
D.   Item Writing
E.   Test Production

With the conclusion of presentation of the developmental aspects of criterion-referenced evaluation, the training program moves to the use of evaluation data for decision-making.

V.   Use of Evaluation Data

A.   Reading Computer-Generated Reports

    B.   Interpretation of Test Data
1. By Individual Student
2. By Objectives or Content Group
3. By Groupings of Students

    C.   Making Decisions Based on Test Data
1. About Individual Students
2. About Objectives or Content Groups
3. About Groups of Students

    D.   Feedback on the Instructional System

    E.   Concept of Validation

    F.   Revision of Evaluation System

    G.   Use of Computers in Evaluation
1. Benefits to Teachers
2. Impact on Classroom Testing and Evaluation

The final section for classroom teachers deals with some of the mechanics of test administration in a classroom. The research conducted in this area of test administration, and reflected in the outline, is a supplement to the intuitive approach upon which most teachers are forced to rely.

    VI.   Administration of Test Program

    A.   Administration of Test Forms

    B.   Compilation of Test Data
1. Various Forms of Test Data
2. Use of Prepared Answer Sheets

    C.   Scoring, Tabulation, and Reporting of Test Data
1. By the Teacher
2. By the Computer

Topical Outline for Administrators

School administrators need to have the broad, overall picture, but do not necessarily need to learn all the mechanics and details that a classroom teacher or test and evaluation specialist must utilize. The overviews presented in the Instructional Development Process and Concept of Evaluation sections are at the concept level and should be known by the administrator in order to give him the overall picture. The same instruction used for teachers and evaluation specialists would be used for school administrators. Therefore, only the titles of these two sections are repeated, rather than all subtopics, for the sake of brevity.

I.   Instructional Development Process

II.   Concept of Evaluation

Many of the instructional topics in evaluation have been consolidated and condensed for the school administrator in this section. He will know what is happening in the evaluation program without having to learn detailed techniques which he will probably not need — such as how to administer a test form to students. Each major section, as represented by a Roman numeral, is numbered consecutively. Therefore, the skip in numbers between II and IX represents sections not applicable to the school administrator.

IX.   Overview of Criterion-Referenced Testing Program

    A.   Decision-Making Using Evaluation Data
    B.   New Evaluation Techniques
    C.   Use of Evaluation Data
    D.   Management of Data

The key issues faced by the school administrator relate to the implementation and management of the evaluation program. This section should teach administrators skills in this particular area of concern.

X.   Management of Evaluation Program

    A.   Personnel
    B.   Budget
    C.   Training
    D.   Management
    E.   Policy
    F.   Support Systems

Topical Outline for Testing and Evaluation Specialists

Many school districts have someone on the staff who can devote time to the details and mechanics of testing. This person may be a guidance counselor, testing director, assistant principal, or a designated teacher in a department or team teaching situation. The following topical outlines reflect the instruction required for this testing and evaluation specialist. The first part of the topical outline is a repeat of all items included in the topical outline for classroom teachers. Only the headings are included, not the specific items under each item, for the sake of brevity. The same objectives and instruction would be used for both teachers and evaluation specialists.

I. Instructional Development Process
II. Concept of Evaluation
III. Performance Curricula
IV. Evaluation Designs
V. Use of Evaluation Data
VI. Administration of Test Program

In addition to the knowledge possessed by teachers, the test and evaluation specialist needs further specific information. The following topics deal with the mechanics of a well-organized testing program that must be attended to by an evaluation specialist, but not by a classroom teacher.

VII. Mechanics of Testing

A. Construction of Criterion-Referenced Test Items
   1. Supply and Selection Items
      a. Multiple Choice
      b. Short Answer
   2. Use of Distractors in Multiple Choice Items
   3. Common Problems in Constructing Multiple Choice Items
   4. Comparison of Criterion-Referenced and Norm-Referenced Rules of Test Construction
   5. Information Required for Criterion-Referenced Test Construction
B. Formation of Test Forms
   1. Item Banking
   2. Test Specifications
   3. Relation of Number of Items to Number of Test Forms
   4. Use of Cards to Construct Test Forms
      a. Equal Test Forms
      b. Parallel Test Forms Using Item Sampling
   5. Numbering Test Forms
   6. Duplication of Test Forms
C. Formation of Student Groups for Testing
   1. Assign Numbers

    2.   Formation of Equal Ability Groups
    3.   Match Students and Groups to Test Forms

    The test specialist also needs to have a logical plan for data management. Decisions must be made about the size and makeup of test groups, such as using all students at one school or all students at a particular grade level in the entire district. Also, a plan is required for data logistics — the movement of evaluation data among classrooms, buildings, and the district offices.

VIII. Data Management

    A.   Assignment of Students to Test Groups
    B.   Makeup of Test Groups
    C.   Data Logistics

Summary

    The success of a criterion-referenced evaluation system is obviously dependent on both the commitment to the use of the data it generates for decision-makers and the skill with which the staff of a district is able to incorporate the evaluation system into program operations. The quality of the preservice evaluation training program affects the commitment and the skill of the staff involved. Therefore, considerable planning must go into the training phase of implementation.

    The skills necessary for implementation have been discussed, as have the resources and training modes to be considered in planning for training. The time necessary for teachers to simply gain an initial exposure to the major skills and concepts of evaluation amounts to above five full six-hour days. Administrators would require a bit less time; testing and evaluation specialists substantially more. In making plans for training, the planners should take these and other time parameters into consideration.

    A well-planned training program will both deepen the commitment to using criterion-referenced evaluation and enhance the competence with which it is utilized. Training in the topics listed above in a variety of instructional modes and in pleasant surroundings conducive to goal-oriented activity may well be the most important component in the implementation of criterion-referenced evaluation.

Chapter 21

Conclusion

This monograph has presented a model for criterion-referenced evaluation in the schools. The contextual settings in which an evaluation system must operate have been briefly illustrated. The types of instructional decisions made by teaching staff and others — and information on which to appropriately base these decisions — have been outlined. The traditional modes of gathering data for decision-making through classroom tests and standardized, norm-referenced tests have been examined and found less than adequate for generating timely, appropriate information. Hence, the need for a different approach to evaluation and measurement became evident and the criteria for an adequate information management system for educational decision-making were clarified. CAM as a model for criterion-referenced evaluation was developed on the basis of these criteria.

The criterion-referenced evaluation model presented in this monograph is first and foremost an information collecting and reporting system, the distinct purpose of which is to provide educational decision-makers with the types of data they need to make decisions within a time framework that renders them effective. The model uses a relatively new testing and measurement technology, criterion-referenced testing, supported by modern data processing technology, to collect, compile, and prepare data for the decision-makers' use. To insure that the appropriate data are delivered to the appropriate decision-makers, modern management technology is used to determine the data needs in terms of the decisions necessary in an educational setting. Extraneous and redundant information can therefore be eliminated before the time and energy to collect it has been spent. Furthermore, the precise information needed is identified beforehand through systematic analysis of the content and structure of a district's educational programs.

The model is designed to fit into the ongoing activities of a district and help

257

it achieve its own goals. No claim is made by the model for the correctness of any particular program content or organization. The model is essentially a process through which the local educational system moves to obtain the information it considers relevant to its decision-makers. Though it is itself content free, the process entailed by its implementation aids the district in defining and articulating its own goals and objectives. Consequently, the model helps the district systematize its own management and organization as well.

The model provides information relevant to the evaluation of students, individually or in groups, of staff, of curriculum, of instructional resources, of organizational structure, and of itself. Thus one process fulfills a variety of educational information needs. The model is flexible enough to operate in a wide variety of specific situations. Because of this flexibility and adaptability, considerable planning and forethought must precede the model's implementation in any given application. Goals and objectives must be articulated, decision-makers must be identified, data processing services must be procured, personnel must be chosen and trained for involvement in the model. The importance of prior planning and coordination cannot be overestimated. Several of the issues and considerations which must be accounted for in the implementation of the model have been discussed in the monograph. Each is important and each new application of the model will involve new, unique, and previously undefined areas of concern for the evaluating agency. As it has been developed and used, the model has acquired the flexibility to allow for these differences among specific users and yet maintain its general applicability and usefulness.

There are a variety of results which might be expected from the application of the model. More precise evaluation of student progress is one result to be expected. Another is more systematic articulation of program goals and objectives. Others are evident throughout the monograph. There have also been many unforeseen results of the model's employment. One has been an increase in student achievement beyond normal expectations. New curriculum materials and staffing patterns have also derived from the experience of using the model. The appearance of unplanned-for results from the model only underscores the need for extensive planning before implementation. It also illustrates the flexibility of the model and the various uses to which it may be put.

Experience with the model's implementation in a variety of settings has led to a number of recommendations. The first is the need for extensiveness and depth of planning mentioned above. Although not every potential problem can be ferreted out beforehand, every possible effort should be made to preplan and document the installation and use of the model in each adopting district. Because planning is so essential, considerable lead-time should be given before the model is actually implemented.

A second recommendation concerns the articulation of goals and objectives. As they are crucial to the model, the definition of the system's goals and objectives should be carried out well in advance of their use in the model. Many teachers have felt they could crystallize their objectives only late in the process, defining merely broad goals until the time for actual instructional lesson planning begins. This kind of planning in stages leads inevitably either to a lack of instruction on some topics or to allowing the resources available to dictate the instructional objectives. The teaching staff should be involved in the articulation of goals and objectives early and fully.

The final recommendation is to involve outside technical expertise in those areas where the local district has not had extensive experience. In any successful application of the model, it will become an integral part of the district using it. It should become central to the district's operation and should never be perceived as an extraneous "add-on" to the instructional function of the district. But the identification of the model with the district should not preclude outside technical expertise where it may benefit achievement of the district's priorities. Objective derivation, testing technology, systems analysis, data processing, staff training, and system maintenance and revision are all areas in which technical assistance from the outside will be valuable to a district newly starting or planning criterion-referenced evaluation. This monograph, as has been pointed out previously, has not purported to be a cookbook for establishing an evaluation system. It should not be used as such, but as a guide to determining the areas for exploration and planning.

Finally, it should be mentioned here that many relevant topics could not be discussed at this time in the monograph. For example, only slight mention has been made of such problems as student attitudes toward testing and using criterion-referenced test data for parent reporting. These and other topics are critical areas involved in effectively operating a criterion-referenced evaluation system. In recent examinations of schools implementing Comprehensive Achievement Monitoring, the test-taking environment was several times noted as an important operational issue which is handled sometimes well and sometimes poorly. In this context, it was observed that teacher attitudes toward the testing process seemed to be of great importance in determining student behavior during testing.

References

Adams, C. Implementation of CAM: Project report. Cheektowaga, N.Y.: Board of Cooperative Educational Services No. 1, Erie County, 1973.

Ammerman, H.L., & Melching, W.H. The derivation, analysis, and classification of objectives. Technical Report No. 66-4, May 1966, George Washington University, Contract No. DA-44-188-ARO-2, Department of the Army.

Aschbacher, P., & Fitzgerald, J. SOBAR field manual I. Los Angeles: University of California at Los Angeles, Center for the Study of Evaluation, 1972.

Dalis, G. T. The effect of precise objectives upon student achievement in health education. Journal of Experimental Education, 1970, 39(2), 20-23.

Duchastek, P. C., & Merrill, P. F. The effects of behavioral objectives on learning: A review of empirical studies. Review of Educational Research, 1973, 43(1), 53-69.

Glaser, R. Instructional technology and the measurement of learning outcomes: Some questions. American Psychologist, 1963, 18, 519-521.

Glaser, R., & Nitko, A. J. Measurement in learning and instruction. In R. L. Thorndike (Ed.), Educational measurement. Washington, D.C.: American Council on Education, 1971.

Gorth, W. P. (Chm.) Monitoring and managing student outcomes by using new computer technology. Symposium presented at the meeting of the American Educational Research Association, New York, February 1971. (Working Paper No. 21, February 1971, University of Massachusetts/Amherst, School of Education, Grant No. 642, C. F. Kettering Foundation.)

Gorth, W. P., Allen, D. W., & Grayson, A. Computer programs for test objective and item banking. Educational and Psychological Measurement, 1971, 31, 245-250.

Gorth, W. P., & Hambleton, R. K. Measurement considerations for criterion-referenced testing and special education. Journal of Special Education, 1973, 6, 303-314.

Gronlund, N. E. Stating behavioral objectives for classroom instruction. New York: Macmillan, 1970.

Gronlund, N. E. Measurement and evaluation in teaching. New York: Macmillan, 1971.

Hartley, H. J. Educational planning-programming-budgeting: A systems approach. Englewood Cliffs, N.J.: Prentice-Hall, 1968.

Kaplan, R., & Simmons, F. The effects of instruction on objects used as orienting stimuli or as summary/review upon prose learning. Paper presented at the meeting of the American Educational Research Association, Chicago, 1974.

Kerlinger, F. N. Foundations of behavioral research. New York: Holt, Rinehart & Winston, 1967.

Kiser, C., & Murphy, J. An operational model for the application of planning-programming-budgeting systems to local school districts. June 1972, New York State Education Department, Board of Cooperative Educational Services No. 1, Erie County, Project No. 99065, U.S. Office of Education.

Kohlberg, L., & Mayer, R. Development as the aim of education. Harvard Educational Review, 1972, 42, 449-497.

Mager, R. F. Preparing instructional objectives. San Francisco: Fearon Publishers, 1962.

National Evaluation Systems, Inc. The CAM3 system. Amherst, Mass.: NES, 1973.

O'Reilly, R. P., Cohen, S. A., & Algozzine, J. Criterion objectives for the bank of objectives, items, and resources in reading. Albany, N.Y.: New York State Education Department, 1973.

Otto, W., & Askov, E. The Wisconsin design for reading skill development: Rationale and guidelines. Minneapolis: National Computer Systems, 1970.

Phi Delta Kappa, Commission on Educational Planning. Workshop packet for educational goals and objectives: A model program for community and professional involvement. Bloomington, Ind.: PDK, 1972.

Pinsky, P. D. Alternative computer configurations for classroom instructional management data processing. In W. P. Gorth (Chm.), Monitoring and managing student outcomes by using new computer technology. Symposium presented at the meeting of the American Educational Research Association, New York, February 1971. (Working Paper No. 21, February 1971, University of Massachusetts/Amherst, School of Education, Grant No. 642, C. F. Kettering Foundation.)

Pinsky, P. D. Mathematical models concerning the measurement of educational achievement levels. Technical Memorandum No. 29, 1972, University of Massachusetts/Amherst, School of Education, Grant No. 642, C. F. Kettering Foundation.

Pinsky, P., White, M. & Gorth, W. An objective and item banking system: paper-based. Albany, N.Y.: New York State Education Department, 1972.

Popham, W.J. (Ed.) Criterion-referenced measurement. Englewood Cliffs, N.J.: Educational Technology Publications, 1971.

Rothkopf, E. L., & Kaplan, R. Exploration of the effect of density and specificity of instructional objectives on learning from text. Journal of Educational Psychology, 1972, 63, 295-302.

Schriber, P. E. Criterion-referenced testing: A comparison of its characteristics in longitudinal testing using item sampling and unit posttesting of achievement. 1973, University of Massachusetts, School of Education, Contract No. C55623, New York State Education Department.

Sequoia Union High School District. CAM project report. Redwood City, Calif.: Author, 1973.

Skager, R. W. The system for objective-based evaluation: Reading. Evaluation Comment, 1971, 3(1), 6-11.

Skinner, B. F. Beyond freedom and dignity. New York: Alfred A. Knopf, 1971.

Stake, R. E. Objectives, priorities, and other judgment data. Review of Educational Research, 1970, 40, 181-212.

Thorndike, R. L. (Ed.) Educational measurement. (2nd ed.) Washington, D.C.: American Council on Education, 1971.

Tuckman, B.W., & Edwards, K.J. A systems model for instructional design and management. Educational Technology, 1971, 11(9), 21-26.

Index